Transwar Asia

SOAS Studies in Modern and Contemporary Japan

SERIES EDITOR
Christopher Gerteis (SOAS, University of London, UK)

EDITORIAL BOARD
Stephen Dodd (SOAS, University of London, UK)
Andrew Gerstle (SOAS, University of London, UK)
Janet Hunter (London School of Economics, UK)
Barak Kushner (University of Cambridge, UK)
Helen Macnaughtan (SOAS, University of London, UK)
Aaron W Moore (University of Edinburgh, UK)
Timon Screech (SOAS, University of London, UK)
Naoko Shimazu (NUS-Yale College, Singapore)

Published in association with the Japan Research Centre at the School of Oriental and African Studies, University of London, UK.

SOAS Studies in Modern and Contemporary Japan features scholarly books on modern and contemporary Japan, showcasing new research monographs as well as translations of scholarship not previously available in English. Its goal is to ensure that current, high quality research on Japan, its history, politics and culture, is made available to an English speaking audience.

Published
Women and Democracy in Cold War Japan, Jan Bardsley
Christianity and Imperialism in Modern Japan, Emily Anderson
The China Problem in Postwar Japan, Robert Hoppens
Media, Propaganda and Politics in 20th Century Japan, The Asahi Shimbun Company (translated by Barak Kushner)
Contemporary Sino-Japanese Relations on Screen, Griseldis Kirsch
Debating Otaku in Contemporary Japan, edited by Patrick W. Galbraith, Thiam Huat Kam and Björn-Ole Kamm
Politics and Power in 20th-Century Japan, Mikuriya Takashi and Nakamura Takafusa (translated by Timothy S. George)
Japanese Taiwan, edited by Andrew Morris

Japan's Postwar Military and Civil Society, Tomoyuki Sasaki
The History of Japanese Psychology, Brian J. McVeigh
Postwar Emigration to South America from Japan and the Ryukyu Islands, Pedro Iacobelli
The Uses of Literature in Modern Japan, Sari Kawana
Post-Fascist Japan, Laura Hein
Mass Media, Consumerism and National Identity in Postwar Japan, Martyn David Smith
Japan's Occupation of Java in the Second World War, Ethan Mark
Gathering for Tea in Modern Japan, Taka Oshikiri
Engineering Asia, Hiromi Mizuno, Aaron S. Moore and John DiMoia
Automobility and the City in Japan and Britain, c. 1955–1990, Simon Gunn and Susan Townsend
The Origins of Modern Japanese Bureaucracy, Yuichiro Shimizu (translated by Amin Ghadimi)
Kenkoku University and the Experience of Pan-Asianism, Yuka Hiruma Kishida
Overcoming Empire in Post-Imperial East Asia, Barak Kushner and Sherzod Muminov
Imperial Japan and Defeat in the Second World War, Peter Wetzler
Gender, Culture, and Disaster in Post-3.11 Japan, Mire Koikari
Empire and Constitution in Modern Japan, Junji Banno (translated by Arthur Stockwin)
A History of Economic Thought in Japan, Hiroshi Kawaguchi and Sumiyo Ishii (translated by Ayuko Tanaka and Tadashi Anno)
Transwar Asia, edited by Reto Hofmann and Max Ward

Transwar Asia

Ideology, Practices, and Institutions, 1920–1960

Edited by
Reto Hofmann and Max Ward

BLOOMSBURY ACADEMIC
LONDON • NEW YORK • OXFORD • NEW DELHI • SYDNEY

BLOOMSBURY ACADEMIC
Bloomsbury Publishing Plc
50 Bedford Square, London, WC1B 3DP, UK
1385 Broadway, New York, NY 10018, USA
29 Earlsfort Terrace, Dublin 2, Ireland

BLOOMSBURY, BLOOMSBURY ACADEMIC and the Diana logo are
trademarks of Bloomsbury Publishing Plc

First published in Great Britain 2022
Paperback edition first published 2023

Copyright © Reto Hofmann and Max Ward 2022

Reto Hofmann and Max Ward have asserted their right under the Copyright, Designs
and Patents Act, 1988, to be identified as Editors of this work.

Cover image: The Greater East Asia Co-Prosperity Sphere
© CPA Media Pte Ltd / Alamy Stock Photo

All rights reserved. No part of this publication may be reproduced or transmitted
in any form or by any means, electronic or mechanical, including photocopying,
recording, or any information storage or retrieval system, without prior
permission in writing from the publishers.

Bloomsbury Publishing Plc does not have any control over, or responsibility for, any
third-party websites referred to or in this book. All internet addresses given in this
book were correct at the time of going to press. The author and publisher regret any
inconvenience caused if addresses have changed or sites have ceased to exist, but
can accept no responsibility for any such changes.

Every effort has been made to trace the copyright holders and obtain permission to
reproduce the copyright material. Please do get in touch with any enquiries or any
information relating to such material or the rights holder. We would be pleased
to rectify any omissions in subsequent editions of this publication should they
be drawn to our attention.

A catalogue record for this book is available from the British Library.

Library of Congress Cataloging-in-Publication Data
Names: Hofmann, Reto, 1975- editor. | Ward, Max M., 1973- editor.
Title: Transwar Asia : ideology, practices, and institutions, 1920–1960 /
edited by Reto Hoffman and Max Ward.
Description: London ; New York : Bloomsbury Academic, 2022. | Series: SOAS
studies in modern and contemporary Japan | Includes bibliographicalreferences and index.
Identifiers: LCCN 2021029890 (print) | LCCN 2021029891 (ebook) |
ISBN 9781350182813 (hardback) | ISBN 9781350182820 (pdf) |
ISBN 9781350182837 (ebook)
Subjects: LCSH: Decolonization–East Asia–History–20th century. | War and
society–East Asia. | East Asia–History. | East Asia–Politics and government.
Classification: LCC DS518 .T725 2022 (print) | LCC DS518 (ebook) | DDC 950.4/1–dc23
LC record available at https://lccn.loc.gov/2021029890
LC ebook record available at https://lccn.loc.gov/2021029891

ISBN: HB: 978-1-3501-8281-3
PB: 978-1-3502-8112-7
ePDF: 978-1-3501-8282-0
eBook: 978-1-3501-8283-7

Typeset by Newgen KnowledgeWorks Pvt. Ltd., Chennai, India

To find out more about our authors and books visit www.bloomsbury.com
and sign up for our newsletters.

To the memory of Aaron S. Moore

Contents

Introduction: The Long Transwar in Asia   1
   Reto Hofmann and Max Ward

Part I   Institutional Transwar Regimes

1   Imperial Shift: Rice and Revolution in Transwar Korea, 1939–1949   17
   Yumi Moon

2   Colonial Militarism in Transwar East Asia: Indigenous Forces and the Three Waves of Militarization   49
   Victor Louzon

3   Occupational Hazards in the Transwar Pacific: Imperialism, the US Military, and Filipino Labor   77
   Colleen Woods

4   University, Landed Class, and Land Reform: Transwar Origins of Private Universities in South Korea, 1920–1960   101
   Do Young Oh

Part II   Ideological Transwar Regimes

5   Resetting China's Conservative Revolution: "People's Livelihood" in 1950s Taiwan   125
   Brian Tsui

6   "*Volksgeist*-ism": Ideational Flows between Europe, Japan, and Indonesia, 1920s–1960s   147
   David Bourchier

7   Reproducing the "Emperor System Within": Transwar Criminal Rehabilitation and Imperial Benevolence in Japan, 1920–1960   169
   Max Ward

Afterword: Transwar as Method   195
   Takashi Fujitani

Bibliography   205
List of Contributors   221
Index   223

Introduction: The Long Transwar in Asia

Reto Hofmann and Max Ward

This volume proposes "transwar" as an analytical category to understand the history of Asia between 1920 and 1960.[1] The term emphasizes the goal to explain some of the important developments in policies, thought, and culture in the 1950s and 1960s not only as outcomes of the Second World War and the collapse of the Japanese Empire, but by situating them within a historical continuum reaching back to the 1920s and the problems that first emerged in those years. This arch possesses an internal coherence that can be distinguished from what came before and after, and which provides for the possibility to trace developments across and between different political contexts and conventional historical periodizations.[2] The transwar is marked by the rise and ebbing of conflicts that first emerged in what Eric Hobsbawm has called the "age of extremes"—democracy versus authoritarianism, imperialism versus anti-colonial nationalism, socialism versus fascism.[3] In response, during the 1920s and 1930s an array of political, cultural, artistic, literary, and philosophical solutions with different political valences were proposed from Indonesia to Japan. Their articulation differed across space but, crucially, was reformulated also across time. If the 1920s gave birth to active nationalist movements, cultural experimentation, revolutionary parties, and the intensification of imperial competition throughout much of Asia, by the 1960s these forces had been transposed into a system of nation-states, new international cultural practices, economic growth plans, and Cold War geopolitics. When seen from this perspective, the 1950s and 1960s appear less a legacy of—or response to—war and empire and more as a chapter in a longue durée of problems that shaped the world and Asia during this complex period. This volume aims to critically reexamine policies, ideas, and practices that had been originally announced as "new" in the 1940s and 1950s within this longue durée, as well as to reassess the claims of "continuity" or "naturalness" that informed the postwar projects of nation-state formation throughout Asia.[4]

To capture these temporal reformulations and spatial negotiations at work in Asia between 1920 and 1960, this volume proposes the concept of "transwar regimes." By "regimes" we understand not only political-economic formations but also a wider array of processes extending to cultural, intellectual, social, and artistic realms, and which together conferred on the transwar period the historical dynamics that distinguished it from what came before and what came after. We contend that this concept can bring together and expand a number of other research agendas on Asia. First, it intersects with the cultural studies of colonial modernity in Asia, as well as with recent works that have explored the deimperialization of the Japanese Empire.[5] Second, it engages with works on the global Cold War by foregrounding the agency of Asians in the selective appropriation of transwar elements in the postwar settlement.[6] Third, it is in dialogue with recent transregional perspectives that trace the circulation of ideas, people, and technologies across Asia and the Pacific in both colonial and postcolonial times.[7] By historicizing the competing imperialisms in Asia since the 1920s and their postwar afterlives, our transwar approach connects the flows of ideas, people, institutional models, and technologies during the Cold War back to the experiences of colonial mobilizations at the hands of Japanese, European, and American imperial powers, and the different sociocultural milieus that existed in and across these empires. Touching on these interconnected levels of analysis, the chapters in this volume, though diverse in their topical and regional focus, serve as examples of the further possibilities for understanding the history of Asia through a transwar lens.

Beyond "Change and Continuity"

The transwar approach we are proposing calls for closer attention to the complex processes by which prewar or colonial ideologies, practices, and institutions were reconfigured *both* for wartime mobilization in the 1930s and 1940s and again in the formation of nation-states and Cold War realignments in the 1950s and 1960s. The uneasy coexistence of "old" and "new" into the postwar period eschews the neatness implied in the framework "change and continuity" that historians commonly use to demarcate the study of this period. Such a historical framework and the political evaluations they informed—such as colonial/postcolonial, fascism/liberalism, militarism/democracy, collaboration/

resistance—make sense from a structuralist perspective but, in their neatness, fail to capture the complicated choices and nuanced experiences of actors on the ground as they confronted these structures.

Take the example of the historiography on Japan. Guided by modernization theory, early English-language studies approached postwar Japan as disconnected from the 1930s and 1940s, wherein Japan, now freed from the purported anomalies of interwar imperialism, militarism, and fascism, returned to its "natural" path of political and economic modernization.[8] Here the interwar and wartime periods were explained away as unfortunate divergences from normative development.[9] This historical demarcation came with the presumption of a political binary between prewar authoritarianism and postwar liberalism, which became the underlying problematic for many early Cold War studies on Japan. By the late 1970s, a new generation of scholars were painting a more complicated picture by not only noting "change and continuity" between the interwar and postwar periods in Japan but also arguing that interwar or wartime remnants actually explained Japan's phenomenal economic growth starting in the 1960s, thus complicating the clear political contrast between the prewar and postwar periods.[10] This scholarship, however, inherited the earlier assumption that 1945 marked a historical divide across which "change and continuity" could be traced.

We would add that outside of studies of Japan, the early scholarship on Asian countries was predicated on similar historical isolations, in which the colonial period represented an anomalous prehistory to the natural development of postcolonial nation-states after 1945. Similar to the Japanese historiographical debates, this narrative was also complicated by later scholars who reassessed colonial developments in the 1930s and 1940s as providing the foundation for postwar economic growth.[11] However, in both versions emphasis was placed on prewar or colonial "legacies" after 1945, as though structural leftovers in themselves were agents in postcolonial development. This historical demarcation produced its own political bifurcations in colonial/postcolonial history, evidenced most clearly in the "resistance and collaboration" framework that informed many early postwar studies of postcolonial nation-state formation in Asia.

One way to move beyond the dichotomy of the "change-and-continuity" approach is to recognize the hybrid nature of transwar regimes. Rather than showing that certain things changed while others remained the same, it is important to explore the underlying problems that continued across the transwar period, and individual or collective efforts to resolve them. Working through the complicated relationship between new and old means to shed light on the constitutive tensions upon which the postwar order was built and that affected long-term historical change in Asia. In other words, the objective is to explore the nuanced transformations of policies, institutions, and ideas starting with their initial inception in the 1920s to their reformulation for war in the 1930s as well as for postcolonial and postimperial nation-state formation in the early years of the Cold War, or what Takashi Fujitani has called "transwar as method" in the afterword. This applies to intellectual, artistic, literary, and cultural transformations as well. Not only were institutions, practices, and ideas continually changing between 1920 and 1960 but they became invested with different political meanings in each context. The challenge of the transwar approach is accounting for these different ideological investments in different political and historical contexts.

"Transwar" in Japanese Historiography

In the 1990s, "postwar Japan" became a historical question in its own right, and scholars started to make passing usage of the term "transwar" when attempting to demarcate the postwar period from what came before and after.[12] However, the objective centered on identifying the "postwar," and as such, "transwar" remained under-conceptualized in these studies—used simply to refer to an empty frame of time between the 1930s and 1950s.

In the past two decades, the scholarship on transwar Japan has expanded to include a wider set of areas and questions. For example, Andrew Gordon has analyzed transformations in the desires and realities of middle-class consumption in metropolitan Japan between the 1920s and 1960s. According to Gordon, if in the 1920s middle-class culture was marked by a gulf between those who aspired toward achieving a "middle-class" lifestyle and the small number of those who could actually afford it, by the 1960s this ratio reversed, as consumer products and leisure activities became more affordable to a wider swath of the Japanese population.[13] Gordon calls this a "transposition" in middle-class culture, which prompts him to identify 1960 as the year in which the "'transwar' gives way to 'postwar' Japan."[14] More recently, other scholars of Japan, including Jonathan Abel, Charlotte Eubanks, and Miriam Kingsberg Kadia, have focused specifically on the transwar period in Japanese history, exploring how particular phenomena such as censorship regimes (Abel), artistic practices (Eubanks), or assumptions about epistemology (Kadia) cultivated during the interwar period continued into the postwar and were practiced or harnessed for different agendas under the Allied Occupation (1945–1952) and beyond.[15] Collectively, these scholars have reflected more deeply on the particular historical dynamics that constituted the transwar experience and which delineated it from other periods of modern Japanese history.

Building from these recent transwar histories of Japan, our aim is to conceptually refine transwar as a historical category, with particular emphasis on the enduring problems that underwrote the intellectual, political, and cultural regimes of Asia between 1920 and 1960. Whereas transwar has been used to explain a particular historical trajectory, we are proposing to bring these various trajectories together in order to understand the transwar as a historical period with its own constitutive problems and dynamics. An important part of that endeavor is to recognize the centrality of imperialism and its postwar traces in the history of modern Asia more broadly.

"Transwar" and the Imperial Turn in Asian Studies

In the studies reviewed above, "transwar" remains largely a category of Japanese *national* history. And yet, transwar regimes were born from and entangled with imperial formations.[16] The transwar approach recognizes that because Japan was an empire before 1945, it set in place links between its colonial possessions and those it occupied during the Second World War, which were reoriented during the Cold War under the hegemony of the United States, as Bruce Cumings has explored.[17] These entanglements open up new possibilities to explore mid-twentieth-century Asia through the competing imperialisms in the region, their different forms and degrees of mobilizations for war, as well as their postwar afterlives. In her chapter, Colleen Woods argues for a transwar "imperial analytic" in order to understand how many developments in the United States' military hegemony in the Pacific were retooled colonial practices from the American Philippines. We believe Woods's idea of transwar imperial analytic can be useful in exploring many of the regional histories of Asia. Thus one central aim of this volume is to extend the term "transwar" from Japanese history to that of Asia in order to consider the extent to which it can open new possibilities for understanding the history of the region as a whole.

We contend that transwar is a useful category for analyzing all of Asia which can bring together what have been disparate studies of colonial/postcolonial national histories, the multiple imperialisms competing in Asia, as well as the civil wars which were concurrent with the Pacific War and which would later become formative experiences in China, Korea, and Southeast Asia. This is to remind us that, as Ernest Mandel has argued in the European context, the problem of imperialism holds the key for understanding "the meaning of World War II" and thus, by extension, the wars in Asia between 1931 and 1953.[18] Of course, the problem of imperialism in Asia was ultimately not resolved but continued into the Cold War, an example of Fujitani's idea in the afterword that 1945 was a historical "junction" between empires. In this transwar history, the Japanese Empire casts a particularly long shadow, as does American hegemony during the Cold War.

A transwar approach can incorporate the discussion of colonial developments from the register of postcolonial/postwar national histories into a longer history in which the imperial and the domestic interact in the flows of people, ideas, capital, and institutions that occurred since the 1920s. Recent work on the transnational ramifications of Japanese and Western imperialism in Asia has made important contributions to this line of enquiry. We are thinking of Aaron S. Moore's groundbreaking work on the infrastructure projects of Japanese engineers between 1930 and 1960, Ethan Mark's analysis of the changing appeal of Japanese pan-Asianism in transwar Indonesia, Takashi Fujitani's exploration of the mobilization of racialized populations in wartime Japan and America and their lasting effects, Barak Kushner's recent collaborations surveying the dismantling of Japan's empire around Asia, as well as Eiichiro Azuma's work on the competing settler colonialisms in the transpacific region.[19] As the chapters of this volume demonstrate, such an approach can be expanded to analyze different scales and multiple levels: from the local, national, and imperial to the transregional. For example, Victor Louzon's chapter traces the influence of Japanese war mobilization across multiple societies, showing how this militarist culture informed independent nation-state formation in the Cold War period. Yumi Moon explores how the American occupation inherited many of the assumptions about Korean rice production from Japan's mobilization of the colonial rice system for war. And David Bourchier traces the permutations of a legal theory he calls *Volksgeist*-ism from Germany and the Netherlands in the nineteenth century, to interwar Japanese legal philosophy, through to how *Volksgeist*-ism informed postcolonial Indonesian legal thinking after 1965. Despite the different levels of analysis, these chapters and others require that we rethink the presumed distinction between Japan's *formal* empire and the United States' *informal* empire during the Cold War, which has guided much of the historiography in Asia. This then raises the question of what kind of dynamics constitute this historical period in Asia.

Toward "Transwar Asia"

This volume is the first attempt to chart the various dynamics that constituted this unique period in Asia. At its most general level, it is to rethink the relationship between the Japanese Empire and American Cold War hegemony in Asia, and how particular processes of nation-state formation in the late 1940s negotiated between these two empires.[20] For example, colonial governance changed over time, and it is important to recognize under what contexts certain policies or institutions were developed, and the dynamics that enabled their availability to be harnessed for new purposes in the postwar or postcolonial contexts. It was thus impossible in 1945 to be firmly "post," whether in Asia or elsewhere. This is to remind us that rather than simply a scholastic exercise, to think "transwar" is to think how actors at the time understood their world and responded to it—whether political leaders, writers, artists, activists, philosophers, or others.

The interwar years gestated a great many innovations to deal with the endemic problems of capitalist and colonial modernity, many of which transcended ideological and geographical boundaries. It is therefore not surprising to see that technologies of rule, bloc economies, ideologies, and welfare policies continuously developed across the temporal span of transwar regimes. For example, as David Bourchier's chapter shows, philosophical questions that were originally posed in the 1920s were given new urgency in the 1940s and then reframed in the 1950s and beyond; as Yumi Moon's chapter explores, institutions that were used to govern a colony were modified for war mobilization and then once again recalibrated to function during the immediate postwar context of occupation and nation-state formation; and as Brian Tsui's chapter explores, long-term political conflicts dating back to the 1920s had been paused during the Pacific War only to be reignited in the late 1940s to influence the postwar political settlement. The challenge is to understand the unique dynamics at work across and between these multiple histories.

That transwar regimes struggled with accommodating new and old becomes evident in the way that societies assigned "1945" a task to divide while, at the same time, they could not avoid a discourse of continuity or repetition. Whether the country lay in ruins and occupied by a foreign power, as in the case of Japan, or whether it embraced the prospect of independence from Western colonialism, as in Indonesia, the sense was that 1945 opened the possibility to reshape the future. But political and cultural discourse alike rested on a vocabulary that evoked a taking back—reconstruction, rebuild, reborn, and so on—which raises the question of discerning how both the "new" and the "continuous" were ideologically imbricated within each other in the postwar/postcolonial settlement. Thus, the transwar approach we are proposing moves beyond the more recent move to recognize "legacies" in postwar nation-state formations. Rather than "legacies," which imply the passive inheritance of prewar material, our transwar approach highlights the importance of "afterlives," an idea that more aptly captures the multiple and often conflicted transformations of ideas, institutions or practices across the changing conditions between 1920 and 1960, while identifying the logics at work in such transformations. The afterlives of prewar or wartime institutions did not continue naturally into the postwar or postcolonial periods but were predicated on specific decisions to harness and retool institutions that had themselves developed over time across different political conditions.

Gordon's logic of transposition mentioned earlier provides one useful approach to conceive the broader historical dynamics at work in the transwar period. Here we suggest others, including the transliteration of ideas into new frameworks, the reformulation of policies, and the recalibration of institutions to meet new conditions. For example, in his chapter Brian Tsui explores the process through which the Guomindang (GMD) "transplanted" its evolving conservative revolution project from mainland China to Taiwan in the 1950s, and the ideological translation this entailed. Tsui concludes that this signified a major "resetting" of the GMD's conservative revolution to a new local and geopolitical context. Similarly, Max Ward analyzes how Japan's prewar criminal rehabilitation system was initially consolidated during wartime and then "recalibrated" in the immediate postwar period, in which the system's earlier ideological associations with the Japanese emperor system was transposed into the postwar idioms of culture, democracy, and liberalism. Terms such as resetting, reformulation, and recalibration can uncover the complicated historical dynamics and political investments across the transwar period, while Fujitani's idea of 1945 as a "junction" between empires can remind us of the larger geopolitical framework within which these dynamics unfolded.

Chapter Outline

Each chapter explores a particular aspect of transwar regimes in Asia between 1920 and 1960. They each focus on what Claudio Pavone has called "channels of continuity," that is, individuals, policies, or institutions that acted as mediators across time.[21] Our hope is that, collectively, the chapters serve as examples of possibilities to develop new research projects on twentieth-century Asia through the historical lens of "transwar." Although we have organized the chapters under themes of institutions and ideas for clarity, such a division is arbitrary since each institution was of course informed by particular ideologies, which themselves transformed as they were institutionalized over time.

Starting the "Institutional Transwar Regimes" section, Yumi Moon's chapter explores the changing dynamics of colonial governance in Korea through the lens of rice control, and the ways in which the US occupation replicated many of the same assumptions and thus same policies that the Japanese governor-general had implemented in colonial Korea for wartime mobilization. Through this transwar history of rice production, Moon shows how a regime of social control evolved in Korea across the wartime divide, arguing for the crucial role of intermediaries such as neighborhood associations in its transformation. In his chapter on transwar Korea, Do Young Oh analyzes an important facet in the transwar reproduction and postwar restoration of class power in South Korea. If in the colonial period Korean elites pursued higher education in Japan's imperial education system, Oh reveals how the landed elites shifted their financial assets to institutions of higher education in response to postwar land reform, which explains the number of South Korean private universities today.

Both Victor Louzon and Colleen Woods focus on the longue durée of militarism in the formation of transwar Asia. Louzon identifies something that might be called "transwar East Asian militarism" in Taiwan, Manchuria, and Korea, illustrating how the militarization of populations under Japanese colonial rule was reenacted in the tumultuous years of the early Cold War. Louzon's chapter importantly reconnects these two periods of militarization and requires us to consider how "militarism"—understood both as a form of rule and social practice—informed both colonial and national forms of mobilizing societies. Pursuing a different question, Colleen Woods's chapter analyzes the labor regime established by the United States in the colonial Philippines, which in the postwar period became a template for staffing US military installations throughout the Pacific. Woods explains not only the ubiquity of Filipino labor in US military installations during the early Cold War but also how the United States turned to employing locals as both a source of cheap labor and a remedy for the socioeconomic difficulties that many of the locales faced after the war.

The chapters collected in the second section titled "Ideological Transwar Regimes" focus on the transliteration of ideas and ideologies across the transwar period in Taiwan, Indonesia, and Japan. Starting off this section, Brian Tsui traces the process through which the GMD "transplated" the ideological foundations of what he calls the GMD's "conservative revolution" from the context of civil war in 1930s China to Cold War Taiwan in the 1950s. Focusing on the importance of anti-communism to the GMD's "conservative revolution," Tsui closely reads Chiang Kai-shek's 1953 revision to Sun Yat-sen's *Three People's Principles* and reveals the ways in which Chiang reinterpreted Sun's text as a "developmentalist, welfarist vision" that accorded more with the GMD's Cold War alignments than it did to Sun's original vision.

In the next chapter, David Bourchier explores the many facets and transwar permutations of a legal theory he calls *Volksgeist*-ism. Arguing that a country's laws must conform to a people's unique national culture, this theory originated in German political and legal thought in the early nineteenth century. *Volksgeist*-ism was adopted by Dutch and Japanese into their colonial and national legal thought, only to be embraced by Indonesian nationalists. Crucially, Bourchier shows how in the 1930s this idea appealed to both Japanese legal scholars and students from colonial Java who anticipated an independent Indonesia. He traces the complex transwar trajectories of this legal theory, showing how it was recast at crucial turning points by a variety of actors—from scholars to politicians—and how it continues to structure Indonesian nationalism up to the present. In the final chapter, Max Ward analyzes the transwar history of criminal rehabilitation in Japan and its changing associations with the emperor system between 1920 and 1960. Whereas criminal rehabilitation programs in Japan are often portrayed as examples of Japan's postwar liberalization, Ward shows how elements of this system were first developed in the 1920s and then consolidated in the crucible of war mobilization in the late 1930s and early 1940s. Ward argues that this transwar system also served to transpose the ideological function of the emperor from prewar sovereign to the postwar symbol of cultural wholeness.

In his afterword, Takashi Fujitani reflects on the chapters in order to elaborate what he calls a "transwar as method" which treats 1945 as a "transit moment" between empires. Fujitani's notion of "transwar as method" recuperates the possibilities stifled by the reimposition of structures of domination and violence in the passage from Japanese imperial power in Asia to US hegemony. Continuity, Fujitani pointedly argues, is not in itself a critical approach to the past. Rather, recognizing how knowledge of the past was shaped by continuities can help historians avoid unduly celebratory narratives and take up what he calls "a past conditional temporal lens" to consider "what might have been" at various moments in Asia between 1920 and 1960.

Notes

1 This book is the product of several years of thinking about the possibility of writing the transwar histories of Asia. In addition to suggestions from the contributors collected in this volume, the editors benefitted from the comments of many other colleagues, including Deokhyo Choi, Namiko Kunimoto, Ethan Mark, and others who attended conference panels and workshops. Lastly, the volume is dedicated to the memory of Aaron S. Moore, colleague, friend, and a pioneer of the kind of critical transwar history of Asia that this book aspires to promote.

2 Here we have in mind what Karatani Kojin has called a "parallax" analysis that focuses on the gaps between different or overlapping historical periodizations. Karatani Kojin, "The Discursive Space of Japan," in *History and Repetition*, trans. Seiji Lippit (New York: Columbia University Press, 2012), 51.

3 Eric Hobsbawm, *Age of Extremes: A History of the World, 1914–1991* (New York: Vintage, 1996). Note the transwar implications of Hobsbawm's historical periodization.

4 Slavoj Žižek warns of misperceptions about the "newness" or "continuity" of historical forms, which for him indicate "the existence of ideology *qua* generative matrix." This ideological matrix can be "discerned in the dialectics of 'old' and 'new,' when an event that announces a wholly new dimension or epoch is (mis)perceived as the continuation of or return to the past, or—the opposite case—when an event that is entirely inscribed in the logic of the existing order is (mis)perceived as a radical rupture." Slavoj Žižek, "The Spectre of Ideology," in *Mapping Ideology*, ed. Slavoj Žižek (London: Verso, 1991), 1.

5 For example, Tani Barlow, ed., *Formations of Colonial Modernity in East Asia* (Durham, NC: Duke University Press, 1997); Barak Kushner and Sherzod Muminov, eds., *The Dismantling of Japan's Empire in East Asia: Deimperialization, Postwar Legitimation and Imperial Afterlife* (London: Routledge, 2018).

6 For example, Odd Westad, *The Global Cold War: Third World Interventions and the Making of Our Times* (Cambridge: Cambridge University Press, 2005); Lisa Yoneyama, *Cold War Ruins: Transpacific Critique of American Justice and Japanese War Crimes* (Durham, NC: Duke University Press, 2016).

7 For example, Eiichiro Azuma, *In Search of Our Frontier: Japanese America and Settler Colonialism in the Construction of Japan's Borderless Empire* (Berkeley: University of California Press, 2019); Janet Alison Hoskins and Viet Thanh Nguyen, eds., *Transpacific Studies: Framing an Emerging Field* (Honolulu: Hawai'i University Press, 2014).

8 Here the classic example is the proceedings from the Conference on Modern Japan published by Princeton University Press in the 1960s and early 1970s. On this conference and series, see Bruce Cumings, "Boundary Displacement: The State,

the Foundations, and Area Studies during and after the Cold War," in *Learning Places: The Afterlives of Area Studies*, ed. Masao Miyoshi and H. D. Harootunian (Durham, NC: Duke University Press, 2002), 261–302; Sebastian Conrad, "'The Colonial Ties Are Liquidated': Modernization Theory, Post-war Japan and the Global Cold War," *Past & Present* 216, no. 1 (August 2012): 181–214.

9 See Edwin O. Reischauer, "What Went Wrong?" in *Dilemmas of Growth in Prewar Japan*, ed. James W. Morley (Princeton, NJ: Princeton University Press, 1971): 489–510.

10 The clearest example of this thesis is Chalmers Johnson, *MITI and the Japanese Miracle: The Growth of Industrial Policy, 1925–1975* (Stanford, CA: Stanford University Press, 1983). For a more nuanced and critical assessment, see John W. Dower, "The Useful War," *Daedalus* 119, no. 3 (Summer 1990): 49–70.

11 For a review and refutation of the colonial legacies in post-1960 South Korean economic development, see Jonghoe Yang, "Colonial Legacy and Modern Economic Growth in Korea: A Critical Examination of Their Relationships," *Development and Society* 33, no. 1 (June 2004): 1–24.

12 For example, see Andrew Gordon, "Conclusion," in *Postwar Japan as History*, ed. Andrew Gordon (Berkeley: University of California Press, 1993), 449–64. On the persistence of Japan's "long postwar," see Carol Gluck, "The Past in the Present," in Gordon, *Postwar Japan as History*, 64–95.

13 Andrew Gordon, "Consumption, Leisure and the Middle Class in Transwar Japan," *Social Science Japan Journal* 10, no. 1 (April 2007): 1–21.

14 Ibid., 2.

15 Jonathan Abel, *Redacted: The Archives of Censorship in Transwar Japan* (Oakland: University of California Press, 2012); Charlotte Eubanks, *The Art of Persistence: Akamatsu Toshiko and the Visual Cultures of Transwar Japan* (Honolulu: Hawai'i University Press, 2019); Miriam Kingsberg Kadia, *Into the Field: Human Scientists of Transwar Japan* (Stanford, CA: Stanford University Press, 2020).

16 This raises the fraught national question that Andre Schmid has warned of when studying the Japanese Empire and its colonial territories. See Andre Schmid, "Colonialism and the 'Korea Problem' in the Historiography of Modern Japan: A Review Article," *Journal of Asian Studies* 59, no. 4 (2000): 951–76. The term "imperial formations" derives from Ann Laura Stoler, "Imperial Debris: Reflections on Ruins and Ruination," *Cultural Anthropology* 23, no. 2 (2008): 191–219, 193.

17 Bruce Cumings, "Japan's Position in the World System," in Gordon, *Postwar Japan as History*, 34–63.

18 Ernest Mandel, *The Meaning of the Second World War* (London: Verso, 1986), 169–75.

19 See Aaron S. Moore, *Constructing East Asia: Technology, Ideology, and Empire in Japan's Wartime Era, 1931–1945* (Stanford, CA: Stanford University Press, 2013); Hiromi Mizuno, Aaron S. Moore, and John DiMoia, eds., *Engineering Asia: Technology, Colonial Development, and the Cold War Order* (London: Bloomsbury, 2020); Ethan Mark, "'Asia's' Transwar Lineage: Nationalism, Marxism, and 'Greater Asia' in an Indonesian Inflection," *Journal of Asian Studies* 65, no. 3 (August 2006): 461–93; Takashi Fujitani, *Race for Empire: Koreans as Japanese and Japanese as Americans during World War II* (Berkeley: University of California Press, 2011); Kushner and Muminov, *The Dismantling of Japan's Empire in East Asia*; Azuma, *In Search of Our Frontier*.

20 This is not to overlook the various European imperial powers in Asia and the different legacies they imparted across the region but to emphasize the serious challenge that the Japanese Empire posed to these powers in the 1930s as well as the United States' dominance in the region during the Cold War.

21 Claudio Pavone, *Alle origini della Repubblica: Scritti su fascismo, antifascismo e continuità dello Stato* (Turin: Bollati Boringhieri, 1995), 14–15.

Part One

Institutional Transwar Regimes

1

Imperial Shift: Rice and Revolution in Transwar Korea, 1939–1949

Yumi Moon

During the Pacific War (1941–1945), feeding soldiers with rice was a "holy" mission for the Japanese wartime administration. The Japanese Empire designated Korea as its rice granary and tightened the system for relaying food and other resources between and among its colonies and newly acquired territories, the Japanese archipelago, and the battlefields. In the final years of the Pacific War, Korea's agricultural and societal interactions changed dramatically to fulfill wartime demands for food and other resources. Then the US occupation forces entered Korea in early September 1945 and abruptly lifted this wartime system. The sudden repeal of the wartime system triggered nationwide popular uprisings throughout 1946. Scholars studying this period have generally identified these widespread Korean protests as symptoms of a "revolution." Without taking a transwar perspective, however, it is difficult to grasp the exact nature of this popular unrest and anxiety in Korea after colonialism.

This chapter examines the rice crisis in wartime Korea and its recurrence in the US occupation period. The rice problem in transwar Korea reveals the material aspects of decolonization and their impacts on people's everyday life. The Japanese Empire rapidly changed its rice control system when a severe drought in 1939 caused famine and disrupted the export of Korean rice to the Japanese archipelago. After liberation, the US military government rejected such state control and left rice issues to the free market. This decision caused a perilous food crisis in South Korea and resulted in widespread protests in 1946. Most of the protests in the first half of 1946 were rather peaceful and occurred in urban areas. In contrast, the harvest-season uprisings were violent, sweeping North and South Kyŏngsang Provinces and Southern Chŏlla Province. I argue in this chapter that the nationwide uprisings in 1946 indicated not so much a left-leaning revolution as a subsistence crisis due to the chaotic transition away from the wartime grain-control system.

In identifying the "transwar" period as a useful historical category, it is important to recognize the enduring impacts of the war on postwar Korean society. The military nature of the US and USSR occupations contributed to preserving some structural elements of Korea's wartime society. While the US and USSR occupations differed in their treatment of the pro-Japanese collaboration of Korean elites, they barely raised the issue of punishing mass-level cooperation with Japan's war activities. Meanwhile, some wartime mobilization networks were refurbished and reconfigured into the new ideological and political systems that the United States and the USSR introduced to Korea. It is ironic that the survival of such networks in South Korea was triggered not by the US occupation's original intention to retrieve such networks but by its rejection of the state maintaining control of the grain economy. During the war, Japan had developed an intricate grain-control system that could be called a "wartime moral community."[1] Here "wartime moral economy" refers to Japan's fraught system of forcibly collecting grain from producers, predicated on the state's "commitment" to maintaining a minimum subsistence level for the whole society. Both the US occupation and Korean leaders in the south decided to purge such a dictatorial system and put their trust in the "democracy" of the free market. Korean grain producers—peasants and landlords alike—rejoiced at the end of the wartime control. Yet confidence in the free market quickly dwindled in early 1946, when serious food crises hit most of the urban areas of South Korea.

The analysis of rice control in this chapter aims at uncovering the diverse origins of the political and popular upheavals in the early years of the US occupation. I argue that the popular uprisings of 1946 had mixed characteristics rather than forecasting a Korean revolution. In describing Korea's volatile situation after liberation, many scholars quote the term "powder keg," found in some records of US officials in Korea at the time. This term was first used in a September 13, 1945, report by John Hodge, the commander of the US occupation in Korea, to Douglas MacArthur, the commander in chief of the US Army Forces in the Pacific. Hodge's report provided a "brief and incomplete picture" of Korea's condition according to his initial observations.[2] Merrell Benninghoff, a US foreign service officer, repeated the term two days later, in his September 15 message to the secretary of state. Benninghoff's report was "substantially the same as that sent by Lieutenant General John R. Hodge, to General Douglas MacArthur."[3] Hodge's use of the term "powder keg" at this point concerned not so much the eruption of a social revolution but serious Korean resentments over the delay in removing the Japanese from Korea and in recovering the immediate independence of Korea.⁴

A transwar approach is indispensable to determining the characteristics both of the popular uprisings in 1946 and of local participants in the protests. Many historians of the US occupation in Korea have emphasized the role of the people's committees and the People's Republic of Korea organized under the leadership of Korean leftists. These historians have criticized the US occupation for disapproving of the People's Republic and for recruiting pro-Japanese collaborators into the government and the police.⁵ However, this interpretation insufficiently scrutinizes how the imperial context—namely, the power shift from the Japanese Empire to the US occupation—caused and reshaped the directions of popular uprisings in Korea after colonialism. A statistical analysis of the 1946 harvest-season protests in the southern provinces reveals a correlation between the uprisings in 1946 and the tenancy disputes of the 1930s, which had occurred within the colonial state's framework for mediating conflicts between tenants and landlords.⁶

Japan's Wartime Control of Rice and the Korean Drought in 1939

The Japanese Empire faced a serious rice shortage in the metropole with its industrialization and the growth of urban population. Before the First World War, Japan was a trade-deficit country, and its three largest imports, after raw cotton, were soybeans (and related products), rice, and sugar. With the expansion of the empire, Japan was able to buy major food items from its colonies. Food imports from outside the empire dropped sharply from the mid-1920s on. Rice from Korea and Taiwan replaced imports from China and Southeast Asia, and the Japanese consumed Taiwanese rather than Javanese sugar. Japan imported 70 percent of its total food imports from its colonies until the mid-1930s.⁷

With colonization, Korea became a subordinate section of the Japanese imperial market.⁸ In the 1920s, Japan transformed colonial Korea into a supply base to satisfy increasing rice demands in the archipelago. The colonial government of Korea conducted a "rice production program" and expanded the size of rice paddies. Between 1921 and 1928, Korea's annual rice exports to Japan increased from 2.4 million bags (sŏk or koku; 1 sŏk = 180.39 liters) to 7.4 million bags, while its total rice production grew from 14.8 million bags to

17.2 million bags. As the massive transfer of rice to Japan brought food shortage to Korea, Manchurian millet filled the gap. The growth of Korean rice exports in the 1920s increased millet imports from Manchuria consistently. According to one study, the destination of 99 percent of Manchurian millet exports was colonial Korea.[9] This development of the imperial food market changed Korea's agricultural production and created "specialization in cereals (rice and millet)" between Korea and Manchuria.

The rice production program in Korea changed in the late 1920s because the cheap rice imported from the colonies reduced the rice price in Japan, angering rice farmers there. In 1921 Japan enacted a "rice law" (*beikokuhō*) that made the Tokyo government regulate the domestic rice market by buying some rice from Japanese farmers and storing it during harvest seasons. However, this law did not control the volume of rice trade from the colonies. Facing the troubles of Japanese farmers, the Tokyo government issued an imperial ordinance in 1928 to restrict imports of foreign rice and applied it to Korea and Taiwan as well. In response, the colonial government in Korea promulgated its own regulation of foreign rice import.[10] However, Japanese rice producers asked for a stronger restriction on rice from the colonies, especially Korean rice. In 1929 the Japanese cabinet therefore organized a "rice investigation committee" (*beikoku chōsa iinkai*) to discuss the "problem" of Korean rice. The committee recommended that the government-general of Korea regulate the monthly volume of Korean rice exported to Japan and issue permits for trading foreign rice in Korea. This decision controlled the seasonal volume of Korean rice exports to Japan.[11]

The Japanese government dramatically changed its rice policy with Korea's great famine in 1939 and the outbreak of the Pacific War. The wartime Japanese leader Ugaki Kazushige (1868–1956) wrote top-secret reports to the Japanese military during the final years of the war. He ruled Korea twice as governor-general (1927, 1931–1936) and was minister of foreign affairs and minister of colonial affairs in 1938. Ugaki did not have an incumbent government position after 1938 but continued advising the Japanese leadership during the war. His report in mid-February 1943 reassessed Japan's situation in the war after its defeat in the Guadalcanal Campaign, the first major victory of the Allied Forces on the Pacific front. Ugaki was optimistic about the war but seriously worried about its material side.[12] He underlined food procurement as the most critical task at hand. According to Ugaki, Japan's procurement depended on the relays of food and other resources within the empire and its new acquired territories. Japan received food from Korea and Manchuria; Manchuria, from Northern

China; Northern China, from Southern China; Southern China, from French China and Thailand; and French China and Thailand, from the South Pacific. He recommended that the Japanese military fight to the death to protect the Japan Strait as a food-supply route to the archipelago and tightly regulate the collection and transportation of resources within the imperial network.[13]

This imperial food network had a weakness. The Japanese government recognized it when a severe drought hit Korea and west Japan in 1939. Mizuta Naomasa (1897–1985), the director of the financial bureau in the colonial government of Korea, stated that the rice harvest in 1939 declined from 24.13 million bags to 14.35 million bags. The gap was approximately 10 million bags—a shortfall that rendered 1.09 million households of Koreans victims of the drought.[14] According to another colonial statistic, the government-general considered relief measures for farm households that had lost 70 percent of their annual harvest to the drought, and 60 percent of Korea's rice farmers belonged to that category.[15]

This famine in Korea alarmed the Tokyo government. Korea sent between 7 million and 10 million bags of rice to Japan annually from 1933 to 1938. The export to Japan declined in 1939 to 395,000 bags—a 93 percent reduction from the previous year. Before this Korean drought, the Ministry of Agriculture in Japan had not tightly controlled the rice market. The ministry expected both an influx of surplus rice from Korea and Japan's swift victory in the Sino-Japanese War.[16] In the 1930s, Ministry of Agriculture officials laid stress on maintaining a stable rice price in Japan. As noted earlier, they regulated the volume of Korean rice export to Japan so as not to drop the rice price and damage the interests of Japanese rice farmers. The Ministry of the Army criticized the existing rice policies because it worried about the unstable rice supply endangering the military's war activities. Local governors in Japan also demanded aggressive rice control because a rice shortage caused unrest and disturbed domestic security in local areas. These factors demanded more coercive measures, including the government's direct purchase of rice from farmers and rice rationing to the people.[17] Between 1939 and 1941, the Tokyo government promulgated several regulations and orders for rice control and eventually adopted the state's coercive collection of rice after the outbreak of the Pacific War. These regulations were synthesized into the "Food Control Law" (*shokuryō kanrihō*) announced in February 1942.[18]

Communicating with the Tokyo government, the colonial state in Korea tried rice-control policies to cope with the impacts of the drought. Colonial officials imposed the official price of rice and increased their regulation of the rice market. The symptoms of rice famine in Korea emerged in the late spring of 1939. In Korea's climate, spring was a season of starvation, when the previous year's fall harvest had been consumed and summer crops were yet to ripen. The newspapers began reporting a shortage of rice in retail stores in late May and early June 1939.[19] The price of rice and other grains climbed to almost 70 percent higher than the prices of the previous year.[20] In Chŏngjin in northern Korea, rice traders could not get rice from the southern regions and decided to import it from Japan to ease the rice shortage in the area.[21] The reports of rice famine continued in major cities and towns of southern Korea. Because retail stores had very little rice, they had consumers line up and restricted them to purchasing 1 or 2 *toe* (1.8 liters) of rice per person on a "first come, first served" basis.[22] The sense of crisis heightened as water shortages prevented farmers from planting rice seedlings on time in the southern grain-belt areas.[23]

The colonial government tried to allay fear by announcing that its rice preserve was around 3.8 million bags, no less than the average annual quantity. They claimed that the rapid rise in the price of rice was disproportionate to the state's supply capacity. They ascribed the rice famine to profit-seeking landlords and merchants hoarding rice for future sales.[24] The Kyŏnggi provincial government first proposed an emergency plan to solve Seoul's rice shortage, given the city's large population.[25] This plan had three key elements. First, the government organized a rice cooperative (*migok chohap*) composed of major rice millers, wholesalers, and retailers in the city. This rice cooperative would form a committee to set a price that the members could accept. The government would approve this committee's price and enforce it as the official price. The committee could meet at its convenience and renegotiate the official price every week or ten days. Second, the government planned to investigate the total quantity of rice available in the province and make policy decisions based on the result of this survey. This required all rice owners to report the amount of rice in their possession. Third, to regulate the behavior of rice traders, Seoul city police decided to summon approximately six hundred rice retailers and request their cooperation with the new policy. Meanwhile, the government would calculate the exact business costs for rice traders and force them to observe the official price. The government would ban any traders from obtaining rice if they violated this official price.[26]

This price control did not solve the rice shortage but did increase the difference between the official price and the market price. Rice owners stopped releasing rice to regular markets. Retailers lowered the quality of rice by mixing bad grains with good ones. Some merchants maintained the official price when police were present but asked a higher price when they were gone. Other merchants hid rice in distant places and took consumers to get the rice only after being paid in advance. Rice purchase became just as secretive, a reporter wrote, as trading opium or stolen goods.[27] People bought rice on the black market at higher prices because it was better than going home empty-handed. Rice disappeared almost entirely from regular markets in August 1939. Rice-related crimes were frequent, such as rice thieves or "greedy" rice traders filling one-third of a rice bag with sand or rock dust. This rice crisis was more troublesome to city dwellers, especially manual workers and the urban poor, than to residents of the countryside.

In September 1939, the colonial government announced "the regulation on the Korean Rice Market Company (*Chosŏn migok sijang chusik hoesaryŏng*)."[28] The governor-general appointed the president and the executive directors of the company. Other rice dealers were prohibited from opening a rice market except in special cases approved by the governor-general, and even the Korean Rice Market Company (*Chosŏn migok sijang chusik hoesa*) needed the governor-general's permission to hold a rice market. Any rice market required that a trader be a member to join rice trades there. Membership involved eligibility criteria and was certified by the governor-general.[29] After shutting down various rice markets, the government opened the first state-controlled rice market in Seoul. Governor-General Minami Jirō attended its opening ceremony in January 1940 and said that the government "should carefully manage the smooth supply of rice with good price in order to avoid any instability to the main diet of the people. The government-general has been communicating with the [Tokyo] government to make the policy consistent between the metropole and the colony."[30]

On December 27, 1939, the colonial government also promulgated "the regulation on rice distribution in Korea" (*migok paegŭp chojŏngnyŏng*) and started rationing rice. *Tonga Ilbo* evaluated that this regulation made Korean rice entirely subject to the state's total mobilization for the war.[31] In comparison to the situation after 1942, the state's rice control between 1939 and 1941 maintained some mediation of private actors. On a practical level, provincial governments were the main agencies of rice control. Each provincial government organized a provincial food-ration cooperative. This cooperative was composed of major mill owners and rice and grain dealers in a province. The provincial cooperative took charge of buying rice and other grains within and outside the province and rationed rice to city-level or prefectural-level food cooperatives. In Kyŏnggi

Province, for instance, the government gathered thirty-three local mill owners and grain dealers and organized the provincial food-ration cooperative. Each member invested 10,000 yen to form the Kyŏnggi cooperative, but its major funding, of 10 million yen, came from the government-controlled Chosen Bank.[32]

Such mediation of private actors meant a deeper intrusion of the colonial state into people's everyday lives—one that would continue to intensify as the war carried on. As noted earlier, the government investigated the amount of each household's rice surplus or shortage. The provincial government ordered the local police and the neighborhood associations in counties and villages to search households under their jurisdiction.[33] After estimating the quantity of rice available in the province, the government ordered rice owners to release rice to the market. If a province had a surplus, the central government assigned its transfer to other provinces that were short of rice. Following this central directive, provincial cooperatives bought rice from farmers or landlords, milled the rice, and sold it to the cooperatives of the designated province.[34] The provincial food-ration cooperatives entrusted district- or prefecture-level cooperatives with rationing rice to the residents of their region.[35]

Private rice owners and dealers were unhappy with this system, especially after the installation of the Korean Rice Market Company. This company monopolized Korean rice export to Japan. The association of rice traders complained. Rice owners and dealers (in cooperatives) spent much money to buy and transport rice from farmers. The Korean Rice Market Company had no such expenses but made a profit simply by exporting the collected rice to Japan. Colonial officials defended this decision because they were under pressure to supply rice in speedy response to the demands of the Japanese military and the Tokyo government.[36] For example, the Tokyo government decided to import 3 million bags of Korean rice in 1940. This was significantly less than Korea's regular export volume but still high for the year after the drought. *Maeil Sinbo*, the official newspaper of the government-general, published the colonial officials' negotiations with Tokyo. They agreed to send 1.5 million bags of Korean rice in exchange for 3 million bags of other grains from Manchuria and Japan.[37] Despite this report, the statistics reveal that Korea ended up sending 3.3 million bags to Japan in 1940.[38] The colonial government had to squeeze an additional 1.53 million bags of rice from the famine-stricken country of Korea to alleviate rice shortage in Japan.

The Outbreak of the Pacific War and the "Blitzkrieg" for Rice Collection in Korea

The Tokyo government delayed its direct purchase of rice until 1942. The Ministry of Agriculture preferred to fill the shortage by importing foreign rice from Southeast Asia and other places. The Ministry of the Army disliked spending foreign currency on purchasing rice because this decreased the military's budget for war procurements. The Ministry of Agriculture managed to overcome such objections by purchasing rice from French Indochina on credit or by bartering to exchange foreign rice for other Japanese goods. During this time, *Maeil Sinbo* printed serial articles on the rice situation that echoed the arguments of the Ministry of the Army. The author of the articles strongly criticized the Ministry of Agriculture and demanded that Korea's rice production and export be increased as an alternative to importing foreign rice. It was only yen that were needed to purchase rice from colonial Korea, he wrote.[39]

Given Governor-General Minami Jirō's ardent devotion to the war effort, colonial officials in Korea were highly motivated to make their food administration receptive to the demands of the wartime empire. Prior to 1942, the colonial government used the terms "the encouragement of [rice] release" (*ch'ulha tongnyŏ*) and "the order to force [rice] release" (*kangje ch'ulha myŏngnyŏng*) to prompt rice producers to sell rice to the agents designated by the government. In some cases, "the regulation on rice distribution" was used as legal grounds to force rice owners to sell rice to the government's agents. In 1940, for instance, the Kangwŏn provincial government decided to purchase all hulled and unhulled rice in the province. The local rice cooperatives purchased rice from rice producers, sent the unhulled rice to Japan for export, and distributed hulled rice within the province.[40] The full-scale collection of rice began in 1942, but the forced sale of rice in Korea to the government's agents was already happening in early 1940.

The government's direct collection of rice and other grains became legal with the Tokyo government's enactment of the February 1942 Food Control Law. The colonial government of Korea conducted rice collection according to this law, while preparing "the regulation on food management in Korea" (*Chosŏn singnyang kwalliryŏng*). The regulation on food management established a semi-governmental monopoly on the rice trade (*chun chŏnmaeje*). The colonial government converted the Korean Rice Market Company into the Korean Food Company (*Chosŏn singnyang yŏngdan*). The regulation made all rice producers, farmers, and landlords legally obliged to submit to the government all surplus rice after keeping the rice needed for their family consumption. The Korean Food Company was the government's agent for purchasing rice from rice producers at the officially set price.[41]

This change reflected the urgent food demands of the empire after the outbreak of the Pacific War. During the war's final years, the rice collection campaigns in Korea were frantic.[42] To achieve the collection goals, the colonial government tried to remove any loopholes in the rice control system.[43] The rhetoric for rice collection became increasingly militant. Colonial officials called rice production and collection a "holy mission" comparable to soldiers' combat on the battlefield. They reduced the daily rice ration per person to half or one-third of the original quantity and encouraged the people to consume substitute foods such as wild edibles. The police punished people if they hid rice or rejected the state orders.

In July 1942, the colonial government started applying some articles of the Food Control Law to Korea. This made it illegal to trade rice and other grains abroad without a government permit and also dissolved the rice-control cooperatives, thereby removing any impact of rice traders on the state control.[44] As a result, the eight hundred rice dealers in Seoul all lost their jobs.[45] In the same month, the government also started changing the rice-rationing system. Previously, retailers distributed rice to consumers at their stores. The state could not entirely control these stores because retailers had their own business interests. The new ration system conglomerated all retail stores and allocated the number of state-controlled stores to each district in proportion to its population.[46]

Prior to this new system, there were three methods of rationing rice. First, people received coupons to use to obtain their rice ration. Second, people went to their regular retail stores and purchased rations at the official price. Third, employees received rice through collective rations from their companies or organizations. Some people who used their regular stores and also received rations at their companies could therefore collect their rice rations more than once. The government started a rice accounting system to remove such double rations. The rice accounting system required that the government learn the exact size of each household because a single rice account was issued to each family. The patriotic neighborhood associations were crucial to running this new system. The government called on the heads of district neighborhood associations and instructed them to organize subdistrict or subcounty associations for inspecting all households in their neighborhoods. The neighborhood associations asked their neighbors to report whether they were getting their rations from their regular retail stores or from the companies where they were employed. Based on the information provided by these associations, the government issued rice-ration accounts to families.[47]

Patriotic neighborhood associations (*aegukpan*) were the lowest units of the Total Mobilization Alliance (*Kungmin ch'ongnyŏk yŏnmaeng*), which organized the masses to support the state's war administration. The neighborhood associations had units in counties, subcounties, villages, and occupational organizations, including government branches, schools, banks, and other institutions. Ten households comprised one base unit of the patriotic association. The number of associations had increased to 380,000 in December 1940.[48] Because many men had gone to war or had day jobs, more women than men were appointed to run the patriotic neighborhood associations. For example, in late 1940, Hokubu Machi (Northern County, in the current Yŏngdŭngp'o area of Seoul) had fourteen thousand residents and 80 patriotic neighborhood associations, most of which were headed by men. By August 1941, 108 of the now 120 neighborhood associations in Hokubu Machi were headed by women,[49] and by 1942, women led 70 percent of the associations throughout Seoul.[50]

During the Pacific War, rice collection campaigns were waged like battles that colonial officials and the people had to win. They were severe and sometimes deadly. In Northern Kyŏngsang Province, the government achieved only 80 percent of the collection goal in May 1942. To complete the remaining 20 percent, the Bureau of Agricultural Affairs mobilized its officials into seven units and organized them into "cheering squads" (*tongnyŏdae*) for rice collection. They carried on a final "blitzkrieg" for rice collection throughout the province between May 9 and May 22 to achieve the goal.[51] Collecting rice as a sort of military campaign in May, the peak of spring famine, must have required a lot of sacrifice and caused resentment among the people in rural areas.

The newspaper reports of the colonial government remained triumphant and moralistic in tone during this time, glorifying the solidarity and virtues of rural society. However, the episodes quoted to celebrate the success were extreme and inhumane. The colonial officials repeated that there was enough food in Korea; people in rural areas should trust the government; the government would never leave farmers to starve. In January 1945, Shiraishi Kōjirō (1897–?), the director of the Bureau of Agriculture and Commerce in the government-general, was interviewed by *Maeil Sinbo*. He again promised sufficient food supplies in Korea. However, the interview revealed that the goal of rice collection had been reduced by 20 percent, that a drought had broken out again, and that the size of the daily rice ration had been further reduced. Shiraishi pleaded with the people to remove black markets at a time when their soldiers were "fighting in hunger, chewing tree roots."[52]

More government reports commended farmers' spiritual devotion to achieving the rice collection goals and destroying the enemy for the victory of the empire.[53] The colonial government allocated the collection quota to individual households but made each village submit its collection goal together. The government assigned responsibility for achieving village collection goals to the heads of village associations (*purak yŏnmaeng*), providing them with some assistance in transporting and inspecting grains. The heads of villages and the clerks of county administrations had their work cut out for them in mobilizing villagers. In Southern Ch'ungnam, the harvest seriously declined in 1944. A county clerk in Chŏngyang, Tomokawa, whose Korean name was Kuchŏn, was responsible for Sindae village in Taep'yŏng subcounty, and the collection quota was 1,200 bags of rice. The village could achieve only 63 percent of its target. He sat down naked in front of the village hall until 10:00 p.m. in the cold winter wind. The worried villagers held a meeting to save him from dying of exposure and promised to submit the rest their quota—a promise they then kept.[54] In another case, a village head named Yoshino worked hard for the rice collection even though his children and wife were very ill. He "won the battle" by completing the village quota, but his two children had to make a "beautiful sacrifice"—meaning death—for the "cause."[55]

In yet another case, in Chŏngdo, Kyŏngsang Province, a poor farmer called Hahey (*p'ap'yŏng yubaek*, a scholar of P'ap'yong) was a tenant and had four sons and two daughters. The first and second sons had left home to work in factories producing war supplies. Hahey finished his collection quota in advance of others and fought the food shortage with wild edible greens. In December 1944, he received an additional quota of rice to submit. He carried the rice left to him to the warehouse for government collection and passed away at its entrance. *Maeil Sinbo* wrote that "the noble spirit of this imperial peasant will travel across Korea's mountains and rivers and unbrokenly fill the hearts of Korean farmers."[56]

The Urban Famine and Rice Protests in US-Occupied South Korea

The US occupation removed the state's rice control in Korea on October 5, 1945, without understanding the complicated wartime system of allocating food to

Koreans. According to the official *History of the United States Army Military Government in Korea*, the military governor, Major General Archer L. Lerch, said at a press conference on October 15, 1946, that the US Army accepted the Korean people's demand to remove all Japanese from responsible positions. The Japanese officials were removed, and as a result the rice collection program collapsed and was replaced by the free market.[57]

In the first euphoric months after liberation, Koreans consumed rice liberally, without the burden of government collection. It was a good harvest year in 1945. The US occupation forces recognized the shortage of food in mid-September 1945 but treated it as a temporary problem caused by the lack of transportation. Hodge wrote that shortage of cereals was due to outshipping by Japan of large quantities of rice after last year's crop. He expected excellent cereal crops in 1945, and the problem in food distribution was due to disruption of railways and lack of motor transportation.[58]

According to the US military document "Rice Situation in Korea," dated December 15, 1945, the US occupation had no worries about rice in Korea and considered exporting Korean rice to solve the food crisis in Japan. The report estimated that the total production of rice, wheat, and other grains in southern Korea was 28,081,000 *koku* and the expected domestic consumption was 23,495,000 *koku*. Therefore, the "surplus for export" from Korea was 4,586,000 *koku*. The report continued that, on October 15, 1945, the US authorities ordered that the Korea Foodstuff Control Corporation (Korean Food Company) of the colonial period be reorganized into Korea Life Necessaries Co. Ltd. (Korean Commodity Company). The agents of the Life Necessaries Corporation had already been provided with the sum of 35 million yen to "briskly purchase rice."[59] The report emphasized the importance of not missing the November–April export season, after which it would be very hard to collect rice despite the expected surplus of 0.8 million tons in Korea. Another report, written by S. Iguchi, the director of general affairs in the US military's central liaison office in Tokyo, also proposed the idea of the US occupation in Korea continuing to export Korean rice to Japan, just as the Japanese Empire had done. Iguchi reported the urgent food shortage among Japanese coal miners to the General Headquarters (GHQ) of the Supreme Commander for the Allied Powers. He requested that the GHQ approve the prompt importation of 10,000 *koku* (15,000 tons) of Korean rice to provide extra rations to the coal miners by March 1946.[60]

This US report misunderstood the food situation in Korea. Koreans sensed the problem in December 1945, as rice disappeared in city markets.[61] Seoul was one of the areas struck hard by this crisis. The mayor of Seoul was initially optimistic, estimating the daily rice demand as 4 *hop* (about 180 ml) per person, or less than 4,800 *sŏk* for the city's total population.⁶² Korean newspapers reported the military government's assessment that transport was in short supply and that the arrival of trucks from the United States would improve the situation.⁶³ However, the rice problems did not improve. The media targeted "immoral" merchants who were hoarding rice for profit. In a radio broadcast, Syngman Rhee accused the Japanese of collaborating with "traitorous" Koreans and sending rice to Japan. He reprimanded brokers on the southern coast who he said were transporting rice to Japan and selling it at a high price there or bartering rice for Japanese tangerines.⁶⁴ Koreans at risk of starvation resented that precious rice was being sent to Japan for tangerines. The smugglers usually contacted Japanese in Tsushima or on the southern coastal areas at night.⁶⁵

Government prosecutors chased illegal profiteers. They raided Seoul's riverside area Map'o and discovered eight thousand bags of rice hidden in a storage depot.⁶⁶ The newspapers printed a photo of rice confiscated by this government raid.⁶⁷ According to the report, the "thick-faced" merchant was Ro Sŏn-jae of Kyŏnggang Trade Company (Kyŏnggang Mulsan) in Map'o. Ro had predicted that the price of rice would rise in winter because the frozen river would hinder rice shipping to Seoul. He had made money after liberation by cheaply purchasing the rice stored for the Japanese Army and selling it at a high price. Looking to profit again, he had collected the rice by borrowing 100 yen from Chohŭng Bank.⁶⁸

In January 1946, Koreans in urban areas were in fear of famine⁶⁹ and requested that the military government change its rice policy. The military government gave up the free-market policy and reverted to rice control. The US military announced that it would set the official price of rice and ration rice to nonfarm households. In February 1946, the government issued Ordinance no. 45 to resume its rice collection, which allowed farmers to keep two *sŏk* of unhulled rice for family consumption and required them to sell the rest to the government. The price of one *sŏk* for government purchase was set as 150 Korean wŏn. The Korean Commodity Company was designated as the agency to manage rice purchases from farmers and also rice distribution in cities. The government instructed the heads of towns and counties and the officers of the agricultural associations (*nonghoe*) to find out how much rice was kept in rural households. If farmers did not follow the order, they would be forced to submit their rice and receive the lower price of 120 wŏn per *sŏk*.⁷⁰ For rationing rice in cities, the military government summoned district heads of patriotic neighborhood associations⁷¹ and requested that the associations investigate the numbers of households and their family conditions in their districts.[72] As in the wartime period, a rice account was required to receive rice rations. For repatriates, district neighborhood associations would examine the size of their households and issue new rice accounts to their families.[73]

Despite such planning, rice rationing did not occur soon because the grain collection in spring had disappointing results. Koreans in urban areas faced starvation throughout the entire year of 1946. They suspected the secret transfer of rice to Japan. The media corroborated such suspicions. *Tonga Ilbo* titled its top column article "Korean Rice Going to West Japan." This article quoted an Associated Press report that Douglas MacArthur had ordered the Japanese government to stop the smuggling of rice and other necessities to Japan from Korea.[74] The US military entrusted the Korean Commodity Company with collecting and rationing rice.

But both farmers and urban residents dreaded the company. As noted earlier, its colonial antecedent, the Korean Food Company, was the agency that had exported Korean rice to Japan during the war. The US occupation leaders asked farmers to cooperate with the rice collection with moral consciousness and patriotism. However, farmers resisted the resumption of rice collection. After liberation, the supply of necessities was unstable and their prices increased. Guns and grenades were available, and armed robbery was frequent in cities. Under such conditions of insecurity, farmers could not simply sacrifice their economic and familial interests for patriotism.[75]

As had been the case during the wartime period, the provincial governments took charge of collecting rice. In February 1946, the Kyŏnggi provincial governor Maurice Lutwack held a meeting at which the Kyŏnggi and Hwanghae governors, magistrates, and police chiefs set the provincial goal for rice collection at 800,000 *sŏk*. The deadline was set for mid-March. The meeting approved a lower goal, 730,000 *sŏk*. The estimated provincial production for the year was already short 130,000 *sŏk* to achieve that goal, and so Lutwack planned to purchase the shortfall from Hwanghae Province.[76] After the meeting, the prefectural governments assessed the quantity of rice production and consumption in their areas and distributed collection quotas to farmers and landlords.[77] The farmers who submitted rice were given priority in buying gasoline, soap, matches, or other necessities. Each household could keep the daily amount of 3 *hop* of rice for each person in the family.[78]

To prevent rice owners from evading their collection duties, the military government punished the sale of rice at rates above the official price, thirty-eight wŏn per *tu* (18 liters), and banned rice from being carried across provincial boundaries. If the police discovered someone other than the government's agents carrying rice across provincial boundaries, they could confiscate the rice.[79] The prosecution bureau of the government opened an economy section to arrest merchants engaging in illegal business and trade. Some Koreans complained that such punishment of free economic activities was "anachronistic" to liberated Korea. The prosecution bureau rejected this, stating that the principle of liberal economy

> is relevant only to a society in which production is smooth and the system of supply and demand well manages the exchange of goods. However, [in Korea] the production system is not functioning … In this transitional stage, we cannot apply the principle of liberal economy. Punishing immoral merchants who … cause economic disorder and price rises is the least the state can do.[80]

As the rice crisis worsened in urban areas, the heads of the neighborhood associations stepped forward, demanding a larger role.[81] In February 1946, the heads of district neighborhood associations petitioned the Seoul city government to distribute rice through the associations to "put out the fire on our feet." They asked that the government confiscate rice hidden in storage and allow people to bring rice in from outside of the city. They also criticized the corrupt activities of rice-ration offices. When thirty *sŏk* of rice were given to a district, the neighborhood associations claimed, the ration offices distributed only ten *sŏk* and the rest disappeared. The neighborhood associations asked that they run the ration offices themselves and fairly distribute rice to residents. The officer of the military government James E. Wilson agreed.[82]

Different approaches were proposed to solve this rice shortage. *Tonga Ilbo* criticized the official price of rice. The author of one of its satirical columns wrote,

> When the "Japs" waged the war, all rice was sent by force to the government. The people suffered from it. After Liberation, rice was blocked by the official price of 38 wŏn per *tu* and was exchanged for Japanese tangerines … Now with the military government law, the police search everybody's attics. The fate of rice is awful. It would be marvelous if the number of the law were 38 [implying that both the official price of rice and the problems of the 38th parallel were sources of pain].[83]

Kim Sŏng-su in the Korean Democratic Party argued that the official rice price was too low in comparison to the price of other commodities, and that farmers were unfairly asked to release rice at a cheap price. Kim demanded the free trade of rice.[84] The Rice Taskforce Committee of the Seoul City, in contrast, did not support the free market and asked that the military government continue the official price of rice and also its rice collection. However, the taskforce wanted to remove restrictions on carrying rice across provincial boundaries for family consumption until the government stabilized the rationing of rice.[85]

The US occupation officers did not fully understand the degree of Korean anxiety in this rice famine. In his press conference in February 1946, Lerch confessed that he had not known until then how serious the food crisis was.[86] When a reporter commented that the government ration for ten days covered only three days of meals, the American officer in charge of the food administration bureau replied that even Americans did not have enough to eat as they were sending food aid abroad. He suggested that Koreans compensate for the shortage of rice by eating vegetables and apples. The headline of the newspaper article on his press conference read thus: "Eat Vegetables and Apples: The Food Administration Officer's Rice Policy."[87] Rice supply in urban areas was dire in spring of 1946. Pirates on a Japanese army boat appeared on the Han River and robbed merchants of their rice.[88] On March 14, 1946, the military government announced a guideline on rationing rice. The daily ration was 2 *hop* of grain per person. Rice rationing and the quantity were to be announced in advance by newspapers and radio broadcasting. To receive rice rations, people needed food-ration accounts with their district associations. The heads of district associations were to inspect the records of ration stations to confirm the fairness of their distribution.[89]

Even after the government's multiple announcements, food rations in March 1946 were delayed for many reasons. When rice rations were not distributed in late March, people started visiting government halls and demanding rice. The heads of district neighborhood associations—women in large numbers—led such protests and asked for meetings with the leaders of the military government, mayors, and governors. Sometimes several thousand people joined such protests in various cities. Because wage earners were most vulnerable in this rice crisis, workers also took collective action. On March 20, 1946, the workers in the print and publishing industries organized an emergency meeting over the food crisis; 120 union members attended this meeting. They demanded an increase in wages for "saving their parents, wives, and children who were wandering the streets in search of food."[90]

Newspaper editorials became grim and desperate toward the end of March. Koreans had been struggling to afford high-priced rice on their small incomes. They had sold all their valuables and exhausted their resources. They were at the stage of risking their very lives for rice. A *Tonga Ilbo* editorial described the situation as one in which the "gate of the tragedy was beginning to open."⁹¹ Many articles described the "horrendous" situation of the people and the spread of rice protests. Workers and employees were absent from their jobs in their search for rice. Students could not go to school because of hunger. Teachers missed school to seek rice in the countryside. If the rice rations did not become available right way, a reporter wrote, the people's miraculous survival over the past three months would finally end in the horrible pit of death.⁹²

More petitions and protests for rice flooded the government halls. Seventy workers of T'aeyang Textile Company visited the military government to meet the chief of the agriculture and commerce bureau; seventy representatives of the Pyŏngmokchŏng neighborhood associations visited the government.⁹³ Three thousand residents of the eight district associations in Seoul crowded the city hall corridors and demanded rice. A reporter wrote,

> It was pitiful to watch women [in the protest] with sick faces swollen from starvation and women with crying babies on their backs standing near the windows of the economic bureau. Madam Wŏn Myŏng Sun and the eighty-eight representatives of district neighborhood associations led this protest. They met Wilson and the mayor, explained their desperate situation, and begged them to solve the food shortage immediately. They returned home after a few hours of protest after the government promised the distribution of rice from April 8.⁹⁴

This food crisis reached a deadly stage in early April. A newspaper article wrote that the protesters said they didn't want to die of hunger before seeing Korea's independence.⁹⁵ On April 1, the employee representatives of Seoul Electric Company, of freight car companies, of taxi companies, and in Yongsan and Yŏngdŭngp'o, and thousands of women camped at the city hall entrance to demand rice.⁹⁶ Many housewives joined the protests.⁹⁷ An article dated April 4, 1946, bemoaned, "We eat breakfast of porridge and pass on dinner. This is none other than famine. The famine protest army (*kia pudae*) crowded the city hall under the rain. This assembly is growing bigger and attracting broader participants. How will the government settle this situation?"⁹⁸

The military government rationed rice for emergency relief on April 8, 1946.⁹⁹ It also permitted the people to carry rice up to 1 *tu* for family consumption.¹⁰⁰ The police ordered officers not to confiscate rice that was carried across provincial boundaries for family use.¹⁰¹ With rationing and the lifting of the ban on rice being carried in from the countryside, the price of rice began to drop. By mid-April 1946, the market price of rice had dropped from 440 wŏn per *tu* to 250 wŏn.[102] The atmosphere changed from one of depression to one of optimism. However, the rice shortage was uneven, and people were tense about rice availability. In Waegwan, when rice in the storage of the former Korean Food Company was being moved to other places, several thousand people came to the company and the prefecture hall on July 23 and protested, shouting, "Where did you take our food? Give us rice!" The police tried to disperse them, but their protests continued.[103]

Urban dwellers could bring rice from the countryside for family consumption but had to receive permits.[104] The neighborhood associations were important in this permit process. Citizens submitted their applications to the neighborhood association and received confirmation from the heads of the associations. Applicants brought confirmed applications to the district (*ku*) government, which issued rice-carry permits. When people received the permits, their neighborhood associations removed the amounts of rice certified for trade from rationing and reported this to their rationing stations. Companies or other organizations underwent a similar process to obtain rice-carry permits.[105]

Rice protests decreased in cities. With the government's grain collection, more serious conflicts emerged in rural areas. The Korean media, both leftists and rightists, recognized the urgency of rice collection. Most journalists were in urban areas that were suffering from rice shortages.[106] The atmosphere in the countryside was different from this urban concern. The peak of rural uprisings in 1946 has been called the October Harvest Uprising or the Taegu Rebellion in Korean history because the most deadly conflicts occurred in Taegu City and its vicinity. The rural protestors considered rice collection at the official price a return to the colonial system. Koreans heard many rumors, for example, that the United States was collecting rice to feed American soldiers; to send to Japan; to ship home to make rice bread in the United States because rice is more nutritious than wheat; or even to send to America because the US military had discovered that some elements in rice were useful for making nuclear bombs.[107]

The US occupation leaders perceived the rural protests as malicious tactics of the "propagandists." John Hodge made an announcement on September 2, 1946, the one-year anniversary of the day when Japan signed the unconditional surrender. He stated that the collection of rice and other grains was necessary to support repatriates, refugees, urban dwellers, and people in need of food. In contrast to the colonial period, he insisted, the military government would guarantee that farmers could keep enough rice for their families' consumption. Hodge indicted some political groups for mobilizing farmers to reject rice collection and for making Koreans believe, through false rumors, that the US occupation was intentionally abusing them. Hodge's words became personal when he criticized the propagandists who were calling the United States a fascist, reactionary, and imperialist country. "To my chagrin," he said, these groups never mentioned the sacrifice of US soldiers and the expense of the US resources marshaled to defeat Japan. He added, "As a person who fought this war against Japan from the beginning, I cannot understand why they consign to silence such great efforts of the United States."[108]

Perhaps Hodge's hostility to the "propagandists" hindered him from understanding the standpoints of rural protesters. The moderate leftist Pae Sŏng-nyong argued that farmers had no incentive to sell rice to the government; rather, they wanted and needed to profit from the gap between the official price and the market price. If the government could keep the market price of rice low during the collection period, farmers would be willing to sell rice to the government. Interestingly, Pae asked whether, in December 1945 or January 1946, Japan had taken Korean rice in exchange for coal. Chi Yong-ŭn, the director of the Food Administration Bureau, answered that no rice had been sent to Japan.[109] On October 12, 1946, the top column article in *Tonga Ilbo* reiterated its preference for a free rice market rather than rice control. The article emphasized that "rice was enough" for Korean consumption. If the government eradicated illegal profiteering and smuggling, the author insisted, there would be no need to enforce rice collection and make farmers feel exploited. If the government forced farmers to submit rice at the official price, farmers would not remain like docile sheep. With some financial measures and a good rice reserve for correcting the market, the author argued, the risk (of relying on free market) wouldn't be greater than the problems of resuming rice collection.[110]

The US military did not accept such recommendations and faced fierce rural protests in fall 1946.[111] In early October, rural protests spread to Kyŏngsang, Chŏlla, parts of Ch'ungchŏng, and Cheju and Kŏje Islands. The majority of the protests concentrated in Northern Kyŏngsang, Southern Kyŏngsang, and Southern Chŏlla Provinces. US military intelligence reported 214 incidents between October 1 and November 20, 1946. Of these, 140 were from the Kyŏngsang areas and 59 from Southern Chŏlla.[112] Different perspectives have been suggested for understanding the characteristics of this harvest uprising. Bruce Cumings charts the areas where protests occurred during this period and emphasizes the leading role of the people's committees and radicalized peasants.[113] Thomas Lee has called the harvest uprisings the "Taegu Insurrection" and questioned the views that identify the protests as revolutionary. He offers a solid analysis, proposing that "the insurrection was essentially a regional rebellion against what was perceived to be an illegitimate extension of state authority."[114] He also emphasizes the importance of the rice collection issue in this uprising. Gi-Wook Shin offers a statistical analysis to understand the historical precedents that influenced this postwar uprising. He analyzed the protest data collected by Cumings together with data on the peasant protests during the colonial period. Shin's discovery is surprising because it reveals that the postwar uprising was connected less with the Red Peasant Union movements influenced by socialists than with the tenancy disputes mediated by the colonial government.[115]

One point to note is that the active adoption of violence by protesters differentiates this harvest uprising from other rice protests during the time. The US military responded to this harvest uprising with armed policemen and soldiers. The confrontation resulted in more casualties among civilians and protesters than among the police. The US occupation established martial law in the central areas where the uprising became violent. Protestors attacked police stations, cut telephone lines, and committed arson and murder. Both the US military and the Korean media highlighted the violent aspects of this uprising. In Hadong, in the Kyŏngsang area, a hundred people attacked the police substation and took guns and ammunition. Six hundred people occupied the Yangsan police station, seriously injured two policemen, and took two guns and thirty bullets. In Pusan, a police station lost thirty-one guns and six hundred bullets. In Chinju, four hundred and fifty people robbed the police station of three guns and forty boxes of shot powder and so on.[116] The police department stated that the CIC and G2 received secret reports that private armies were being organized in Kunsan and other areas.

The US occupation leaders targeted the "propagandists" as having fomented violence behind the scenes. Calling them "agitators," "anarchists," and "liars," John Hodge seemed almost obsessed with explaining the falsity of their messages on the US occupation. He broadcast his speeches on the radio and said that the food stock in southern Korea was low; he had been making great efforts to "get food shipped to Korea" and had prohibited "Korean food stocks to leave Korea or be eaten by the Americans." With great hostility, he accused the "agitators" of using "the food situation as a basis to tell vicious lies designated to stir good Korean people into mass violence."[117]

The military governor Lerch also criticized a party of "propagandists" who were provoking violent incidents in southern Korea. Like Hodge, he argued that food shortage was fundamental in this crisis. He asked Korean farmers to cooperate with the government and make rice available to feed all Koreans in the south. Protestors targeted the police because they were assisting the government's rice collection. In Northern Kyŏngsang, the local police took charge of collecting summer grains in 1946. Lerch acknowledged the deep resentment of Koreans toward the conduct of the police during the colonial period. He claimed that the police had been reformed under the military government, which did not run the "high police" for political oppression; in addition, fewer than 20 percent of current policemen had been in the colonial police. These former colonial policemen could accept democratic ideas, Lerch insisted. He promised to purge those who were deeply Japanized in thought and behavior.[118]

The October Uprisings shocked Korean society after colonialism. The cruelty of the violence left Koreans at a loss. If they were dissatisfied with the US military government, the author of an article asked, why did they try to get something by shedding the blood of their fellow citizens?[119] Even though the organizers of the incident were arrested, this could not bring back the people who had been drawn into the pit of death, the author lamented.[120] The media were also sympathetic, stating that the true reasons for the Taegu uprising lay in the difficult living situations of Koreans. They were bitterly disillusioned about liberation. If the people had not been suffering from unbelievable hardships of life, a columnist wrote, they could not have been mindlessly stirred up by agitations.[121]

In the face of the strong rural resistance, the US military leaders and Korean elites debated whether the US military government should continue rice collection. Most Korean leaders—even the minister of agriculture of the military government Lee Hun-gu, who held a PhD from Columbia University in New York—argued that Korea must have surplus rice because it was no longer sending several million bags of rice to Japan each year. However, the US military reassessed the total rice production in Korea and concluded that this abundance of Korean rice was a myth. *The History of the United States Army Military Government in Korea* states:

> True it was that no rice was to be exported to Japan, but the Military Government was unaware that Koreans had come to consider rice a luxury grain and had depended for the bulk of their diet on other grains which were imported from China and Manchuria ... the sad fact emerged that Korea was simply not a food surplus country. Even if no rice had been smuggled to Japan, and if all hoarded supplies had been brought to the market, there still would have been barely enough rice for Korean needs.[122]

The Japanese Empire had privileged the Japanese by transferring Korean rice to Japan and in doing so had created the myth of a rice surplus in Korea. Korean leaders had internalized this rhetoric and repeated this premise in attempting to solve the rice crisis under the US occupation. Lerch received many petitions from Korean leaders. The petitioners agreed at one point that they had plenty of rice in Korea. Lerch thought that this optimism had made Koreans fall prey to bad propagandists. He explained that grain was in short supply. The main reason was the lack of fertilizer during and after the war. Agricultural production per square mile had decreased. Second, more than two million Koreans had repatriated to South Korea by the fall 1946. Third, the trade routes for importing grains from Manchuria were shut down.[123] According to US assessment, the rice demand in South Korea should be more than twenty-five million *sŏk* for liberal consumption, but the harvests in 1946 were only twelve or thirteen million *sŏk*. Therefore, to stop famine, the government collection of rice was inevitable.[124]

Eventually, the US eased the rice crisis through forcible rice collection, food aid, and imports of foreign rice from Brazil, California, Burma, and elsewhere. One of the main differences between the Japanese colonial rule and the US occupation in Korea was the latter's material abundance and its generous allocation of resources to alleviate Korea's internal and external crises. The wartime grain trade of Japan was directed to maintain the economic and political hierarchy of the empire and its stability. It supplied Manchurian millet to Korea in order to transfer Korean rice to Japanese consumers and imperial soldiers on the battlegrounds. Japan's wartime administration did not drop the role of extracting resources for the empire even while it invested some resources in its colonies and occupied areas. In comparison, the US occupation, at least in postwar Korea, did not consider Korea's economic value significant to their Korea policy. They were more concerned to make Korea's new regime compatible with the ideological orientations of the United States. The US government approved aid of $2,500 million to the US military government. Korean leftists argued that the sum would be Korea's debt, but Hodge denied this.[125] The Associated Press reported that the International Emergency Food Relief Committee was allocating 50,000 tons of food to Korea and 245,000 tons to China.[126] Large-scale rural protests did not recur in 1947 and 1948. Armed conflicts occurred on Cheju and in Yŏsu-Sunchŏn, but the characteristics of these protests differed from those of the harvest uprisings of 1946. The military government stated that it had never sent rice to the United States or Japan and that it was importing 32,000 tons of grain monthly from the United States. The military government set the total goal of rice collection at 4,358,000 *sŏk* and divided that into provincial goals. They were: North Chŏlla, 798,000 *sŏk*; Southern Chŏlla, 750,000; Southern Kyŏngsang, 600,000; Northern Kyŏngsang, 720,000; Northern Ch'ungchŏng,

180,000; Southern Ch'ungch'ŏng, 470,000; Kyŏnggi, 775,000; Kangwŏn, 600,000; and Cheju, 5,000.[127]

The collection goal was 50 percent of the quantity imposed by the wartime colonial government. Once the collection was over, farmers could sell rice to anyone who was not an illegal trader. The military government spent approximately 20 million wŏn to make up the budget deficit. They bought rice in the countryside at a high price and rationed it in cities at a low price.[128] This US policy gave farmers some room to sell some surplus rice on the market, so the market trade of rice gradually recovered.[129] Lerch repeated that the military government's objective was not to lose a single Korean life to famine that winter.[130] The Korean media supported this rhetoric.

From spring 1947 on, rice, clothing, firewood, and other goods were abundant in the markets. However, the problem was the lower buying power of citizens due to inflation, low wages, and unemployment. A relatively stable ration made the rice price decline and rice was available in the market, but the price did not dip below 510 wŏn per *tu* (*mal*).[131] More articles now criticized the government about the high price of goods. The supply of rice and necessities was great, but their prices were too high for citizens to afford.[132]

Individual rice accounts began to be issued on April 1, 1947.[133] In February 1947, Seoul city prepared to issue resident cards to citizens to determine the population trends and for future elections. Those who were fifteen years and older registered themselves, while younger people were registered by their head of household. In addition, rice accounts were issued to individuals rather than to families. These resident cards and individual rice accounts were aimed at reducing the country's "ghost population."[134] The arrival of 4,500 tons of rice from Burma was reported. About 50,000 tons were to be imported from Indochina, Brazil, Burma, and Thailand, approximately 9 tons of which had already arrived in Korea.[135]

The newspapers reported that 0.48 million tons of food and grain were imported from the United States—180,848 tons in 1946 and 304,605 tons from January to August 1947. The newspaper *Tonga Ilbo* worried about the damage to Korea's agricultural base.[136] Such a massive supply of grain stabilized the higher rice price during the rainy season and changed the psychology of consumers and rice owners. The price went down again in August 1947.[137] The military government recovered the original quantity of the daily ration—2 *hop* and 5 *chak*.[138] Rice collection in 1947 was much better. The purchasing price increased. A press observation team visited Southern Chŏlla to report on the atmosphere there. In comparison to the protests in October 1946, farmers understood the government's policy and cooperated with the rice collection. In Northern

Chŏlla, the submission of spring crops was 100 percent complete by mid-August, while Southern Chŏlla finished it by mid-September. The quotas for fall harvest collection were not yet set. But the governor was confident about achieving the collection goal without many difficulties.[139] This relative success of rice collection in 1947 and 1948 indicates that the rural society offered a certain degree of cooperation with the US occupation and created order from the resentful protests in 1946.

Conclusion

The popular unrest in Korea in 1946 was a reaction to the chaotic transition from the Japanese wartime system. It was paradoxical that the rice crisis restored the role of local neighborhood associations without provoking many political accusations of pro-Japanese collaboration. Despite the national agenda to purge collaborators, this issue was compartmentalized from everyday administrative efforts to solve the food crisis. Women in neighborhood associations led rice protests in many urban areas. Further study is needed to clarify the leadership of the rural uprisings and their directions. I assume that the existing village associations played a certain role in both the harvest uprisings and the subsequent rice collection by the military government. The type of mass protests seen in 1946 were not repeated in 1947 and 1948.

The US occupation inherited the institutions of Japan's wartime system and had to deal with the psychology, mythology, and expectations of Koreans who had lived through Japan's wartime mobilization. Korea's transition from the wartime system unfolded in many areas, and the food crisis in 1946 was a symptom of such transition. The US occupation did not understand how Korea's food economy had been subordinated to the imperial trade network or how the colonial state had regulated almost all Korean actors in the government-controlled system to procure resources for the war. To solve the subsistence crisis it therefore had on its hands, the US occupation restored some wartime policies, practices, and mobilizational networks. Simultaneously, the US military government and its officials tried to "reform" the existing institutions and behavior of Koreans according to their own ideological orientation. The material abundance of the United States made the transition possible, albeit gradual. Under the US occupation, various institutions were modified, hybridized, and created, and they together formed a postcolonial regime in Korea.

For instance, even though the US occupation endorsed the administrative role of the neighborhood associations, US military officials wanted to ensure that the associations had "democratic" characteristics. In October 1946, the governor of Kyŏnggi Province, Colonel Anderson, wrote a document entitled "How an Election Is Held," which described how the government was to guide neighborhood associations to hold an election and vote on certain issues. First, the government was to hold a meeting of prefecture magistrates. They would be given information as to what would be voted on and then received the printed and sample ballots. Then the magistrates were to call a meeting of county heads (*myŏnjang*) and give them the same information. Next, the county heads would hold a meeting of subcounty heads (*kujang*), who in turn called the heads of the neighborhood associations (*panjang*). Each neighborhood association unit (*pan*) consisted of about ten families. The neighborhood associations were to hold an election, and each head of a member family was to vote.[140] The military government indeed held an election to choose the heads of neighborhood associations. In December 1946, 556 heads of county (*tong*) neighborhood associations were elected in Seoul, and 8 county heads refused to have elections. Hodge supposedly removed these heads who refused to hold elections.[141]

Some of these county heads were conservative, but their use of neighborhood associations for political objectives was prohibited and punished if discovered. For instance, one county head forced the members of that county's neighborhood associations to pay 100 wŏn each to Syngman Rhee in support of his travels. Such contributions required the permission of the police, and the head's behavior was investigated by the city government.[142] In another case, in the election of legislators, several newspapers printed an advertisement, in the name of the alliance of the county neighborhood associations, nominating nationalist politicians, including a leader of the Korean provisional government named Cho So-ang. The county association alliance made an official announcement that this was the act of several county heads, not the consensus of the association.[143]

How the people's committees coped with this restoration of neighborhood associations and their enhanced representation by election remains to be studied. This change may well have challenged the status of the people's committees and created complicated political situations in many local areas. The story told in this chapter is more complex than the US occupation's choice of pro-Japanese collaborators over members of the leftist people's committees. I suppose that such restoration of neighborhood associations in different forms also occurred in North Korea under the Soviet occupation.[144]

Notes

1. On moral economy, see James C. Scott, *The Moral Economy of the Peasant: Rebellion and Subsistence in Southeast Asia* (New Haven, CT: Yale University Press, 1976); E. P. Thompson, "The Moral Economy of the English Crowd in the Eighteenth Century," *Past & Present* 50 (February 1971): 76–136.
2. John Hodge, "Conditions in Korea," September 13, 1945, from John R. Hodge, *Mi kunjŏnggi chŏngbo charyojip*, vol. 3 (Ch'unch'ŏn: Hallim Taehakkyo Asia Munhwa Yŏn'guso, 1995).
3. H. Merrell Benninghoff, "The Present Situation in Korea," September 15, 1945, from Hodge, *Mi kunjŏnggi chŏngbo charyojip*, vol. 3.
4. Hodge wrote,

   The best way to describe southern Korea at present is to state that the area is a powder keg ready to explode upon application of a spark. I discovered today that Korean translations, including translations of the proclamations, have translated the words "in due course" announced in the Cairo Agreement to the words or meaning "in a few days" or "very soon" … This thought of immediate independence and immediate sweeping out of the Japs has dominated their minds. Disappointment in the fact that there is any delay is great. (Hodge, "Conditions in Korea," September 13, 1945)

5. Bruce Cumings, *The Origins of the Korean War*, 2 vols. (Princeton, NJ: Princeton University Press, 1981–1990).
6. Gi-Wook Shin, "The Historical Making of Collective Action: The Korean Peasant Uprisings of 1946," *American Journal of Sociology* 99, no. 6 (May 1994): 1596–624.
7. Kazuo Hori, "The Formation of Capitalism in East Asia," in *Economic Activities under the Japanese Empire*, ed. Minoru Sawai (Japan: Springer, 2016), 24–5.
8. Yusuke Takeuchi, "The Shifting Axis of Specialization within the Japanese Empire: A Study of Railway Distribution of Cereals in Colonial Korea," in Sawai, *Economic Activities under the Japanese Empire*, 52.
9. Ibid., 55.
10. Kim Sŏn-mi, "1930 nyŏndae migok chŏngch'aek kwa singminji chijuje ŭi chŏn'gae," *Pusan Sahak* 18 (1994): 501–2.
11. Ibid., 504–6.
12. Ugaki Kazushige Bunsho (hereafter UB), "kibi shinshun ni okeru jikyoku taikan" (February 1943), file no. 234. This document is located in Modern Japan Political History Materials Room, the National Diet Library of Japan.
13. UB, "shokan no henei" (July 1943), file no. 244.
14. "Chosŏn hanhae taech'aek kwa kuje sanghwang ŭl sŏlmyŏng," *Maeil Sinbo* (hereafter MS), February 24, 1940.

15 Yi Song-sun, *Ilcheha chŏnsi nongŏp chŏngch'aek kwa nongch'on kyŏngje* (Seoul: Sŏnin, 2008), 66.
16 Oda Yoshiyuki, *Sengo Shokuryō Gyōsei No Kigen: Senchū, Sengo No Shokuryō Kiki o Meguru Seiji to Gyōsei* (Tōkyō: Keiō Gijuku Daigaku Shuppankai, 2012), 13–18.
17 Ibid., 20–34.
18 Ibid., 65–70.
19 "Osu e ssalgigŭn," *Tonga Ilbo* (hereafter TI), May 31, 1939; "Osu chibang paengmika p'oktŭng," TI, June 1, 1939.
20 "Miga poda p'oktŭng hanŭn chapkok," TI, June 12, 1939.
21 "Namjosŏnmi tannyŏmhago sinsŏk esŏ ilmi iip," TI, June 19, 1939.
22 "Ssal kigŭn," TI, June 27, 1939.
23 "Chŏngmi hanch'ŏn p'oktŭng," TI, July 8, 1939.
24 "Maejŏm maesŏk ŭl chŏltae kŭmji," TI, July 15, 1939.
25 "Kyŏngsŏng ŭi miga chojŏlch'aek wansŏng," TI, July 16, 1939.
26 Ibid.
27 "Ssal kigŭn ap'yŏn chŏrŏm milmaemae," TI, August 10, 1939.
28 Yi Song-sun, *Ilcheha chŏnsi nongŏp chŏngch'aek kwa nongch'on kyŏngje*, 85.
29 The imperial ordinance of the governor-general of Korea, no. 23, enacted on September 27, 1939.
30 "Taemang ŭi kyŏngsŏng yŏnchwi kŭm 4 il e kaejangsik," MS, January 5, 1940.
31 "Singnyang hwakpo e kangnyŏkhan kukkajŏk t'ongje wansŏng," TI, December 28, 1939.
32 "Kunbu en ilindang sadu kyŏngsŏng inch'ŏn ŭn p'aldu," MS, January 12, 1940.
33 "Migok sojiryang ch'ŏngju kun esŏ chosa," MS, January 19, 1940.
34 "Chŏnsŏn e chŏngbi toen singnyang paegŭp kiku hyŏnhwang," MS, February 1, 1940.
35 Ibid.; "Tonae migok chŏnbu maesang chŏnp'yo na hogŭn t'ongjangje ro pogŭp," MS, February 2, 1940; "Migok t'ongje wiban t'ongch'ŏnsŏ ŏmjung ch'wije," MS, February 5, 1940.
36 "Kongnyŏn pandae kaeŭich'i anko kijŏng pangch'im taero," MS, January 30, 1940.
37 "Singnyang munje wa chosŏnmi," MS, January 7, 1940.
38 Chŏn Kang-su, "1940 nyŏndae han'guk ŭi migok t'ongje chŏngch'aek: haebang chŏnhugan ŭi pikyo punsŏk ŭl chungsimŭro," *Kyŏngje Sahak* 19 (December 1995): 226; Yi Song-sun, *Ilcheha chŏnsi nongŏp chŏngch'aek kwa nongch'on kyŏngje*, 103.
39 "Singnyang munje wa chosŏnmi," MS, January 10, 1940.
40 "Tonae migok chŏnbu maesang," MS, February 3, 1940.
41 The imperial ordinance of the government-general of Korea, no. 44, enacted on August 9, 1943.

42 "Singnyangsobi rŭl hamnihwa," MS, March 24, 1942; "Kakpu sanŏppujang sojip singnyang munje hyŏpŭi," MS, March 24, 1942; "Singnyang ŭi kin'gŭp ch'aek hwangnip," MS, April 9, 1942.
43 "Pujŏng migok maech'ulp'yo ŏmsa," MS, March 31, 1942.
44 "Singnyang kwallipŏp ilbu chŏgyong," MS, July 2, 1942.
45 "Migok ŏpcha chŏngni munje," MS, August 16, 1942.
46 "Migok somaejŏm haptong ŭl kyehoek," MS, June 17, 1942.
47 "Tan'gok tanch'e paegŭp p'yeji," MS, June 26, 1942.
48 Yi Chong-min, "Chŏnsiha aegukpan chojik kwa tosi ui ilsangt'ongje," *Tongbang Hakchi* 124 (2004): 840–5.
49 Higuchi Yūichi, "Taiheiyō sensō ka no josei dōin- aikokuhan o chusinni," *Chōsen Shi Kenkyūkai ronbunshū* 32 (1994): 119–38. Translated in Korean by Hong Chong pi'l, "T'aep'yŏngyang chŏnjaengjung ilche ŭi yŏsŏng dongwŏn," *Myŏngji Saron* 10 (1999): 32.
50 Yi Chong-min, "Chŏnsiha aegukpan chojik kwa tosi ui ilsangt'ongje," 873.
51 "Migok kongch'ul ch'ongnyŏkjŏn," MS, May 11, 1942.
52 "Kŭmnyŏndo singnyangjŏn e igija," MS, January 9, 1945.
53 "Tomin ŭn punt'uhara," MS, January 10, 1945.
54 "Migok kongch'ul hyŏnji pogo: ch'ungbukp'yŏn," MS, January 21, 1945.
55 Ibid.
56 "Migok kongch'ul hyŏnji pogo: kyŏngbuk p'yŏn," MS, January 21, 1945.
57 USAMGIK, *History of the United States Army Military Government in Korea* [microform], compiled 1946–1948 (Washington, DC: Library of Congress, Photoduplication Service, 1977), vols 3 and 4, chapter 6, 16.
58 Hodge, "Conditions in Korea," September 13, 1945.
59 GHQ/SCAP Records, RG 331, box no. 6432, folder no. 10, "Rice Situation in Korea," December 15, 1945.
60 GHQ/SCAP Records, RG 331, box no. 6432, folder no. 10, From: Central Liaison Office, Tokyo, to General Headquarters of the Supreme Commander for Allied Forces, "Importation of Rice from Korea for Coal Miners," December 13, 1945.
61 "Yanggok kwa sit'an ponaera," TI, December 6, 1945.
62 Ibid.
63 "Miguk ch'urŏk paektae suip," TI, December 7, 1945.
64 "Ssal taeil milsuch'ul malla," TI, December 7, 1945.
65 "Chosŏnmi rŭl milgam kwa kyohwanhan," TI, February 7, 1946.
66 "Kŏmsadae tongwŏn maejŏm mich'anggo chŏkpal," TI, December 9, 1945; "P'alchŏnsŏk ŭnnik haetta t'allo," TI, December 10, 1945.
67 "P'alchŏnsŏk ŭnnik haetta t'allo," TI, December 10, 1945.
68 Ibid.
69 "Hyujit'ong," TI, January 3, 1946.

70 "Chŏngjo kangje maesang ŭl silsi," TI, February 2, 1946.
71 "Singnyang paegŭp silsi kyŏlchŏng," TI, January 19, 1946.
72 "Yanggok ŭn ikkŏnman paegŭp chiji," TI, January 6, 1946.
73 "Singnyang paegŭp silsi kyŏlchŏng," TI, January 19, 1946.
74 "Chosŏnmi sŏilbon ŭro," TI, January 31, 1946.
75 "Hyujit'ong," TI, January 5, 1946; "Kansang ŭi ŭnnikmi kangbang," TI, January 15, 1946.
76 "3 wŏl 15 il kkaji p'alsimmansŏk sujip," TI, February 5, 1946.
77 Ibid.
78 Ibid.
79 "Tado waŭi migok unban ŭl ŏmgŭm," TI, February 10, 1946.
80 "Akchil moribae en sahyŏng," TI, February 11, 1946.
81 "Kakpan ŭl t'onghayŏ paegŭphara," TI, February 12, 1946.
82 Ibid.
83 "Hyujit'ong," TI, February 4, 1946.
84 "Mi kongjŏngga ch'ŏlp'yehara," TI, February 13, 1946.
85 "Chayu pan'gok hŏyonghara," TI, February 13, 1946.
86 "Harodo yŏyu tulsu ŏmnŭn," TI, February 17, 1946.
87 "Ch'aeso wa kwasil mŏgŭra," TI, September 19, 1946.
88 "Han'gang yŏnan e haejŏksŏn ch'ulmol," TI, March 5, 1946.
89 "Singnyang paegŭp pangch'im kunjŏngch'ŏng t'ŭkpyŏl pangch'im," TI, March 14, 1946.
90 "Ch'ulp'an nodongjohap ŭi purŭjijŭm," TI, March 22, 1946.
91 "Singnyang ŭi wigi rŭl kŭkpokhara," TI, March 30, 1946.
92 "Wigi e chingmyŏn!" TI, March 30, 1946.
93 "Ssal tallago kunjŏngch'ŏng e swaedo," TI, March 30, 1946.
94 "Tŭrŏnna, ssal tallanŭn ausŏng sori!" TI, March 30, 1946.
95 "Kigŭn! Ssal dao ssal," TI, April 2, 1946.
96 Ibid.
97 "Aeso ŭi yŏnsoksŏn," TI, April 3, 1946.
98 "Hyujit'ong," TI, April 4, 1946.
99 "Hanhap tchari ŭnggŭmmi p'alil putŏ ilche paegŭp," TI, April 5, 1946.
100 Ibid.
101 "Chang kyŏngch'al pujang tam," TI, April 5, 1946.
102 "Nakhasan t'an ssal kap," TI, April 9, 1946; "Ssal ssal naerinŭn ssalgap," TI, April 25, 1946.
103 "Singnyang yŏng ŭi paengmi panch'ul," TI, July 23, 1946.
104 "Hŏga toenŭn chayu panip," TI, April 10, 1946.
105 Ibid.
106 "Hagok sujip ŭl kanghaeng hara," TI, August 8, 1946; "Hoengsŏl susŏl," TI, August 10, 1946.

107 "P'agoe nŭn tongnip ŭl panghae," TI, November 11, 1946; "Ssal sujp, ch'ungnam ŭn wŏllaero kakto ŭi ch'ian taegae hwakpo," *Kyŏng Hyang Sinmun* (hereafter KH), November 22, 1946.
108 "Sŏndongga ŭi ŏnhaeng ŭl taejung ŭn kamsihara," TI, September 3, 1946.
109 "Singnyang nan haegyŏl ŭi haeksim ŭn?" KH, October 8, 1946. The US permission of rice carries was suspended during the collection period.
110 "Migok chŏngch'aek ŭi chaegŏmt'o rŭl yomang," TI, October 12, 1946.
111 "Hwaktaehwa hanŭn kakchi soyo," TI, October 11, 1946; "Pubunjŏk ŭro misin," KH, October 11, 1946.
112 Thomas H. Lee, "The Origins of the Taegu Insurrection of 1946" (Harvard, BA Honors thesis, 1990), 97–8.
113 Cumings, *The Origins of the Korean War*.
114 Lee, "The Origins of the Taegu Insurrection of 1946," 13.
115 Gi-Wook Shin, "The Historical Making of Collective Action."
116 "Hwantae hanŭn kakchi soyo," TI, October 11, 1946.
117 John Hodge, "Warning against Agitators and Propagandists," October 14, 1946, from Hodge, *Mi kunjŏnggi chŏngbo charyojip*, vol. 3. This statement was delivered on radio.
118 "Kakto e haltang han ssal sujip ŭn myŏngnyŏn 2 wŏl 15 il kkajiro," TI, October 16, 1946.
119 "Hoengsŏl susŏl," TI, October 17, 1946.
120 Ibid.
121 "Yŏjŏk," KH, October 20, 1946.
122 USAMGIK, *History of the United States Army Military Government in Korea* [microform], vols. 3 and 4, chapter 6, 36–7.
123 "Sujip ŭn paegŭp ŭi mot'ae," TI, October 24, 1946.
124 Ibid.; "Namjosŏn ŭi singnyang taech'aek e taehaya lŏch'wi changgwan sŏngmyŏng," KH, October 24, 1946.
125 "P'agoe nŭn tongnip ŭl panghae," TI, November 12, 1946.
126 "Namchosŏn e ssal omant'on paejŏng," KH, January 14, 1947.
127 "Ssal sujip mokp'yo nŭn sasamoman p'alch'ŏn sŏk," TI, October 18, 1946.
128 "Ssal kongch'ul e ch'aegim suryang tahamyŏn chayu maemae hŏgahanda," TI, October 16, 1946.
129 Chŏn Kang-su, "1940 nyŏndae han'guk ŭi migok t'ongje chŏngch'aek: haebang chŏnhugan ŭi pikyo punsŏkŭl chungsimŭro," *Kyŏngje Sahak* 19 (1995): 229–31.
130 "Kia rŭl ŏpsi hagi wiham i ssal sujip kyehoewk ŭi iyu," KH, October 12, 1946.
131 "Ŏlmana ttŏrŏjŏnna," TI, March 4, 1947.
132 "Chŏkpal munje ŏdero? Tŭnnŭnga?" TI, March 6, 1947; "Ssal kapsŭn chŏrak toeŏ choŭna," KH, March 22, 1947; "Chŏrak ilto ŭi miga," TI, March 29, 1947.
133 "T'ongjang kaeinbyŏllo 4 wŏl 1 ilbut'ŏ sijak," TI, March 13, 1947; "Kaeinbyŏl t'ongjang silsi," KH, March 13, 1947.

134 "Simin ege kongminjŭng, ssal t'ongjangdo kaeinbyŏllo," TI, February 12, 1947.
135 "Piruma esŏ ssal sach'ŏnt'on," TI, May 18, 1947.
136 "Miguk sŏ kajŏon singnyang 48 mant'on tolp'a," TI, August 26, 1947.
137 "Ssal 560 wŏn taero chŏrak," TI, August 31, 1947.
138 "Sŏulsi singnyang chŭngbaeryang," KH, September 5, 1947; "12 hoebun ssal paegŭp chongjŏn taero 2 hap 5 chak," TI, September 5, 1947.
139 "Namchosŏn hyŏnji pogo," TI, September 13, 1947.
140 Charles A. Anderson, "How an Election Is Held in Korea," October 1, 1946, from Hodge, *Mi kunjŏnggi chŏngbo charyojip*.
141 "Paniphan changjak ŭn semin e paegŭp," KH, December 19, 1946.
142 Ibid.
143 "Ch'ongŭi nŭn anida," KH, December 21, 1946.
144 Suzy Kim, "Revolutionary Mothers: Women in the North Korean Revolution, 1945–1950," *Comparative Studies in Society and History* 52, no. 4 (2010): 749–50.

2

Colonial Militarism in Transwar East Asia: Indigenous Forces and the Three Waves of Militarization

Victor Louzon

In Japanese political culture, militarism seems to be an indisputable casualty of 1945: despite the transwar continuities highlighted in this volume, it would be hard to deny that the power and prestige of the military declined drastically in postwar Japan, under the combined effects of American occupation, traumatic war memories, growing pacifism, and the outsourcing of national security to the United States. Nonetheless, this account is roughly accurate only if we forget that Japan had an empire. Shifting focus from the former metropole to its erstwhile possessions in East Asia yields a strikingly different picture: while Japan was entering its interminable "postwar" (*sengo*), Taiwan, Korea, and Northeast China (Manchuria) experienced into the 1950s and even 1960s intense processes of militarization, if by that term we mean state attempts to diffuse in society values and modes of behavior associated with modern armies. To be sure, these processes responded to the geopolitical and political conditions of the early Cold War in East Asia. In some respects, however, they also built upon late colonial developments.

Indeed, mere repression and exploitation do not capture the range of transformations brought about by "total war" (*sōryokusen*) in the colonies. Militarism and empire were intimately connected: Louise Young has shown that the conquest of Manchuria was a laboratory and a catalyst for "hyper-militarism" at home.[1] But there was also an ambitious effort at exporting this militarism to Japan's colonies—among colonized subjects themselves, not only Japanese settlers. In the past decade, research has devoted more attention to this enterprise.[2] I argue that its breadth allows us to speak of a shift toward "colonial militarization" (considered as a process) or "colonial militarism" (considered as a project). In these territories, militarization should thus be considered a transwar (and, accordingly, transimperial) phenomenon, stretching at least from the 1930s to the 1950s.

But the colonial era proper, though decisive, was a moment in a longer trajectory. To appreciate the turn in colonial policy in the 1930s, as well as understand the ideas it tapped into, its relative success, and its longer-term effects, we need to go yet further back in time. It was the period of the First Sino-Japanese War that saw the concurrent and connected emergence of militarization projects and Japanese imperialism in East Asia. For our purpose, Carter Eckert's idea of "three waves" of militarization can therefore be extended from Korea (to which he applied it) to East Asia writ large. Each wave corresponded to an episode of war mobilization as well as a transformation of imperial relations in the region; despite these ebbs and flows, each wave also built upon the previous one.

This chapter traces this history, building on secondary and primary source research. In order to narrow down my field of inquiry, I will mostly focus on a central feature of militarization: the training of colonial populations for war in Korea, Taiwan, and Manchukuo, particularly the recruitment of colonial soldiers and to a lesser extent paramilitaries, as well as the transwar trajectory of these men and policies.[3]

The First Wave of Militarization in East Asia and the Era of Japanese Hegemony

At the end of the nineteenth century, East Asia was engulfed in a "global wave of militarization."[4] In an increasingly competitive and dangerous international environment, two beliefs spread among reformist or revolutionary political and intellectual leaders in Japan, China, and Korea: first, that armies had to be reformed on the model of European militaries; second, that societies needed to be imbued with the virtues of discipline, dedication, and vigor associated with modern armies. This militarization of political imaginaries was most precocious and thorough in late Meiji Japan, where influential authors elaborated, in the late 1880s and the 1890s, a neo-traditional ideology presenting Japan as an inherently martial nation endowed with the spirit of *bushidō*.[5] Yet the phenomenon was pan-East Asian in scope. The disastrous First Sino-Japanese War of 1894–1895 convinced many Chinese reformers, inside and outside government circles, that it was necessary to create "New Armies" and use them as a crucible to make the whole male population more capable and willing to take up arms for their country, like Japan had done.[6] Similarly, in Korea, China's defeat empowered those reformers who wished to strengthen the army, "seen increasingly as a repository of martial virtues that were valuable, indeed indispensable, for personal character development and for the preservation and development of the nation, both conceived largely in hypermasculinized terms."[7] Japan played a central role in this process: as a successful model of military modernization, as a threat, and as a filter for Western ideas, translated and adapted into a "Sino-Japanese lexicon" (J. Fogel) easily appropriated by Chinese and Korean elites.

Despite this entanglement, late-Meiji promoters of militarization reactivated and radicalized the long-standing idea that Japan's "martial nature" made it stand apart from its Chinese and Korean neighbors' excessive and debilitating focus on "civilian" qualities. Somewhat like the *Kultur* of the German bourgeoisie (as opposed to the *Zivilisation* of the Frenchified aristocracy) in Norbert Elias's classic analysis, the purported *bushidō* tradition of the Japanese samurai class was reimagined as a "national" attribute—universal within Japan's boundaries, absent without.[8] Furthermore, this exceptionalism provided one rationalization among many for Japan's superiority and sometimes rule over its neighbors. *Bushidō* theorists were often proponents of imperial expansion: in a dog-eat-dog world where national survival was predicated on military strength abroad and disciplined patriotism at home, the argument went, a-martial peoples were less qualified to self-govern.[9]

Japan, the fountainhead of East Asian militarization, thus actively thwarted this very militarization process in its newly acquired colonial territories, Taiwan and Korea. In Taiwan, ceded by the Qing Empire in 1895, the fledgling reform of the Chinese Army was nipped in the bud by the Japanese takeover. In Korea, this first wave of militarization was interrupted after the Japanese protectorate was established, culminating in the abolition of the Korean Army in 1907. Colonial authorities prudently abstained from training the Taiwanese and Korean populations for war. They did make use of local auxiliaries in their pacification of Taiwan and Korea, but those were progressively replaced by the police, led by Japanese officers; the military proper was kept a purely Japanese institution. Although security concerns drove this disarmament, it also had broader ideological and political ramifications. Izawa Shūji, the first minister of academic affairs under the Government-General of Taiwan (GGT), pleaded against applying the Meiji Constitution to—hence imposing conscription on—the colony invoking cultural differences. The poor reception of Japanese textbooks, he argued, was due to the fact that they glorified militarism, a value anathema to the island's Han majority population, who also feared Japanese education was but a preparation for military service.[10] Such was the trade-off: the Taiwanese should neither be granted political rights nor be asked to fight for the empire.

The image of Han Chinese and Koreans as insufficiently warlike for their own good became a recurring cliché in what Takashi Fujitani calls the "vast reservoir of Japanese Orientalist knowledge." A related prejudice was that colonized men were effeminate by the militarized standards of masculinity that had spread in many industrialized societies in the late nineteenth century. Korea's long-standing subservience to great powers was said to have fostered a "diplomatic personality" type (*gaikōteki seikaku*), and Han Chinese and Koreans alike were routinely depicted as "bookish and weak" (*bunjaku*).[11] This allowed for some exceptions: for instance, a 1905 article in the *Taiwan nichi nichi shinpo*, the newspaper of the GGT, contrasted Taiwan's hakka minority with the minnan majority. The latter, the article read, have a "quiet temperament and often engage in commerce. They are of the literary type, indulge in poetry, like luxury, and are rather prone to bookish weakness (*wenruo*)." The hakka, on the other hand, "often have a fierce temper … They are farmers, do not shy away from hard labor; they can almost be said to possess the 'warrior style' (*wushi feng*) of the Japanese."[12] These flattering remarks, however, were reserved—just like in the British Empire—for a minority of "martial races."

Nor did Japanese authorities make efforts to rectify this supposed effeminacy. The promotion of martial virtues, increasingly prevalent in the metropolitan school system, was conspicuously absent from colonial education, which had distinctly Confucian, peaceful inclinations. Taiwanese schoolchildren were urged to follow the example of Wu Feng, a virtuous seventeenth-century scholar who sacrificed his life to persuade fierce autochthonous Austronesians to give up head-hunting;[13] Koreans were encouraged to see themselves as docile economic producers. This divergence continued under the so-called Taishō democracy: in the metropole, the post–First World War decline in military spending was compensated by the expansion of military training in schools; this measure did not concern the colonies, despite the pleas of Korean nationalists who thought it would serve their pre-annexation agenda of militarization.[14]

In Manchuria, where Japan held predominant influence after the Russo-Japanese War (1904–1905) but little direct political power until the 1931 invasion, military modernization continued under the stewardship of local strongman Zhang Zuolin. Yet when the state of Manchukuo was created by the Japanese

Army in 1932, its official ideology rested on the "Kingly Way," a neo-traditional ideal of government by moral example and harmony between the races. In the long run, it was supposed to make Manchukuo a "paradise" (*rakudo*) and a driving force of world peace. This implied that militaristic ideals were not to be promoted, except for Japanese settler youth: education for "Manchurians" (Chinese) mostly emphasized the region's Confucian heritage.[15] The pastoral image of the rural population that was promoted, reinforced by preexisting clichés about the Han race's distaste for military affairs, was contrasted with the depredations of the Chinese "warlords" the Japanese were claiming to save the region from.[16] The problem—and a major difference with Taiwan and Korea— was that Manchuria remained a hotbed of armed resistance and banditry until the end of the decade. Rampant insecurity and the desire to maintain the fiction of independence led the Japanese to recycle part of the surrendered Chinese Northeast Armies into a "Manchukuo Army." However, it was viewed merely as a necessary evil, and this unreliable force, whose prestige was very low, was gradually downsized in the 1930s.

Japan's East Asian Empire in the Second Wave of Militarization

This overall aversion to militarizing colonial societies changed in the 1930s, when they became increasingly mobilized in Japan's military ventures by an increasing "hyper-militarist" overlord. The initiative for this second wave of militarization came from colonial, rather than metropolitan authorities. The Japanese Korean Army seems to have first considered enrolling Korean soldiers in 1932, after the Manchurian Incident. What enabled it to overcome Tokyo's initial reticence was the full-blown invasion of China in 1937 and the support of the Government-General of Korea (GGK), which pointed out progress in the Koreans' willingness to fight for Japan, for example, in Manchuria, where their performance did not compare unfavorably with that of "metropolitans" (*naichijin*).[17] A volunteer system was created in 1938 and replaced in 1944 by military conscription. In total, between 286,000 and 367,000 Koreans (out of 24 million) served in the Imperial Army, out of which around 200,000 did as soldiers (mostly in the infantry) and the rest as porters or auxiliaries.[18]

In Taiwan as well, the enrollment of local soldiers had been advocated by some members of the conservative colonial elite since the late 1920s for reasons that echoed those of their Korean counterparts: military service was seen as a corollary of greater equality between the metropole (*naichi*) and the colony (*gaichi*). Just like in Korea, this idea was rejected by Japanese settlers and metropolitan authorities. After the Manchurian Incident, however, the Taiwan Army assumed a more assertive role in colonial affairs, as it strove to turn Taiwan into a participant in "total mobilization" (*sōdōin*). Following seventeen years of civilian rule, the position of governor-general was also placed back in military hands in 1936 with the nomination of Admiral Kobayashi Seizō. Kobayashi and the Taiwan Army successfully pushed for the recruitment of colonial soldiers, although it happened later than in Korea, for there was wariness about arming a Han Chinese population while Japan was at war in China.[19] Taiwanese porters and auxiliaries started working in the Imperial Army in 1938, a volunteer system was decided in 1941 (before Pearl Harbor) and implemented in 1942, and conscription was imposed in January 1945, partly to prepare for a potential American landing on the island. It is estimated that 207,000 Taiwanese men served as soldiers or auxiliaries.[20]

In the officially independent Manchukuo, non-Japanese were targeted for enrollment in the "national" Manchukuo Army, not the Imperial Army. However, this force underwent far-ranging transformations in the 1930s. The first Manchukuo Army, recruited among the lower classes of society, included a significant number of outlaws, its loyalty was doubtful, and it tended to perform poorly on the field. Faced with these problems, the Kwantung Army proceeded to reform it, making it, in a sense, more overtly colonial: Japanese officers poured in starting around 1935; by the end of the Second World War, they were more numerous than "Manchurian" ones from the rank of major downward.[21] Conscription was implemented in 1940. Its goal was not to recruit a large army (the number of soldiers was gradually reduced to sixty thousand in 1941, before being hastily expanded again in the last months of the war), so the experience of military service was not as widespread as in Korea or Taiwan. It was rather to improve the quality of recruits through careful selection, enhance the prestige, and improve the social makeup of the army.[22] The task of internal pacification being more or less completed by 1940, the role of this reformed military was now to protect the borders of Manchukuo and later intervene in Northern China alongside Japanese forces.

In Taiwan, Korea, and Manchukuo, the recruitment of soldiers went along with the proliferation of paramilitary organizations. The case of Youth Leagues, studied by Sayaka Chatani, is particularly telling: these organizations, which had been institutionalized in the metropole and progressively extended to

Taiwan and Korea, swelled in numbers during the Second World War. They also became increasingly militarized, with uniforms and drills becoming a feature of their members' daily life, and were turned into a tool for mobilization under conditions of total war, as well as a recruiting pool for colonial soldiers.[23]

In Manchukuo, the authorities first used existing Chinese youth organizations, themselves a legacy of East Asia's first wave of militarization. Although, in the early 1930s, one of their missions was to help maintain local order against guerillas and bandits, the authorities strove to deemphasize the militaristic element in their training, which was blamed for having fostered "xenophobic" (i.e., anti-Japanese) biases before the 1931 invasion. For instance, in Fengtian Province, the name "Children Army" (*tongzijun*), as the Chinese boy scouts were known, was deemed too bellicose: the organization was rechristened "Children Corps" (*tongzituan*) and given peaceful Mencian mottoes. "Youth Leagues" (*seinendan*), at first a blanket label given to a variety of preexisting groups, were similarly defanged.[24] For the Japanese backers of the new regime, these organizations were not meant to mobilize young men behind a nation in arms, whether Manchukuo or Japan.

This started to change around 1937, when youth groups were uniformized and brought under the umbrella of the Kyōwakai, a mass organization whose function was notably to "mobilize, train and organize the whole nation."[25] It seems, however, that in practice the mobilization of Manchukuoan youth was always geared toward production more than combat, and that the Kyōwakai did not play a major role in preparing youth for military service.[26] Nevertheless, the difference with Taiwan and Korea was more in degree than nature: in the colonies proper, labor performed by youth organizations was also presented as a type of patriotic duty, and a common feature of these structures was a pervasive militarization of organization and aesthetics.[27]

The training of colonial soldiers and expansion of paramilitary youth groups were not merely a pragmatic response to a shortage of men: as B. Palmer points out, the first measures in that direction were considered as soon as the invasion of Manchuria, *before* Japan's continental expansion put too much of a drain on the country's manpower.[28] Military and paramilitary mobilization was piece and parcel of a broader transformation of colonial policy, which one could term a "militaristic-imperial program." The movement toward more aggressive assimilationism in the 1930s is usually referred to as *kōminka* (imperialization, literally "the transformation [of colonized people] into imperial subjects"), an official term in Taiwan and Korea, also used by extension for Manchukuo. Within *kōminka*, cultural and linguistic assimilation was inseparable from two related objectives: strengthening the colonial subjects' loyalty to the emperor of Japan and turning them into enthusiastic participants in the war effort. This implied, among other things, having them incorporate the martial values promoted by the Imperial Army, in direct contradiction with the thrust of colonial education and propaganda before the 1930s but in accordance with the resurgence of *bushidō* ideology in the metropole.[29]

This major shift was particularly evident in the realm of education. In Taiwan, after the full-blown invasion of China in 1937, school curricula and "social education" (i.e. education delivered through other channels, such as youth organizations, the arts, etc.) were largely subordinated to the goal of increasing the population's "military strength" (*senryoku*); "training" (*rensei*) young minds and bodies to that purpose became an all-pervasive goal and slogan.[30] In schools, the heroic deeds (past and present) of the Imperial Army were now exalted as something Taiwanese students could be part and proud of.[31] The same process unfolded in Korea, where the GGK acceded to the elite request that military training be extended to indigenous schools in 1934. This was followed by a more pervasive militarization of education: from the late 1930s on, stories of Japanese military heroism superseded depictions of peaceful indigenous mores in textbooks, students were trained in Japanese martial arts, and school life was regimented, with uniforms and bugle calls becoming features of daily life.[32] In Manchukuo, the militaristic-imperial program existed, but it was counterbalanced both by a preexisting ideological commitment to the "Kingly Way" and by the resistance of liberal Japanese educators, so the turn was never quite as sharp as in Taiwan and Korea.[33] It was nevertheless palpable from the late 1930s and above all early 1940s. In urban schools at least, prayers for fallen soldiers and Japan's victory were introduced. Japanese military instructors became more numerous and feared, and students were asked to salute the flag and their elders and stand at attention whenever someone shouted "Long live the emperor." Boys had their heads shaven, and school uniforms were modified according to military templates.[34] As for physical education, it was reinforced with a view to strengthen young men for production and war, with Japanese martial arts now gaining pride of place in the curriculum.[35] It should be noted that the militaristic-imperial program was never applied to "puppet armies" in China proper, where the Japanese were content with absorbing preexisting forces, which they did not try to train, let alone indoctrinate.[36] In that respect too, Manchukuo, although not quite a colony, was much more closely integrated with Japan than a mere collaborationist state: it fully participated in colonial militarism, in both its practical and ideological dimensions.

War Mobilization, Militarism, and the Mutation of Colonial Relations

In the mind of its promoters, colonial militarism entailed a transformation of the relationship between the metropole and the peripheries of the empire. Fujitani has described this, for Korea, as a shift from exclusionary to inclusive practice of imperial power; the same could be said about Taiwan. In both territories, Japanese rule under conditions of war mobilization was undoubtedly more repressive than in the comparatively liberal 1920s—"cultural policy" (*bunka seiji*) in Korea, and civilian rule in Taiwan. Nonetheless, new duties (fighting for the empire at the risk of one's life) implied new rights: colonial hierarchies remained clear-cut, but some discriminatory measures were somewhat relaxed, such as the de facto prohibition of mixed marriages or school segregation. Official discourse emphasized the organic unity of metropole and colony (the term *gaichi* was abandoned in 1945), and colonial subjects were granted a modicum of political rights, culminating in the opening of seats for Korea and Taiwan in the House of Peers, although harshening authoritarianism rendered this partial enfranchisement moot. The biopolitical attention of the state was also extended to larger parts of the colonial populace, now made up of potential soldiers.[37] On paper, the status of Manchukuo relative to Japan was enhanced as well, its "sovereignty" affirmed through the abolition of extraterritoriality in 1937. However, the "unity of purpose" (*ittoku isshin*) between the two countries made this independence purely formal—and since colonial discrimination was officially nonexistent, the authorities could hardly display their generosity by reducing it.

What should be stressed is that the greater inclusiveness of colonial rule was not only due to measures meant to compensate or prepare the population for military service. To some extent, it also resided in military mobilization itself. Colonial authorities presented it as an opportunity for colonized young men to assert their worth and rightful place in the empire by demonstrating their bravery and loyalty to the emperor: the "*bushidō* spirit," long reserved to the *naichijin* and a sign of their superiority, was now an avenue theoretically open to all young men through *kōminka*.

Beyond the mere steps of drill and enrollment, this required a thorough transformation of one's self. Colonial subjects had to be guided through this conversion, in which subjective Japanization and militarization were closely intermeshed. A good example of this project is a handbook published in

Taiwan in 1944 for young indigenous men eligible for military service. Through dialogues, short texts, and letter patterns written in elementary Japanese, potential conscripts were taught how to become worthy "soldiers of the empire" (*teikoku gunjin*). This was presented not only as a patriotic duty but also a personal achievement, since the inspection assessed both a young man's physical health and his "spirit"—a staple of wartime discourse, the "Japanese spirit" (*Nippon seishin*) being the mysterious quality that would allow indigenous youth to be as one with all "Japanese men" (*Nippon danshi*). The handbook was also a tool for young men to learn Army Japanese, particularly the personal pronouns and titles which they would use in their new role.[38] As C. Eckert has shown, this "conversion" was also at the heart of training in the Manchukuo Military Academy (MMA), although it targeted a much narrower, carefully selected elite.[39]

None of this detracts from the fact that the increased brutality of Japanese rule under hyper-militarism, accompanied by exacting demands in goods and labor (including sexual labor in the case of the comfort women), was strongly resented. Nevertheless, research published in the past decade has painted a picture more complex than the resistance narratives that flourished in Korea, the Republic of China (ROC) and the People's Republic of China (PRC) after independence was regained. Projects of colonial militarization found an echo in parts of the Korean, Taiwanese, and, to a lesser extent, Manchukuoan populations. The Imperial Army had no difficulty recruiting: in Taiwan and Korea, the number of volunteers far exceeded that of available positions, and although this "volunteer fever" was partly spurred by coercion, oral history reveals that enlistment was indeed desirable for many young men. Even in Manchukuo, where enthusiasm was significantly lower (see below), applicants to military academies faced fierce competition, as the trade of arms was considered a good career after the Manchukuo Army was reformed.[40] Of course, this zeal generally had mobiles more mundane than the grandiose reasons put forward by Japanese propaganda. Joining the army in different capacities (as well as militarized youth groups, as S. Chatani has shown) was a path of upward mobility for many young men. In Korea and Taiwan, soldiers mostly hailed from farmer families (although applicants from the lowest classes were kept at bay).[41] The Japanese military opened new opportunities for them, whether in their homeland or the empire. Particularly toward the end of the war, there was also a cost of *not* joining the army, since the alternative was often conscript labor of some kind.

Enlistment also came along with a more symbolic promotion. On the one hand, the recruit's status within indigenous society was improved at several levels. The first level was generational. The militarization of colonial society went hand in hand with a state-sanctioned valorization of youth (*seinen*) that took an unprecedented intensity in the 1930s: for the promoters of *kōminka*, youth were key in transforming society in accordance with the goals of Japanization, "imperialization," and militarization. A privileged target of state mobilization and discourse via the expanding education system, they were tasked with "educating" their elders, naturally more attached to their precolonial upbringings and culture.[42] In relatively gerontocratic agrarian societies, this was a stark reversal of generational hierarchies. The second level was social and local. Being accepted in the Imperial Army was presented by the state, and experienced by many, as a proof of personal worth that conferred prestige within the local community but also accrued to that community. This was manifested in the solemn send-off parties organized by local authorities for enlisted men. For modest rural youth, such state and community recognition was much harder to come by in the 1920s: colonial militarism provided new shortcuts to social status.[43] Third, the extension of military service and *bushidō* discourse to the colonies allowed a form of revirilization: no longer presented as weak and effeminate, indigenous young men could now be accepted in the community of militarized, Japanese manliness. The price was high—joining the ranks of Japan's "expendable male bodies"[44]—but the reward not negligible.[45]

On the other hand, the militarization of colonial societies also affected the soldiers' place in the empire. Again, three dimensions can be distinguished for analytical purposes (they were closely intermeshed in practice). First, the hierarchical divide between military men and civilians, so central to Japanese hyper-militarism, never completely overrode the line between *naichijin* and indigenous subjects, but it did complicate it. For example, in Korea and Taiwan, the prestige of the military compelled policemen, even Japanese ones, to treat indigenous recruits with new respect.[46] Furthermore, there was no official racial divide in the Imperial Army, which spread indigenous soldiers in units of *naichijin*. Although the Manchukuo Army was a separate institution, it was also a multinational one, and mixing between Japanese and "Manchurians" at the company level happened toward the end of the war.[47] As for racial relations in Manchukuo's military academies, they were hierarchical and tense, but institutions such as the MMA did provide a playing field where cadets of different ethnicities could compete, a rare opportunity in the world of civilian "laymen."[48]

Second, Japan's expansion in the 1930s and early 1940s changed the relative position of its older East Asian colonies in a multilayered empire. Seiji Shirane has shown how the Southern Advance (*nanshin*) into South China and Southeast Asia turned Taiwan into a secondary imperial center.[49] This was particularly the case for those Taiwanese who served in the Imperial Army, who could sometimes experience the status of sub-imperial overlords in occupied territories.[50] This renegotiation of imperial hierarchies was also palpable in the imperial crossroads that was Manchukuo: in the military academies of the puppet state, Koreans could aspire to ranks and functions that would have remained out of reach in their native lands.[51]

Last, and least measurably, the recruitment of indigenous soldiers and the "imperial-militaristic program" that accompanied it led to a compression of colonial horizons of expectation. As Fujitani, following Dipesh Chakrabarty, stresses, the official discourse in Korea (or for that matter Taiwan) consigned colonized people to "an imaginary waiting room": they were never ready *yet* for full equality with the *naichijin*.[52] It should be emphasized that this justification of colonial hierarchies fitted the self-perception of Japan as a civilizing influence in the late Meiji period but also in the somewhat more liberal Taisho and early Showa eras: the assimilation (*dōka*) that was supposed to lead, in the minds of metropolitan and indigenous reformers, to the extension of metropolitan law to the colonies (*naichi enchō*) was thought of as a gradual progress toward modernity which primarily concerned an elite educated stratum. The anti-intellectualist ideology of hyper-militarism overturned this gradualist/elitist view of assimilation: one became an "imperial subject" not so much through arduous learning as through a leap of faith, sacrifice, and obedience that everyone was theoretically capable of. The Taiwanese author Zhou Jinbo's short story "The Volunteer Soldier" (1941) illustrates this. A friendly debate pits Zhang Minggui, who received higher education in Japan, against his less learned friend Gao Jinliu, who believes he can become Japanese by wholeheartedly performing simple rituals: "by clapping our hands, we are living a faith. It's a question of faith. It's the faith we can become fully Japanese. … We clap our hands when we accept a meal. We clap our hands when we go into battle." Finally, Gao joins the Imperial Army as a volunteer, proving the superiority of his point of view.[53]

The partial success that colonial militarism met among male youth seems to have been least evident in the Chinese majority population of Manchukuo. Anti-Japanese resentment was widespread in the Manchukuo Army and military academies, and, as a rule, the militaristic-imperial program was received with cynicism.[54] To some extent, this difference with Taiwan and Korea is induced by a bias in the sources: the narrative of anti-Japanese resistance still imposed by the PRC shapes narratives of the Manchukuo era, notably oral history.

However, even allowing for this asymmetry, distaste for Japanese-led military mobilization was clearly stronger than in the colonies proper. One reason for this discrepancy was the short duration, shaky foundations, and, consequently, more erratic violence of Japanese rule in Manchukuo: for a twenty-year-old man in 1940, Chinese rule and education was still a living memory and the demise of Japan a credible perspective. For young Koreans and Taiwanese, joining the army was a way of improving one's lot in an apparently robust Japanese order. Their "Manchurian" counterparts could hope to see the end of it. Oral history suggests that they were not impervious to the conceptions of heroism and virility conveyed by colonial militarism.[55] Nonetheless, its aesthetic appeal was probably, and its political appeal certainly, lesser than in Korea and Taiwan.

Former Colonial Soldiers in the Third Wave of Militarization

The news of Japan's surrender did not bode well for colonial soldiers, who faced a sudden and messy demobilization.[56] In Manchukuo, overrun by the Soviet Army in August 1945, superior officers were deported to Siberia and up to 150,000 soldiers were interned, although others took advantage of the chaos to flee or go underground (often as whole units).[57] In China proper, Taiwanese soldiers were sent by their new compatriots to prisoner-of-war camps, sometimes for months.[58] In Taiwan and Korea, most soldiers simply left their dissolved units and returned home. Colonial soldiers came back to impoverished homelands, where they struggled to find employment. As indigenous soldiers of a defeated and dissolved empire, they could expect no support or recognition for their sacrifice, and they experienced a steep deterioration of their social status. Worse, they bore the stigma of collaboration. From a legal perspective, it was decided they had committed no crime by fighting under the Japanese flag: Korea and Taiwan were officially Japanese, and although the ROC had never recognized the statehood of Manchukuo, it did not target its foot soldiers for prosecution (as opposed to some high-ranking bureaucrats).[59] Politically, however, they had a target on their back, and many knew it—the violence against Japanese officers that occurred upon war's end in Manchukuo was an attempt at reclaiming a kind of political virginity, as much as an expression of pent-up hatred.[60]

Nevertheless, the skills acquired under Japanese-spurred militarization soon proved useful again: sovereignty transfers, economic crisis, and the collapse of colonial police plunged postwar societies in rampant insecurity. In spite of their awkward political position, ex-soldiers or paramilitaries took matters into their own hands and consequently were not fully demobilized. In Taiwan, many joined self-defense organizations, where they found employment, a renewed role in local communities, and an opportunity to revive peer groups developed during the war.[61] In Korea, demobilized men stepped in en masse to replace demoralized police in the first weeks after the Japanese surrender. The units they formed took names reminiscent of Japanese militarization—a fresh memory—such as "youth brigades" or "self-defense brigades."[62] The authorities often had little choice but to co-opt these groups to maintain local order and/or to resist political challengers. In the course of a few months, Korean militias were tentatively brought under the purview of the "people's committees," local organs formed to prepare for independence. In Taiwan, the beleaguered Chinese police absorbed many local self-defense groups in late 1945 to early 1946.[63] In Manchuria, as soon as August 1945, Nationalist (KMT) authorities ordered what was left of Manchukuo authorities to organize surviving units of the Manchukuo Army, police, and local militias into "local [peace] preservation committees," in an attempt to thwart a complete takeover by the Communist Party (CCP), which the Soviet Army had allowed to gain a head start in the region.[64]

Indeed, militarized young men were caught up in what could be termed a third wave of militarization in East Asia. This wave closely followed the second one and involved some of the same protagonists, but its context and political stakes were different. States and contenders for state power now competed to fill the political void left by the dismantling of the Japanese Empire, a postcolonial struggle also embedded in the great power rivalry and ideological enmity of the nascent Cold War. Imperial Japan had left behind not only weapons and political chaos, but also a pool of young men and teenagers with some measure of military training and a social status damaged by postwar conditions. This made them useful for competing political forces and available for remobilization; however, their role in postwar struggles was bound to be problematic, since all major contenders claimed the mantle of anti-colonial legitimacy.

In the late 1940s, these factors played out differently in the three territories considered. This was due to the way colonial rule and militarization had been experienced but also, and more importantly, to the nature of the power struggle that followed Japan's defeat in each region. In Northeast China (Manchuria), an overt civil war pitted the KMT and the CCP: the legacy of colonial militarization was a tactical asset in the short term but a political liability for both parties. In South Korea, the new government had to build an army from scratch and faced unrest that vas violent but stopped short of civil war; it was thus both incentivized and free to redeploy the skills of ex-colonial forces against its political enemies. In Taiwan, the Chinese governorate that "liberated" the island soon proved inept; when discontent erupted in a short, spontaneous revolt, the legacy of colonial militarization was remobilized against the authorities.

Civil War and "Political Banditry" in Manchuria

China's Northeast, which concentrated Japanese industry and military equipment, became the key battlefield of the Chinese civil war. Ex-colonial forces were a precious asset in its first phase: the efficiency of Japanese repression had left few other available fighters, while both the KMT and the CCP lacked adequate forces in that region. The KMT government claimed the allegiance of surviving Manchukuo Army units, by and large successfully, since most officers recognized their legitimacy and were anti-communist. Recycling collaborationist forces nonetheless posed a political problem. It was justified by framing the civil war as the prolongment of the War of Resistance: since the "red bandits" were attacking the motherland on behalf of their Soviet masters, the very limited purge of puppet forces was a patriotic laxness. Fighting the communists was even presented as a way to "make amends" (*zixin*) for former Manchukuo soldiers.[65]

The CCP railed against these "underground armies" (*dixiajun*), but it could not, at first, shun this source of manpower either: when they entered Manchuria, communist troops absorbed at least seventy-five thousand ex-Manchukuo soldiers, who made up as much as 40 percent of some units (ex-Manchukuo paramilitaries and police also joined various communist-led militias).[66] They were eager to find new employment, and communist leaders wondered at the ease with which they recruited in the Northeast: as the joke went, a non-commissioned officer who took a bathroom break found his platoon constituted when he returned.[67]

It turned out this was building on shaky grounds: after the National Army entered Manchuria in November 1945, and even more after the Soviet Army left in the spring of 1946, many Manchukuo officers rebelled with their men. The communists replied with fierce counterinsurgency campaigns against "political bandits" (*zhengzhi tufei*), a disqualifying term used to refer to ex-Manchukuo forces, local militias, and outlaws loyal to the KMT. Now, the past of ex-Manchukuo soldiers was held against them more systematically.

For example, in Tonghua, near the Korean border, communist authorities still invited them to make amends (*zixin*) by joining their forces in November 1945. After some of them (along with demobilized Japanese soldiers), spurred by KMT agents, rose up in February 1946, they were brutally suppressed and accused of trying to "restore the puppet (*wei*) political power of Manchukuo."[68] The CCP did not stop enrolling ex-puppet soldiers, but wholesale absorption was abandoned: they were now sprinkled in existing units, recalcitrant leaders were executed, and the rank and file "reformed" much more thoroughly, all the more that ideological problems such as officer brutality, "individual heroism," and contempt for civilians were partly identified as hangovers of Manchukuo Army culture.[69] It is no coincidence that vast campaign of army rectification (*zhengjun*) that started in late 1947 in all "liberated" areas was first experimented in the Northeast in late 1946: it was required by the unreliability of communist armies in that region, of which the presence of ex-Manchukuo soldiers and policemen was an important factor (by contrast, former forced laborers in the Manchukuo era were considered allies in the rectification movement).[70]

On the Nationalist side, too, the arrival of reinforcements from other provinces, starting in 1946, reduced the reliance on ex-Manchukuo troops. Nonetheless, their total demobilization was no more an option than for the communists, if only because of the risk that they would become bandits or sell their services to the CCP: those not absorbed in the National Army largely staffed semi-regular "peace preservation corps."[71]

The Second Life Paramilitarism in South Korea

Until 1950, Korea south of the 38th parallel also underwent sharp political polarization, although not to the point of civil war. I will focus here on the South, because its case is better documented but also because the legacy of colonial militarization was less obvious in the North. It does seem that North Korean authorities absorbed ex-colonial soldiers, and may have found some inspiration in Japanese wartime mobilization techniques.[72] However, on that matter, the Korean communists mostly followed the Soviet model and could also tap into a pool of veteran guerillas from Manchuria, as well as Soviet-trained cadres.[73] They could thus afford to purge colonial officers and, more broadly, do away with the legacy of Japanese militarization to a degree their southern opponents could not. The latter had little background in armed resistance, no troops of their own, and no alternative model for mobilizing society for war. To them, ex-colonial forces were vital for a potential clash with the North and, more pressingly, hostile forces in the South.

In addition to groups devoted to maintaining local order, around fifteen "private armies" emerged in the South after August 1945, often made up of ex-colonial soldiers: the largest one boasted tens of thousands of members, and although its figureheads were nationalist politicians, its actual founders and leaders were Korean officers of the Imperial Army.[74] The US occupation authorities looked upon these armies with wariness, and dissolved several, but they also used them as recruiting pools for the Constabulary, created in January 1946 as a prelude to an actual South Korean Army. This continuity was perceptible in the tactical culture of the men, for instance, in their proclivity for bayonet charge, which came from their Japanese training and puzzled American officers.[75]

In addition to this, social factors such as unemployment and the influx of returnees from Japan and refugees from North Korea, combined with the polarization and brutalization of political life, created fertile ground for the resurgence of paramilitarism. Armed youth corps, most of them squarely on the right, flourished after a wave of anti-government riots in the fall of 1946. These riots convinced US authorities that communists controlled the People's Committees and that right-wing youth corps were a necessary evil. Sponsored by political forces and the police, they broke up strikes or attacked left-wing activists. Although that was an impossible legacy to claim for nationalist organizations, youth corps culture clearly bore the mark of Japanese paramilitarism (the Chinese "Blue Shirts" were also a reference, as were European fascist paramilitary groups).[76] Right-wing youth corps were extremely violent. On the Southern island of Jeju, where protests against taxes and police brutality evolved into a left-wing armed uprising in 1948–1949, they played a key role in the repression, and their exactions against combatants and non-combatants alike became infamous. Particularly brutal was the Northwest Youth Corps, an organization that provided North Korean refugees with protection, charismatic leaders, and, last but not least, the opportunity to take revenge on presumed "Reds."[77]

Paramilitary youth groups were progressively incorporated in the Constabulary and, after the Republic of Korea (ROK) was established in 1948, in the army of the new regime. Meanwhile, their leaders took up high-ranking positions. One (Yi Pŏmsŏk) became Syngman Rhee's first prime minister and minister of defense and had high schools build anti-communist, paramilitary Student Defense Corps, as well as implement military and spiritual training curriculum: this was a striking return to the wartime militarization of youth, without Japanese cultural assimilation.[78]

Reenacting War Mobilization in Taiwan

As opposed to Manchuria or even South Korea, KMT authorities had little competition in Taiwan, where communist presence was weak. Nonetheless, haphazard economic policy and corruption rapidly eroded their legitimacy after the takeover. Governor Chen Yi and his subordinates found it convenient to disqualify local criticisms as antipatriotic, since the Formosans had been "liberated" by China despite having taken part in the Japanese war effort. The island's colonial legacy was also used as a reason to delay local self-rule and staff all high-ranking positions with mainlanders. Furthermore, hasty efforts at erasing Japanese cultural influence devaluated the skills developed in colonial times—the prohibition of Japanese in official documents even effectively barred many Taiwanese from public life. These measures were met with a mixture of resentment and cynicism, for the governorate failed to inspire awe. Its insistence on China's military victory over Japan as a source of legitimacy did not square with the Taiwanese experience of the rag-tag National Army, which paled before the relatively untried Japanese Taiwan Army. The KMT regime, while denouncing Japanese "militarism," had had its own militarization program since the 1930s and moved to implement it on the island after the war, but without success: efforts at training Taiwanese students were perceived as a joke after the GGT's much more thorough measures.

Contempt for the new rulers formed an explosive cocktail with economic dissatisfaction and political frustration among Taiwanese elites. In late 1947, a case of police brutality Taipei triggered protests that degenerated into riots, then into a short island-wide uprising: official buildings and many mainland Chinese were attacked by the furious population, unchecked by deliquescent police and overspread armed forces. The "February 28 Incident," as it is known, was short-lived: the authorities only lost control of the island for a dozen of days, before reinforcements sent from the mainland crushed the unrest in bloodshed.

During the Incident, prominent Taiwanese formed "Resolution Committees" to press for greater local and provincial autonomy. At the grassroots, however, mobilization took a different aspect. Tens of thousands of young men took to the streets. Most had experienced wartime militarization, directly or vicariously depending on age.[79] Former soldiers of the Imperial Army and, less measurably, members of paramilitary Japanese organizations played a major role, since their organizational and, to some extent, fighting skills could be put to use. Some Resolution Committees called upon them to maintain order, and more radical leaders (some of them communist) tried to rally them for armed struggle, but their mobilization mostly happened at the grassroots level, through networks inherited from military camaraderie or wartime mass organizations. Schools, which were privileged sites of militarization during the war, were often chosen as headquarters by "rebel" groups, who seized the training weapons left there by the Japanese when they could not find real ones. For those Taiwanese sympathetic to the revolt, ex-soldiers had an obligation to take the lead. This was sometimes experienced as peer pressure to take part in suicidal action, but it could also be a way, for colonial veterans, to re-experience the sense of worth and virility that had been taken away from them: in Chiayi, for instance, it was female students who called the names of local veterans on the radio, urging them to step forward. Beyond veterans, the aesthetics of wartime mobilization were adopted by many rebels, who used Japanese Army terminology to name their "units," sang Japanese military songs, wore borrowed Japanese uniforms, and so on. Several survivors still mentioned, decades later, the "Japanese spirit" that led them to take up arms.

This had little to do with actual nostalgia for colonial rule. Rather, it was driven by spite against the governorate's Chinese nationalist discourse and by the simpler fact that, for many young Taiwanese men, Japanese military aesthetics still were the most readily available model for asserting one's heroism and rightful role in society. In spite of this, and of the rebellion's limited lethality, this mimicry was an aggravating circumstance in the eyes of KMT authorities. The disproportionate suppression of the Incident (thousands were killed) particularly targeted Taiwanese elite, but also men presumed to have served in the Imperial Army, many of whom hurriedly destroyed or buried their wartime souvenirs, such as uniforms or swords. This violence was designed to terrify the Taiwanese society into submission, cleanse it of its Japanese "militarist" mentality, and eliminate a greater number of colonial collaborators—in official eyes, the revolt had shown that the postwar purge had been insufficiently thorough. After the Incident, the authorities accelerated the absorption of ex-colonial soldiers in the National Army (sometimes by force), both to use them in the civil war against the communists and to dilute their specific identity in a broader collective.[80]

After 1950: Legacies, Continuities, Disavowals

In the 1950s, ex-colonial soldiers and paramilitaries were suppressed or incorporated in the armed forces of South Korea, the ROC, and the PRC. The consolidation of state authority and the ageing out of these men reduced their relative importance. This does not mean that the legacy of colonial militarization vanished in these three territories, but it became less visible, absorbed as it was into national programs of mass mobilization and militarization spurred by region-wide, interrelated crises, such as the Korean War and cross-strait standoffs.

The ROC launched a massive campaign of militarization in the 1950s to resist a looming PRC takeover threat and, on paper, plan for a reconquest of the mainland. That effort was even more intense than that of the GGT (resulting, notably, in a standing army of six hundred thousand men), but it did build on measures taken during colonial times.[81] Hwang Jyn-lin describes the legacy of Japanese militarization in the 1930s–1940s as a "gift" (*enhui*) to the 1950s KMT, ranging from material infrastructures to generalized military training in schools, and more generally a preparedness for island defense that stretched back to threats of a US landing. It should be noted that Chinese military leaders tasked with injecting fresh blood into the war-fatigued National Army consciously tried to bank on the prestige of soldiering among Taiwanese youth, by recreating some of the rituals introduced by the Japanese, such as solemn send-offs. From the standpoint of the islanders, the continuity must have been striking.[82] ROC authorities went as far as recruiting Japanese officers to help train their army. The "White Group," as it was called, was kept secret. It seems that Chiang Kai-shek used it to counterbalance American influence but also because he felt more familiar with Japanese methods: he had, after all, been trained in Japan in the 1900s, during the first wave of East Asian militarization.[83]

Due to Cold War divides, Japanese legacies were erased more thoroughly in Northeast China. Yet, from the standpoint of its inhabitants, the intense militarization the region underwent in the 1950s was partly a prolongment of an experience that had begun under Manchukuo authorities. Even by the standards of PRC militarized socialism, the Northeast was singled out because of its proximity to the theater of the Korean War—in this respect, 1949 was not a cleaner break than 1945. Like the Japanese before them, although on a much-expanded scale, the Chinese communists enrolled large parts of the civilian population into "people's militias" (*minbing*), a term that progressively replaced the diverse appellations for existing paramilitary groups. Militias served as a tool of mass mobilization to fight against enemies, both internal (spies, counterrevolutionaries, bandits, etc.) and external: they were tasked with propagating "anti-imperialism" and convincing an exhausted population that going to fight in Korea was glorious (they were a recruiting pool for "volunteers" themselves). Despite this evident de facto continuity at the policy level, the actual remnants of Manchukuo forces continued to pose problems, the rapid expansion of people's militias leading to the absorption of "enemy and puppet personnel." These unreliable elements were, officially at least, purged in the political campaigns of the early 1950s along with "bandits," "landlords," and members of "secret societies" (over one hundred thousand militiamen were excluded). Afterward, they fade away from the records, probably because of their age. Militarization did not abate with the end of the Korean War: the first Taiwan Strait Crisis in 1958 and the Great Leap Forward led to yet another expansion of militias, which sometimes replaced existing units of production and education and were subjected to levels of militarized discipline, aesthetics, and collective life later condemned as a "leftist deviation."[84]

Last, the ROK remained, after the Korean War, a militarized state constantly bracing for a new clash with the North. Drills for students survived the end of the conflict, and the large standing army (comparable in size with that of the ROC) was recruited through a military service system that "drew largely on colonial precedents and continental European ... models"—conscription, first introduced in 1943 by the Japanese, was effectively resumed by the new regime after 1948. But it was easy for the upper classes to evade their obligations through legal or illegal means, which gravely tarnished the prestige of the army and the credibility of state-led militarization. Restoring them was Park Chung-hee's self-appointed mission after his coup in 1961. He "tightened implementation of the conscription laws and started a large-scale indoctrination campaign aimed at winning ideological hegemony for the 'national defense state,'" with significant success.[85] As C. Eckert has begun to demonstrate, Park's commitment to the militarization of Korean society came directly from his military experience under colonial rule, particularly in Manchukuo, and he was quite candid about it.[86]

This is not to say that East Asian militarization was purely Japanese in its inception: it was, rather, a variant of a global trend, with Japan serving as a regional interface. Precisely because they were directly subordinated to Japan, colonial and semi-colonial lands such as Taiwan, Korea, and later Manchukuo were relatively insulated from state-led militarization until the late 1930s, when they became the target of an intense "militaristic-imperial program" in the context of Japan's efforts at mobilizing and consolidating its East Asian empire. In 1945, this convergence with the Japanese main islands became a stark divergence: instead of undergoing a thorough demilitarization like the former metropole, these societies were subjected to continued militarization, although under different, postcolonial political powers. Ex-colonial soldiers and paramilitaries, although they bore the stain of "collaboration," were remobilized in different capacities in the highly fluid postwar years. But the transwar history of militarization did not stop with the ageing out of these men: it continued well into the 1950s and even 1960s, in the context of intense Cold War tensions. Colonial legacies of militarization become harder to weigh with the passing of years, but cases such as Park Chung-hee suggest that they remained consequential well into the 1960s. However, in his willingness to acknowledge them, Park would remain an exception: in postwar East Asia, just like during the "first wave" of the late nineteenth century, militarization projects were so closely tied with nationalism that their Japanese heritage was unavowable, at least until the liberalization of the public sphere in South Korea and Taiwan in the late twentieth century.

Notes

1 Louise Young, "When Fascism Met Empire in Japanese-Occupied Manchuria," *Journal of Global History* 12, no. 2 (July 2017): 274–96.
2 For example, see Carter Eckert, *Park Chung-hee and Modern Korea: The Roots of Militarism, 1866–1945* (Cambridge, MA: Harvard University Press, 2016); Takashi Fujitani, *Race for Empire: Koreans as Japanese and Japanese as Americans during World War II* (Berkeley: University of California Press, 2011).
3 Japan also sponsored local forces in occupied Southeast Asia, where it displaced European colonial powers. But these forces, albeit tightly controlled by occupation authorities, came along with the promise of independence. Japan's older colonial possessions had no such perspective; there, militarization was to be pursued *within* the Japanese Empire. One could argue that the puppet state of Manchukuo fits the Southeast Asian model better than the Taiwanese/Korean one. However, the open-endedness of Manchukuo's "union" with Japan, cultural commonalities, and human circulation all plead for considering these three East Asian territories together.
4 Eckert, *Park Chung-hee and Modern Korea*, 45.
5 Oleg Benesch, *Inventing the Way of the Samurai: Nationalism, Internationalism, and Bushido in Modern Japan* (Oxford: Oxford University Press, 2014).
6 Oleg Benesch, "The Samurai Next Door: Chinese Examinations of the Japanese Martial Spirit," *Extrême-Orient Extrême-Occident* 38 (2014): 129–68.
7 Eckert, *Park Chung-hee and Modern Korea*, 38–51.
8 Norbert Elias, *The Civilizing Process* (Oxford: Blackwell, 2000), 5–30.
9 Benesch, *Inventing the Way of the Samurai*, 17–18, 67–72, 78, 90–103.
10 Faye Yuan Kleeman, *Under an Imperial Sun: Japanese Colonial Literature of Taiwan and the South* (Honolulu: University of Hawai'i Press, 2005), 138–9.

11 Fujitani, *Race for Empire*, 45, 55–7.
12 Lin Cheng-hui, *Taiwan kejia de xingsu licheng: Qing dai zhi zhanhou de zhuisuo* (Taipei: Guoli Taiwan daxue chuban zhongxin, 2015), 300.
13 Komagome Takeshi, *Shokuminchi teikoku Nihon no bunka tōgō* (Tokyo: Iwanami shoten, 1996), 166–73.
14 Eckert, *Park Chung-hee and Modern Korea*, 56–61.
15 Andrew Hall, "The Word Is Mightier than the Throne: Bucking Colonial Education Trends in Manchukuo," *Journal of Asian Studies* 68, no. 3 (August 2009): 895–925, 896.
16 For example, see Usui Shigeru, *Nan Manshū no nōson* (Tokyo: Chijin shokan, 1940), 135.
17 Fujitani, *Race for Empire*, 40–6.
18 Brandon Palmer, *Fighting for the Enemy: Koreans in Japan's War, 1937–1945* (Seattle: University of Washington Press, 2013), 42–4, 123–5, 136.
19 Kondō Masami, *Sōryokusen to Taiwan: Nihon shokuminchi hōkai no kenkyū* (Tokyo: Tōsui shobo, 1996), 16–60.
20 Lin Jiwen, *Riben juTai moqi (1930–1945): zhanzheng dongyuan tixi zhi yanjiu* (Taipei: Daoxiang, 1996), 225.
21 Fu Dazhong, *Wei Manzhouguo jun jianshi* (Changchun: Jilin wenshi chubanshe, 1999), 1–6.
22 Kozawa Shinkō, *Hishi Manshūkoku gun: Nikkei gunkan no yakuwari* (Tokyo: Kashiwa shobō, 1976), 169–72.
23 Sayaka Chatani, *Nation-Empire: Ideology and Rural Youth Mobilization in Japan and Its Colonies* (Ithaca, NY: Cornell University Press, 2018), 170–1, 209–14.
24 "Fengtian sheng gongshu jiaoyu ting lijiao ke 'Lijiao gaiyao,'" in *"Manshū-Manshūkoku" kyōiku shiryō shūsei*, vol. 11 (Tokyo: Emuti shuppan, 1993), 441–774, 521–3, 540–2.
25 Shimizu Ryōtarō, "Manshūkoku tōchi kikō ni okeru senden/senfu kōsaku," *Senshi kenkyū nenpō* 17 (2014): 49–75, 62–3.
26 I thank Filippo Dornetti for this information. For a case study, see Filippo Dornetti, "Chiiki shakai ni okeru Manshūkoku Kyōwakai no tenkai to nōmin no dōkō: Hōten shō Bujun ken wo chūshin ni," *Mita gakkai zasshi* 110 (2017): 83–107.
27 Chatani, *Nation-Empire*, 153.
28 Palmer, *Fighting for the Enemy*, 46.
29 Benesch, *Inventing the Way of the Samurai*, 174–213.
30 For example, see *Taiwan no shakai kyōiku* (Taipei: Taiwan sōtokufu, 1942), 4; *Rensei no michi: kokumin rensei no shidō ni tsuite* (Taipei: Taiwan sōtokufu kokumin seishin kenkyūjo, 1942).

31 For example, see *Renshō no kōgun* (Taipei: Taiwan sōtokufu bunkyōkyoku shakaika, 1937).
32 Eckert, *Park Chung-hee and Modern Korea*, 62–8.
33 Hall, "The Word Is Mightier than the Throne."
34 For example, see the recollections of Qu Bingshan, Xue Lanshi, and Zhang Dewei, *Wo suo zhidao de Wei Man zhengquan* (Beijing: Zhongguo wenshi chubanshe, 2017), 456–526.
35 Yamazaki Itarō, "Manshūkoku oyobi Hoku-Shi ni okeru minzoku taiiku to sono genjō narabini shisetsu ni tsuite," *Shina kenkyū* (May 1940), in *"Manshū-Manshūkoku" kyōiku shiryō shūsei*, vol. 14, 727–85.
36 Liu Hsi-ming, *Weijun: Qiangquan jingzhu xia de zuzi (1937–1949)* (Taipei: Daoxiang, 2011).
37 Fujitani, *Race for Empire*, 68–73.
38 *Sōtei dokuhon* (Taipei: Taiwan sōtokufu, 1944).
39 Eckert, *Park Chung-hee and Modern Korea*, particularly 274–310.
40 Diary of Shi Mingru, January 8, 1938, in *Zheyin shenshen: yi ge Wei Man junguan de riji*, vol. 1 (Changchun: Jilin sheng zhengxie wenshiziliao weiyuanhui, 2011), 6.
41 For Korea, see Fujitani, *Race for Empire*, 262–5.
42 For example, see *Sōtei dokuhon*, 80–5.
43 Chatani, *Nation-Empire*, 15. It helped that in the metropole itself, the promoters of *bushidō* ideology had long idealized the countryside, supposedly uncorrupted by modernity. Benesch, *Inventing the Way of the Samurai*, 122.
44 Komagome Takeshi and J. A. Mangan, "Militarism, Sacrifice and Emperor Worship: The Expendable Male Body in Fascist Japanese Martial Culture," *International Journal of the History of Sport* 16, no. 4 (1999): 181–204.
45 Chatani, *Nation-Empire*, 174; Eckert, *Park Chung-hee and Modern Korea*, 82–3.
46 For example, see Xiao Jinhai (1996), in *Zou guo liang ge shidai de ren: Taiwan Riben bing*, ed. Ts'ai Hui-yu (Taipei: Academia Sinica, 2008), 108.
47 Sha Qing, "Zhong, Ri xuesheng helian hou," in *Ai'ai Changbai: WeiMan junxiao xuesheng huiyilu*, ed. Li Tiancheng (Changchun: Jilin sheng qingnian yundong shi gong zuo weiyuanhui, 2000), 25–9.
48 Eckert, *Park Chung-hee and Modern Korea*, 92.
49 Seiji Shirane, "Mediated Empire: Colonial Taiwan in Japan's Imperial Expansion into South China and Southeast Asia, 1895–1945" (PhD diss., Princeton University, 2014).
50 For example, see Zheng Chunhe (1997), in Ts'ai, *Zou guo liang ge shidai de ren*, 58.
51 This was also true of internal colonial hierarchies: Taiwanese Austronesians were given greater consideration once their "martial" qualities were judged useful.

52 Fujitani, *Race for Empire*, 52–3. The phrase comes from Dipesh Chakrabarty, *Provincializing Europe: Postcolonial Thought and Historical Difference* (Princeton, NJ: Princeton University Press, 2000), 8.
53 Zhou Jinbo, "Shiganhei," trans. Hiroaki Sato, in *Taiwan Literature: English Translation Series* 37 (2016): 3–22, 18–19; Leo Ching, *Becoming "Japanese": Colonial Taiwan and the Politics of Identity Formation* (Berkeley: University of California Press, 2001), 115–17.
54 For example, in the diary of Shi Mingru, a cadet at the Fengtian military academy (see *Zheyin shenshen*).
55 For example, see Li Tiancheng, "WeiMan junguan xuexiao jianjie," in *Ai'ai Changbai*, 1–16.
56 Up to fifty thousand Koreans and around thirty thousand Taiwanese were killed in the Japanese military. To my knowledge, there are no reliable figures for the Manchukuo Army.
57 Liu, *Weijun*, 446.
58 Tang Xiyong, "Tuoli kunjing: zhanhou chuqi Hainandao zhi Taiwanren de fanTai," *Taiwan shi yanjiu* 12 (2005): 167–208.
59 Former colonial subjects could be charged for individual war crimes.
60 This was particularly the case for ethnic minorities who had been singled out for privileged treatment and now feared retaliation from the Han majority. For example, see Zhengzhu'erzhabu, "Weiman di shi junguanqu suoshu budui touxiang Sulian Hongjun de jingguo," in *WeiMan fuwang*, ed. Sun Bang (Changchun: Jilin renmin chubanshe, 1993), 423–7.
61 For example, see Cai Mingchuan (1994) in Hsu Hsueh-chi, *Gaoxiong shi Er'erba xiangguan renwu fangwen jilu*, vol. 1 (Taipei: Academia Sinica, 1995).
62 Bruce Cumings, *The Origins of the Korean War: Liberation and the Emergence of Separate Regimes, 1945–1947* (Princeton, NJ: Princeton University Press, 1981), 73.
63 "Taiwan yi nian lai zhi jingwu," Archives of the Institute of Modern History, Academia Sinica, 228/01/01/020.
64 Liu, *Weijun*, 466–72.
65 Xiong Shihui, "Shenyang shi fulao shishen zhaodaihui xunci," April 14, 1946, in Xiong Shihui Papers, Columbia University, MS#0642, 1.
66 Steven Levine, *Anvil of Victory: The Communist Revolution in Manchuria, 1945–1948* (New York: Columbia University Press, 1987), 104; Liu, *Weijun*, 504–5.
67 Wang Chaoguang, *He yu zhan de jueze: Zhanhou Guomindang de Dongbei juece* (Beijing: Renmin daxue chubanshe, 2016), 52.
68 "Gao weijing weijun shu," *Tonghua ribao*, November 10, 1945; "Tonghua zhidui silingbu Ru Fuyi canmouzhang xiang Tonghua quanti tongbao guangbo jianghua," *Tonghua ribao*, February 7, 1946, in *Jiefang zhanzheng shiqi de Tonghua* (Tonghua: Tonghua shiwei dangshi yanjiushi, 2000), 44–5, 571–2.

69 "Dongbei ju guanyu Dongbei jiaofei gongzuo baogao," April 10, 1947, in *Heilongjiang dangshi ziliao*, vol. 8 (Harbin: Heilongjiang shengwei dangshi gongzuo weiyuanhui, 1986), 15–19; "Dongbei yezhan budui zhengwu yundong zongjie" (*c.* June 1948), in *Xin shi zhengjun yundong* (Beijing: Jiefangjun chubanshe, 1995), 295–308.
70 Zhou Huan, "Huiyi dongbei yezhanjun de xin shi zhengjun yundong" (August 1990), in *Xin shi zhengjun yundong*, 697–711.
71 Taiwan National Archives, 0035/581.28/5090, "Wei diancheng Dongbei shoubian budui chuli qingxing kenqi jianhe shizun," November 21, 1946; Academia Historica, 002-020400-00002-114, digest of telegrams from Du Yuming and Xiong Shihui transferred to Jiang Jieshi, May 23, 1947.
72 Suzy Kim, *Everyday Life in the North Korean Revolution, 1945–1950* (Ithaca, NY: Cornell University Press, 2013), 44, 116–19.
73 Fyodor Tertitskiy, "Study of Soviet Influence on the Formation of the North Korean Army," *Acta Koreana* 20, no. 1 (2017): 195–219.
74 Cumings, *The Origins of the Korean War*, 68–81.
75 Robert K. Sawyer, *Military Advisors in Korea: KMAG in Peace and War* (Washington, DC: Center of Military History, 1962), 11–15, 25.
76 Mark Gayn, *Japan Diary* (New York: W. Sloane, 1948), 435–8.
77 *The Jeju 4.3 Incident Investigation Report* (Jeju-si: Jeju 4.3 Peace Foundation, 2014), 117, 178–9, 197–209.
78 Kim Bong-jin, "Paramilitary Politics under the USAMGIK and the Establishment of the Republic of Korea," *Korea Journal* 43, no. 2 (2003): 289–322, 308–9.
79 The following points are drawn from Victor Louzon, "From Japanese Soldiers to Chinese Rebels: War Experience and Remobilization during the 1947 Taiwanese Rebellion," *Journal of Asian Studies* 77, no. 1 (February 2018): 161–79; V. Louzon, "Colonial Legacy and War Aftermaths in Taiwan, 1945–1947," in *In the Ruins of the Japanese Empire: Imperial Violence, State Destruction, and the Reordering of Modern East Asia*, ed. Barak Kushner and Andrew Levidis (Hong Kong: Hong Kong University Press, 2020), 76–97.
80 Xu Zhaorong, *Taiji laobing de xie lei hen* (Taipei: Qianwei, 1995), 29, 335–56.
81 An exception was the island of Jinmen, which Japan had not colonized. Michael Szonyi, *Cold War Island: Quemoy on the Frontline* (New York: Cambridge University Press, 2008).
82 Hwang Jyn-lin, *Zhanzheng, shenti, xiandaixing: Jindai Taiwan de junshi zhili yu shenti, 1895–2005* (Taipei: Lianjing, 2009), 79–163.
83 Barak Kushner, "Ghosts of the Japanese Imperial Army: The 'White Group' (*Baituan*) and Early Post-war Sino-Japanese Relations," *Past & Present* 218, no. 8 (2013): 117–50.
84 *Dongbei minbing sanshiwu nian* (1949–1984) (Shenyang: Shenyang junqu silingbu dongyuanbu, 1985), 4–19.

85 Vladimir Tikhonov, "Militarism and Anti-militarism in South Korea: 'Militarized Masculinity' and the Conscientious Objector Movement," *Japan Focus* 7, no. 12 (2009) (https://apjjf.org/-Vladimir-Tikhonov/3087/article.html).

86 This will be explored in greater depth in the sequel to his *Park Chung-hee and Modern Korea*.

3

Occupational Hazards in the Transwar Pacific: Imperialism, the US Military, and Filipino Labor

Colleen Woods

The US military's employment of Filipino contract laborers on the islands of Okinawa and Guam after the Second World War illustrates one way that US imperial power adapted in the postwar era in response to Philippine independence in 1946 and the broader global trend toward decolonization. This deployment of Filipino labor not only benefited the expansion of US imperial power in the Pacific, it also reengaged an older system wherein the US military relied on Filipinos to construct and maintain military sites. However, conventional understandings of both the postwar Philippines and the US military presence in the Pacific during the Cold War largely ignore the importance of imported Filipino labor. What is more, while scholars of Philippine labor migration note the importance of colonial-era migration to the United States, they often date the beginning of large-scale Filipino migration in the Marcos era, overlooking post–Second World War precedents.[1] But the beginnings of this contract labor system are even earlier: indeed, when the US military and private contractors integrated Filipino laborers into the postwar Pacific labor market, they were building upon and adapting uneven political and economic relationships that had been in place since at least 1898. Though it is not uncommon for scholars working in the fields of Asian American and cultural studies to take a longer chronological view, connecting colonial and postcolonial history, historical scholarship, with some exceptions, remains largely focused on either the US colonial *or* the postcolonial periods in the Philippines.[2] In this chapter I argue that using a transwar imperial analytic reveals how important Filipino workers had become to the US military by the onset of the Cold War and how the expanding military power reformulated colonial labor systems to meet the needs of the Cold War–era American Empire. As I've written elsewhere, in hiring Filipinos to work on US military bases in the Philippines at lower wages than American workers, the US military exploited a global political and economic system based on wage inequalities.³ In employing Filipino laborers to work on other US military sites around the region—Guam, Okinawa, and Wake Island—and at much lower pay than other workers, the US military showed the importance of economic inequality for extending US military power.⁴ The chapter also reveals that the expansion of US military power in the Pacific, even after Philippine independence, required the services of a Philippine workforce.

The United States took over the Philippine archipelago from Spain in 1898 and held it, under different arrangements, until 1946. On the question of colonial labor, previous scholars have shown that the US Army compelled Filipinos to work as early as 1899, continuing to employ Spanish colonial tactics of coercion well into the twentieth century, albeit with tactics adapted for the wage-labor market.⁵ However, this scholarship usually emphasizes labor as connected to US colonialism's other "civilizing efforts" and can imply a top-down application of colonial power that supposedly terminated with independence.⁶ Connecting colonial and postwar labor dynamics, on the contrary, demonstrates the ways in which local populations were made part of the US imperial project. The conventional "postwar" analytic is inadequate to capture these continuities of US imperial power before and after 1945. Instead, in this chapter, I deploy a "transwar" approach that focuses on the imperial dynamics of military contract labor across the post–Second World War Pacific region to illuminate the legacies and adaptations of US imperial power in the Pacific.

Colonial Labor

In 1926, American president Calvin Coolidge appointed Carmi Thompson, an Ohio Republican, veteran of the Spanish-American War, and "highly successful businessman, with stakes in banking, coal, newspapers, and the iron-ore industry," to conduct a survey on the "economic and internal political conditions of the Philippine Islands."⁷ With the price of rubber rising in the United States, Coolidge was under pressure by the American Rubber Association to revise the land laws in the Philippines so that American corporations such as the Ohio-based Goodyear Tire Company could develop rubber plantations on the southern Philippine island of Mindanao.⁸ To perform the job, Coolidge selected

Thompson, a politician who already shared the president's view that Philippine independence would need to be "postponed for some time to come," as the United States' island colony was a growing economic asset.[9]

Thompson's subsequent report on his three months of travel centered on the economic prospects of the Philippines but also included an unexpected consideration of "the capacity of the Filipinos as workmen." While touring the construction site for a "new naval hospital" in Cavite, southwest of Manila, Thompson had observed "several thousand [Filipinos] employed in the navy yard." This was notable to him because he had not expected to see evidence of such labor capacity on the islands. He remarked in his report that "Filipinos were good workers," which would be just what the labor-intensive rubber industry wanted to hear. A piece in the *New York Times* focusing on Thompson's visit to the American naval yard appeared in July 1926, just as Congress was debating the Bacon Bill, legislation that sought to separate the southern islands from the rest of the Philippines and create a new territory where American corporations could develop rubber plantations.[10] Although Thompson's remarks on Filipino labor applied only to those workers he met at Cavite, the *Times* considered his assessment newsworthy, as "naturally, the labor question [was] important to the development of the rubber industry."[11] The newspaper also considered it important to emphasize that Thompson had seen *thousands* of Filipino laborers employed at the site.

To be sure, it was not unique to find Filipinos working either for or alongside the US military in the archipelago. As scholars have noted, Filipinos began serving as "carriers" or cargadores for the US Army in the islands as early as 1899. Other scholars have argued that the shift from Spanish to American colonial rule did not result in the complete dissolution of Spanish colonial systems, largely because Americans adapted aspects of Spanish rule, including coercing Filipino labor to support US colonial development.[12] But the American colonizers believed that the creation of a "wage-labor market"— as opposed to what Americans believed was a "feudal" Spanish labor system— would compel Filipino workers to sell their labor, an important distinction between the two colonial styles.[13] Yet, even after the early colonial period— when the US Army forced Filipinos to work on road-construction projects— the touted "market forces" did not produce the results Americans imagined. For example, a 1923 editorial in the Philippine branch of the American Chamber of Commerce's journal noted that the "real labor problem in the Philippines" was rooted in the inability to "induce the people to work."[14] This question of "motivation" was all important because convincing Filipinos to labor for the US government—as well as private companies—was, as Greg Bankoff has written, critical to the success of colonial development and US government projects.[15]

Explicit colonial rule by the United States would continue until the 1935 Tydings-McDuffie Act, which transitioned the Philippines to Commonwealth status, and then independence in 1946. Up until then, however, according to the paternalistic ideology of the US civilizing mission, Filipinos were still in a period of "tutelage," much like the island colony as a whole.[16] With proper oversight and training, Americans expected that Filipino workers would one day be as efficient and ambitious as Americans. In fact, the idea that American colonization was not rooted in exploitation but was instead aimed at "developing" Filipino capacities remained a critical ideology of American imperial power. A major step toward democratic "maturity" and independence would be when the positions held by US colonial administrators would be held by Filipinos, the process of which was called "Filipinization."

Not dissimilar from the ways that Americans in the early years of colonial rule sought to explain US rule in the Philippines as benevolent—by distinguishing the American system from the former Spanish system—during the 1920s and 1930s colonial officials continued to believe and promote the idea that the transference of an American-style capitalist system to the Philippines and Southeast Asia was, as Anne Foster has argued, a force for good and a model for successful colonial rule.[17] Indeed, aiming to score points against competing imperial powers, former governor general of the Philippines William Cameron Forbes argued that "the greatest fundamental divergence of American practice from that of other colonizing countries" was "the treatment of labor" in the Philippines.[18]

To be sure, Forbes's comments were not merely aimed at other imperial powers—Forbes was a central figure in a campaign to undo the effects of Filipinization policies, which had increasingly delegated the day-to-day running of the colonial state to Filipinos in "preparation" for self-rule. By 1926, for example, the Philippine civil service was comprised of 470 Americans and 18,246 Filipinos.[19] Yet Forbes contended that the programs in industrial education meant to "enable the laborer to learn and apply scientific methods" and inspire "the laborer [to look] for better things" had not gone far enough. Forbes and the collective of anti-Filipinization advocates—which included the US-Philippine business lobby—maintained that the economic and labor system of American colonization was meant to model free-trade and democratic ideals and thereby improve the Filipino workers' lot. But the important issue of labor—"the greatest fundamental divergence of American practice" from other colonial powers—could not be trusted in the hands of Filipinos, whom Forbes considered to be entrenched in *caciquism*, the (Spanish colonial) concept by which elites exploited the Philippine *tao* (common man).[20]

Despite Forbes' misgivings, the Filipinization project was largely successful, especially in terms of increased Filipino employment and earnings.[21] Thompson's 1926 tour of the Cavite Naval Yard illustrates some of these effects and bolstered the impression of American benevolence. In 1928, the Port of Manila reported that the "thirty-three years of American sovereignty" had been a "constructive co-partnership designed to enable the Filipino to develop" and had resulted in greatly improved "standards of living."[22]

Racialized Wages

At least initially, Americans found Filipino laborers wanting in the islands. Citing labor shortages, in the first decade of colonial rule, some employers—including the naval forces at Cavite—turned to hiring Chinese laborers instead.[23] But the idea that, as American Federation of Labor (AFL) commissioner Edward Rosenberg—who traveled to the Philippines to assess labor conditions in the islands in 1903—put it, "there was a great scarcity of labor in the Philippines Islands" was patently false. Rosenberg claimed that there was "an unlimited supply of cheap Chinese labor."[24] The perception of a labor shortage—which was really a *Filipino labor* shortage—and the controversy over hiring Chinese laborers were based on racialized assumptions that had persisted across the islands' transfer from Spanish to US colony and were exacerbated by turn-of-the-century US anti-Asian prejudice.[25]

According to Rosenberg in 1903, when it came to employment with the US government at the marine engineering department at the Cavite Naval Yard, Chinese workers received "the same wages as Filipinos with equal skill." Yet he also expressed concerns that, with their "cheap as he can live" standard of living, Chinese laborers would have the effect of "reducing the already small wages of the Filipinos," an assessment that undoubtedly reflected the AFL's concern that US annexation of the Philippines would enable Chinese laborers to migrate to the United States.[26] However, the notion that workers' wages could be determined by a racialized "standard of living" was not unfounded in the colonial Philippines. As Bankoff demonstrates, during the first decades of American rule employers frequently made "interethnic comparisons between groups of workers on the basis of their productivity," using assumptions of race and "fitness" to determine groups' relative "competitiveness" in the job market.[27] This conventionalized the hiring of Filipinos at lower rates than workers from the United States, not just the exportation of Americans' anti-Chinese labor practices. Moreover, the establishment of differential wages ensured Filipinos (as well as Philippine Chinese workers) would remain poorer vis-à-vis Americans living in the continental United States, thereby reifying Filipinos' favorably low (for US employers) "standard of living."[28]

As Rosenberg observed in the colonial era—and as was the case in the postwar era as well—the US military and civilian employers put Philippine racial, ethnic, and national identities to use in determining wages and pitting workers against one another, although the connection across colonial and prewar labor practices is usually obscured. Nonetheless, the US Cold War military complex retained and expanded the exploitative and explicitly racist practices of wage differentials dating to the colonial period, reformulated to a situation in which labor and the US Empire now spanned the Pacific.

Although the economic depression of the 1930s would stall some US military construction projects in the Philippines, by 1940 the extreme expansion of American military infrastructure in the buildup to the war meant a significant engagement of Filipino labor. Between 1940 and 1945, the Naval Bureau of Docks and Yards "built or supervised the building of more than four hundred advance bases for the Navy across the globe, including in the Philippines, Guam, and Okinawa."[29] Filipinos were involved in these US-led labor projects throughout and even after independence in 1946. Indeed, the Philippines and Filipino labor—modeled on the colonial labor regime—served as the engine of US imperial expansion in the Pacific.

Building the New Era

In early 1946, the American social worker Irene Murphy wrote to her brother-in-law Frank Murphy, a sitting Supreme Court justice and former high commissioner to the Philippine Commonwealth, to tell him of her shock at witnessing Manila in ruins. The city was "absolutely crucified," she wrote, with "yawning black holes and jutting twisted facades."[30] Irene had just returned to the Philippines for the first time in ten years; from 1933 to 1936 she had coordinated social events for her husband's brother, a lifelong bachelor, when he was the top US colonial official in Manila. In 1946, Irene returned to Manila to serve as the assistant to the executive director of Philippine War Relief Inc. (PWR), a private organization founded in 1944 by "leading citizens interested in the Philippines," most of whom had spent time working in the American colonial state in the Philippines.[31] Having spent the war years in the United States, the experience of seeing the destroyed colonial city first-hand elicited in Murphy a visceral reaction—a recognition of the grim on-the-ground realities and human costs of the Pacific War. She recounted to Frank that "the first true view of Manila from the airport made a swish in my insides that put me to bed."[32]

In vividly describing her first encounter with a devastated postwar Manila, Murphy focused her description, in particular, on a single building: the Legislative Building, one in a trio that also included the Finance and Agricultural Buildings, all built according to famed American architect Daniel Burnham's master plan for Manila.[33] The building, designed in the same neoclassical style as many US federal buildings, was a physical monument to the myth that Americans annexed the Philippines only in order to guide Filipinos on the civilizational path toward modern democratic governance. Although the fighting between US and Japanese forces destroyed nearly 65 percent of Manila, it was the sight of the Legislative Building that had particularly disturbed Murphy: "It took the P.I. [Philippine Islands] and the U.S.A. 40 years to achieve something like that building," she lamented.[34] The idea that Filipinos and Americans had built the Philippines together was one in which Murphy clearly felt a keen sense of pride. From this perspective, the Legislative Building, like US colonialism in the islands, had been a laborious, but worthy, mutual undertaking. Murphy's grief illustrates a colonial ideology that the Americans and Filipinos had *cooperatively* built the Philippines—the nation and its buildings, roads, rails, and schools—together. Moreover, while Murphy would characterize the postwar moment as a "new world" or, as one *Washington Post* piece put it, "the beginning of a new era" in which "Filipinos will have a great opportunity to demonstrate the fruits of democracy and freedom in the Far East," the American military would, in particular, continue to rely on Filipino laborers in the belief that Americans and Filipinos were building a "safer" Pacific together.[35]

The war had resulted in cataclysmic damage to the Philippines; the estimate that 61 percent of total property had been destroyed did not include damage done to land, natural resources, or human life. In fact, the damages enumerated in the Philippines by various postwar surveys were considered second only to the damages in Poland among the allied nations. In March 1946, five months before the United States relinquished sovereignty over the islands, the American Red Cross reported that, in addition to widespread famine in the mountain province of Luzon, "indications point to other famine possibilities in islands over the next ten months."[36] Relief workers estimated a 40 percent reduction in the planting of staple crops—whose harvest would not only provide food for the population but be sold in order to finance future agricultural production.[37] Shortages of food, medicine, adequate housing, and employment plagued relief organizations such as the Red Cross and PWR, as well as the US military civil affairs units and the Philippine commonwealth.

The displacement of tens of thousands of civilians—an estimated 100,000 people just in greater Manila area were rendered homeless by the war—and the near complete destruction of agriculture, livestock, and industry left Filipinos workers with few options. Furthermore, in 1947, a commercial attaché at the US embassy in Manila admitted that, due to the displacements caused by the war and Japanese occupation, the "unemployment situation [remained] obscure." The embassy estimated that at least 1.5 million Filipinos were unemployed, out of a total population of close to 20 million.[38]

Undoubtedly, employment opportunities with the US military enabled Filipino workers to earn a living.[39] Indeed, by 1948, one Philippine official told the *Manila Chronicle* that jobs provided by the US military, as well as "the hiring of laborers by private contracts," had minimized "the appalling high rate of unemployment in the Philippines."[40] Still, the US military did not seek to hire Filipinos out of a sense of altruism or even as part of a plan to aid the Philippines in postwar reconstruction. As during the colonial period, the US military sought out Filipino laborers because they quite simply cost less than hiring Americans.

Initially, the US military hired Filipino laborers to work on sites in the islands. In April 1945, the Construction Corps of the Philippines, or CONCOR, was specifically created by US Army engineers so that the institution could "make more effective use of Filipino labor."[41] Within five months CONCOR employed over thirty-seven thousand Filipino civilians. While some duties with CONCOR dovetailed with war rehabilitation work, such as maintaining roads and public utilities, other tasks found Filipinos working on improving and expanding US military sites in the island. For example, in a July 22, 1945, *New York Times* article titled "We Build a Base Surpassing All Others," journalist Lindesay Parrott described the large-scale constructions projects underway in the Philippines. During the war, the islands had been envisioned by Douglas MacArthur as a "site for staging the bulk of the American armies" for a planned invasion of Japan; after the war, as Parrott described, army engineers and naval Seabees still worked to fulfill the army's plan to construct "the maximum number of bases the Philippines can hold." Though Parrott credited US military engineers and construction workers with the success, he also noted that the army and navy in the Philippines combined "employ[ed] close to 150,000 Filipino workers."[42]

Cold War Expansion

The outbreak of the Korean War led to a tripling in US military spending, and Truman's adoption of Cold War policy set forth in NSC-48 and NSC-68 provided the ideological justification the Truman administration needed to seek an increased military budget from Congress for the US military's expansion.[43] The military's ability to extend its geographical reach did not come cheap, and the allotted budget for the military was significantly lower than that allocated during the Second World War.[44] Therefore, in order to maintain and expand its imperial position in the Pacific, US military officials looked for ways to cut costs. One of the ways they did so was by procuring an inexpensive labor force. Beginning in 1947, the US Navy and Army stretched the defense budgets—and private companies increased their profits—by recruiting and circulating Filipino laborers around the Pacific.

In May 1947, the office of Douglas MacArthur, the commander in chief of the Far East (CINCFE), issued a statement to the Philippine-Ryukyus Command (PHILRYCOM) and the Marianas-Bonins Command (MARBO) that offered a potential strategy to stretch US military allocations: PHILRYCOM, a subordinate command under the authority of the CINCFE, would recruit Filipinos for employment in "the construction, operation, and maintenance of military installations" in Okinawa. MacArthur's headquarters informed the lower commands that it was "desirable that Filipino labor be provided as soon as possible to permit contract work" in order to "eliminate costly importation of United States labor in lower grade positions."[45] The CINCFE explicitly recommended hiring Filipino laborers in place of "continentals," that is to say, workers from the United States, who were paid a premium for their labor on the islands.

Military officials recognized, however, that the newly independent Philippine Republic had sovereignty over decisions about who could exit and enter Philippine territory, meaning that Philippine independence had imposed limitations on the legal mobility of Filipino laborers. The US military could, and indeed did, request the use of Philippine soldiers in postwar occupations, including nearly six thousand troops to the island of Okinawa. Because the Philippines had, through independence, gained sovereignty over foreign and immigration policies, in order to transport civilian laborers, the US military and private contractors sought the help of the US embassy in Manila and the Philippine government.[46] In 1947, the US Army requested that the Philippine Department of Labor and Foreign Affairs approve their recruitment of Filipinos for employment in "the construction, operation, and maintenance of military installations" in Okinawa.[47] Later that year, Nathaniel Davis of the US embassy wrote to Bernabe Africa, the Philippine secretary of labor and foreign affairs, to indicate that the US military "foresaw a need for about 8,000 laborers to be employed directly by the United States outside of the Philippines including the Marianas islands, Okinawa, and elsewhere in the Pacific."[48] Within three days Secretary Africa had responded, granting the US Army permission to recruit and ship laborers to locations outside the Philippines. This correspondence between the embassy officers and the secretary acted as a treaty, or agreement, between the United States and the Philippines, and it dictated the terms of employment for "labor recruited in the Philippines either by the Army or Navy or by contractors under the jurisdiction of the Army or Navy."[49] At the end of August 1947, Lieutenant General Whitehead, commander of Far East Air Forces, informed his subordinates that "Filipino Nationals" would "provide an immediate supply of skilled and semi-skilled labor" in areas other than Japan or Korea. He explained that Filipinos could be employed "at minimum cost as compared to the operational cost when utilizing American personnel."[50] As Whitehead explained it, the plan was simply a rational cost-saving measure the military had to employ in order to stay within its allocated budget.

Soon, Filipinos were traveling to work on US military projects across the Pacific, including Guam, Wake Island, Saipan, and a base on the island of Okinawa. Thus, only one year after Philippine independence, the Philippine government negotiated a diplomatic agreement that would serve as the labor contract for the thousands of Filipino laborers hired by the US military and US military contractors to work on US military bases in the name of securing the "Free World's security" in the Pacific.

To be sure, large-scale changes—including Philippine independence, rising decolonization movements, and the hardening boundaries of Cold War geopolitics—as well as small ones—such as changes in working conditions—posed new challenges and opportunities for both private corporations and workers in the years after the Second World War. Nonetheless, the recruitment of low-wage Filipino labor by US military contractors—even after Philippine independence altered the status of Filipinos in relation to the United States—essentially built on and, at times, adapted a system of labor that had been crafted during the US colonial occupation of the islands. Yet, unlike during the colonial period, the formal labor agreement between the US and Philippine governments allowed US officials and contractors to argue that Philippine politicians had agreed to the current relationship through diplomacy rather than imperial coercion. When the Philippine Department of Labor and Foreign Affairs secretary approved a request from the US Army to recruit Filipinos for employment in "the construction, operation, and maintenance of military installations" in Okinawa in 1947—that is to say, a year after the Philippines gained independence from the United States—the island's own government was agreeing to help the US military expand its imperial hold over other Pacific territories.[51]

While the US Army had, both in the colonial period and during the war, employed civilian labor in the Philippines, many of the new construction tasks formerly performed by US servicemen were transferred to private companies in the form of exclusive military contracts. Because recruiting civilian Filipino workers through the military directly was not enough to answer the demand, the Philippine state partnered with these private companies to export labor for US military projects in the postwar Pacific. Stevedoring, which had been performed by the US Army since the end of the war, for example, was taken over by the low-wage paying Luzon Stevedore Company.[52] Privately owned military contractors like Luzon Stevedore or Visayan Stevedore Company (VISTRANCO) used the same placement processes as the military and quickly transformed Filipino laborers into workers for US military and capital expansion in the Pacific.[53]

Government contracts were a boon to private construction companies, many of which already had experience in working with the US government on large-scale engineering and construction projects.[54] Though some workers were employed directly by either the US Army or Navy, in many cases, Filipinos laboring outside of the Philippines worked for private contractors.

The Luzon Stevedore Company, a company with long-standing ties with the US military, was, according to a 1948 US embassy memo to the US secretary of state, "responsible for 80 percent of the labor done by Filipinos on Guam."[55] In addition to exploiting the labor of Filipino workers, American business interests also generated capital through the process of transporting laborers; companies could earn a profit every time a new migrant traveled to a Pacific military installation. When the US military and private contractors integrated Filipino laborers into the US military economy during the colonial era and then during the postwar Pacific labor market, they built upon, adapted, and continued the uneven political and economic relationship between the United States, the Pacific islands, and the Philippines.

Furthermore, because wages and other working conditions were established through diplomatic channels, any alteration required a new round of negotiations. Thus, ironically, Philippine independence made it easier for the US military and private contractors to justify lower wages and therefore continue to exploit the colonial-era wage inequality.[56] In this manner, the transwar labor regime that had been elaborated in the colonial era—with its wage differentials and lower "standard of living" for Filipinos—continued, with the help of Philippine politicians, even after Philippine independence and was a crucial cost-saving measure for the US military at the start of the Cold War.

Occupational Hazards

On September 21, 1952, the *New York Times* published "Report on Okinawa: A Rampart We Built," by George Barrett, a foreign correspondent who the year before had set himself apart from other journalists by publishing an unflinching and graphic account of the Republic of Korea's military strike on a village in the southern province of South Gyeongsang.[57] During the war, Barrett chronicled the devastating effects of some US-led bombing missions on Korean villages, many of which originated from Kadena Air Base in Okinawa.[58] His September 1952 report was thus prompted by a desire to investigate where the strikes on Korea had originated. However, in contrast to Barrett's pieces on the Korean War, which arguably blurred the neat and moralistic boundaries of Cold War violence that US policymakers sought to maintain, his extended piece on the US military's "$500,000,000 construction project" on the island of Okinawa worked to naturalize the US military's transformation of a former Japanese colony into the "the key American air base in the Fast East."[59]

Okinawa Island, the largest in the Ryukyu island chain southwest of Japan, had been the site of one of the deadliest battles in the Pacific War. That devastation, according to Barrett, resulted in a "savage transfer of title" for the island from the Japanese Empire to occupying Americans. While the rest of Occupied Japan reverted to Japanese sovereignty in April of 1952, the United States kept control of the southern islands, including Iwo Jima and Okinawa, where it retained a large, and growing, strategic military presence. "What was still only recently a lonely, weed-ravaged memorial to the 12,520 Americans and 110,000 Japanese who died" there in 1945 had now become, Barrett observed, "a rivet-hammering, rock-blasting, $500,000,000 construction project." The "savage title" transferred through warfare and abundant US military budgets explained how Okinawa had become home to airfields now perfectly positioned "for the B29s that take off each day to pound North Korea."[60]

If Barrett saw the US occupation of Okinawa as, in part, territory won through war, the US military expanded this logic into one of "national security" and protection against potential war in order to justify its presence in the Pacific. Like Barrett, the US military often referenced the need—should war come again— "for the gargantuan eight-engine heavies that can carry atom bombs against any target on the surface of our planet." Yet, rather than dwelling on the strategic or geopolitical dimensions of US-controlled Okinawa, or "the political future" of the former Japanese colony, Barrett's article invites readers to marvel at the size and scope of a construction project that was "roughly equivalent to building a city the size of Indianapolis from scratch."[61] Sketching a scene described as an "magical transplanting of whole American communities," Barrett lavished detail on the new "suburban housing developments" that featured schools, department stores, and theatres as well as "winding roads, flagstone walks and 'picket' fences" made of bamboo. He marveled at how the US military had transformed a "barrier-reefed outpost [that] was little more than a wasteland when the last war ended" into both the "Gibraltar of the Pacific" and a home away from home for American service members and their families.[62]

Yet despite Barrett's attention to the details of "modern kitchens" and bamboo fences, his article only briefly mentions the workers who hammered, rock-blasted, and cemented the project into place: the "construction gangs" comprised of American, Okinawan, Japanese, and Filipino laborers. It was not particularly uncommon for the US military to employ civilian workers from nearby communities but, by the immediate postwar era, neither was the presence of Filipino laborers working on US military construction projects outside of the Philippines unique. Clearly, the presence of Filipino workers on US bases in the Pacific had become so routine that Barrett did not even think to explain the presence of these overseas foreign workers in Okinawa. So naturalized was the imperial labor regime that Barrett—the hard-hitting investigative journalist— could not even see it.

By the early 1950s, after receiving complaints from Philippine workers around the Pacific, the Philippine government issued a request to the US State Department regarding migrant labor. Citing "discriminatory wage differentials" as a central concern, the Philippine government demanded to renegotiate the 1947 labor agreement. The US military and military contractors categorized labor and determined wages based on the nationality of workers, resulting in a system in which Americans, Filipinos, and Okinawans would be paid dramatically different wages for the same job.[63] To give an example of wage differentials, the US Air Force paid Ryukyuan plumbers, a relatively skilled position, $0.15, Filipino plumbers $0.76, and Americans $2.37 for each hour of work.[64]

In response, the US military used the logic of national or international security to justify the fortification of US military presence in the Pacific *and* the system of wage differentials. As I've written elsewhere, the topic of wage differentials was discussed in a series of 1956 Congressional hearings regarding the application of the "Fair Labor and Standards Act in Certain Territories, Possessions, and Oversea Areas of the United States," during which the Department of Defense (DOD) lobbied to ensure that the US military and US military contractors remained exempt.[65] In the hearings, Rear Admiral Joel. D. Parks stated that the DOD was interested in "stretching the defense dollars as far as they will go," noting that "the amount of money which can be spent for nation defense [was] limited." He defined this limit as "the amount of money this country can afford or the national economy can afford." Paying higher wages to Filipino laborers, a topic on which he spoke directly during his testimony, meant "something else [was] going to have to be cut out of defense." Though he did not say so explicitly, Parks communicated that the enormous presence of the US military around the world in the 1950s depended on the continued exploitation of Filipino workers.[66] Furthermore, when faced with complaints, the DOD argued that the costs of the US military's global security role had to be shared. Indeed, a 1957 DOD position paper on the renegotiation of the 1947 Philippine labor agreement makes clear the kind of pressure the US military was willing to put on the Philippine state in order to maintain its access to low-wage workers, when it reminded Philippine political leaders that any adaptation to the wage scale would result in increased rates of "unemployment and loss of dollar exchange" in the Philippines. The DOD also urged negotiators to emphasize the fact that "US bases surrounding the Philippine islands" afford "protection to the Philippine Islands proper."[67]

Labor complaints were not limited to imported Filipino workers. In Okinawa, US military and civilian occupation officials had to address the resentment Ryukyuan laborers felt toward Filipino laborers. The political, economic, and social conditions in the Ryukyuan islands, which were incorporated into the Japanese nation-state in 1879, posed a different set of problems than those faced by the US military on the island of Guam. Beginning in 1949, the US occupation in Okinawa began instituting English-language training and technical training in order to eventually replace Filipino laborers with less costly Ryukyuan laborers. This was particularly important to civilian occupation officials who recognized the impact that the US military's expropriation of land had on the Okinawa labor market. According to a 1955 study, seventy-five thousand Okinawans labored for the US military, 80 percent of whom had "been driven out from the rural communities through land expropriations."[68] A recent International Confederation of Free Trade Unions report had also criticized the wage inequality there. It was the DOD's position that replacing Filipinos with Ryukyuan laborers on Okinawa would get rid of the problem of wage differentials and, from the point of view of the US military, the forced repatriation of Filipino laborers was consistent with the terms under which Filipinos had been hired to work overseas. According to the explanation provided by J. E. Moore, lieutenant general in the US Army and high commissioner of the Ryukyu Islands to the US ambassador to the Philippines, it had been necessary in the early occupation years to bring in "qualified [Filipino] personnel to assist in the rehabilitation and operational work" because Okinawa's almost exclusively agrarian economy had meant that there was a "totally inadequate number of trained and experienced workers" on site for the US military to hire.[69] The military and the occupation government had, however, always planned to train Ryukyuans as part of a broader development plan for the island.

In fact, in November of 1948 CINCFE wrote to the Department of the Army on the "employment of native labor" in "non-occupation projects" to argue that hiring Ryukyuans in Okinawa would come at "no expense to the United States." The "several thousand civilians, mostly Filipinos," who were employed in the construction, maintenance, and operation of US military installations came at "a heavy dollar cost to the US—far in excess of native labor costs."[70] By this, CINCFE was referring to the US military's policy of paying laborers in high-value US dollars, not the devalued local currency. CINCFE suggested paying Ryukyuan laborers in yen purchased through appropriated funds.[71] Further, hiring local workers would benefit the Ryukyuan population, as "labor is practically the only commodity the Ryukan [sic] people now have to sell." This was not, however, because the destroyed agrarian economy left them unable "to produce themselves an adequate supply of consumer goods" but, as the letter admits, because of "the fact that one third of the total cultivatable land in Okinawa is used by our military and naval forces."[72] This new plan would increase prospects of the Ryukyuan economy particularly in agriculture and fisheries. Indeed, the US military's presence had—according to a 1955 Congressional hearing—acquired 17 percent of farmland and in the process dispossessed upward of fifty thousand Ryukyuan families. Thus, transitioning Filipinos out of jobs in Okinawa would open up positions for the local population who the US military and civilian occupation had committed to training.⁷³

There were further complaints raised about "wage differentials," unemployment, and labor mobility across the American Trust Territory of the Pacific Islands (TTPI), Hawaii Territory, and Guam. In October 1949, the new civilian governor of Guam wrote to Oren Long, the secretary of Hawaii, requesting the "most recent numbers on unemployment in the Territory of Hawaii." In particular, Governor Carlton Skinner wanted to know if there were any categories of labor available for employment. "As you probably know," Skinner wrote, "much of the labor force on the Island of Guam consists of [an] alien group—Filipinos." The California-born governor assumed that the Filipino group had been hired when there was a labor shortage in the United States, and the nation had sent the workers to Guam in an effort to shift "the emphasis of employment of U.S. citizens or residents of other U.S. territories."⁷⁴ In fact, in March of 1949, Hawaii's secretary Long had already written to the director of the Office of the Territories and Island Possessions, a part of the Department of the Interior, to suggest that the thirty-three thousand unemployed workers on the Hawaiian Islands could replace the "ten or fifteen thousand Filipinos" working on Guam.⁷⁵

Underemployment was an issue across US-held territories in the late 1940s, and the US military's decision to import Filipino laborers eventually rankled civilian officials who were attempting to deal with unemployment problems in US territories. In 1949, for example, the governor of Guam demanded to have "evidence of the non-availability of citizens of Guam, citizens of the United States, citizens of the Marianas, or other islands of the trust territory."⁷⁶ In February of 1950, Ingram M. Stainback, the territorial governor of Hawaii, asked the director of interior to inquire with the navy if Hawaiian laborers could fill the jobs currently filled by Filipinos on Guam.⁷⁷ Civilian governors in US-controlled territories did not necessarily object to individuals migrating between US territories as much as they did to the practice of hiring Filipinos—citizens from an independent country—for US military work. For example, in 1950, R. S. Herman, the acting governor of Guam, contacted the high commissioner of the TTPI to share his support for the mobility of workers from the TTPI, which included the Mariana, Marshall, and Caroline Islands, and noted that "at present time, large numbers of aliens [are] employed at various places." Herman also "recognized that other areas [than Guam] are in need of cash income earned by such a group," and he suggested to the TTPI high commissioner that "our interests and commitments would best be served by making available employment opportunities to local inhabitants and Trust Territory inhabitants first." He added that "free movement of Trust Territory residents for work is necessary to avoid instituting features of the forced contract labor system which has been seen an ugly excrescence of colonialism in the last two hundred years."⁷⁸ Not in so many words, the governor recognized the continuities of the United States' colonial labor system in the Pacific.

Conclusion

In late July 1957, Salvador Ancheta and Luis Roldan, leaders of the Filipino Returnees from Okinawa Association, drafted a letter to the Philippine secretary of foreign affairs (Felixberto Serrano) and the US ambassador in Manila (Charles Bohlen). Both men had, in 1947, traveled to Okinawa to work for the US Armed Forces. Seven years later, in 1954, both were deported from Okinawa as part of an effort to reduce the military's reliance on third-country nationals (a category that did include US citizens) and increase hiring from what the military termed as "local labor pools."⁷⁹

In the seven-page-long letter, Ancheta and Roldan detailed their grievances, including the forced separation from their spouses, women whom they had met while laboring on Okinawa, and their children. The deportees had been forced to leave the island on short notice, leaving them with insufficient time to arrange for travel documents for family members. For most of the individuals in the Filipino Returnees from Okinawa Association, the forced separation from their spouses and children ranked highest on their list of grievances. Moreover, according to Roldan and Ancheta, many Filipinos wanted to stay in Okinawa. Even Filipinos who were legally married to Ryukyuan women were not allowed to stay in the island, and this was even if they found a job with a commercial firm. Harassment by the Ryukyuan police also ranked among their list of grievances, but the Filipino returnees argued that the US military and US civil administration—not the Ryukyuan government—were to blame. Ancheta and Roldan argued that after "ten long years of loyal and faithful service to the United States Armed Forces" the military had launched a "systematic punitive campaign aimed solely to persecute and discriminate the very same Filipino workhorses" who had made the military's achievements in Okinawa "PHYSICALLY possible."⁸⁰ In short, Roldan and Ancheta argued that the Filipino workers faced discrimination and exploitation on multiple fronts, and they knew that this was tied to the success of the US military in the Pacific.

While Philippine officials viewed the labor arrangement with the US military and private contractors as a means of addressing unemployment in the archipelago, US military officials saw it as a way to stretch budgets based on a discriminatory pay system based on race and nationality. Filipino laborers who worked on US military installations deepened an existing transpacific imperial pattern whereby state and capital interests collaborated to recruit and exploit pools of low-wage workers and to keep pay low across the Pacific "labor pool." Previously, US colonization had provided the state and private capital a way to access and mobilize Filipino laborers, although usually these workers were headed to the US mainland (such as the California agricultural workers). However, the new political context of the postwar Pacific, including the event of Philippine independence, posed new challenges to the previous colonial division of labor. Cold War ideology made it easier for private constructors and the US military to adapt to the challenges posed by Philippine independence. Moreover, the US incorporation of Pacific territories meant that Filipino laborers found themselves laboring for Cold War "national security" in places neither formally colonized nor fully independent. As I've described elsewhere, perhaps counterintuitively, the expansion of US military power also politicized workers in new ways. The experience of working for the US military or US military contractors led some workers to demand more rights and protections from the Philippine state, the United States, and even the United Nations.[81]

Yet even as some Filipinos, Ryukyuan, and Americans fought to include contracted workers under the United States Fair Labor Standards Act of 1949, their efforts for justice relied on the colonial relationship between the United States, the Philippines, and Okinawa staying in place.

American politicians, the US military, and military contractors believed that the employment opportunities created by the expansion of the US military in the Pacific ultimately benefitted everyone involved; by positioning bases in the Pacific as central to "international security," American officials argued that Filipino or Ryukyuan laborers worked for their own security, not just US interests. Nonetheless, in the case of Okinawa, these comments reveal how a free-market labor regime was created through the expropriation of Ryukyuan land and the flooding of the labor market with agricultural workers; in the case of the Philippines, it depended on an international agreement between two sovereign states that was enforced through contracts with individual workers. In both cases, the argument of cooperation and security obscured relations of power. To be clear, the logic of fiscal necessity does not explain the US military's reliance on Filipino workers in Okinawa, because the expansion of the US military overseas is not just about the free-market allure of contract labor: it is also about the ways in which US imperial power expanded under the guise of "global or international security" and on the back of a colonial legacy.

Notes

1 Scholarship on labor migration during the colonial period includes the following: Joanna Poblete, *Islanders in the Empire: Filipino and Puerto Rican Laborers in Hawai'i* (Urbana: University of Illinois Press, 2014); Dorothy Fujita-Rony, *American Workers, Colonial Power: Philippine Seattle and the Transpacific West, 1919–1941* (Berkeley: University of California Press, 2003); Rick Baldoz, *The Third Asiatic Invasion: Empire and Migration in Filipino America, 1898–1946* (New York: New York University Press, 2011); and Catherine Choy, *Empire of Care: Nursing and Migration in Filipino American History* (Durham, NC: Duke University Press, 2003). Examples of recent work on Philippine export labor include the following: Robyn Magalit Rodriguez, *Migrants for Export: How the Philippine State Brokers Labor to the World* (Minneapolis: University of Minnesota Press, 2010); Filomeno V. Aguilar Jr., *Migration Revolution: Philippine Nationhood and Class Relations in a Globalized Age* (Singapore: National University of Singapore Press, 2014); Kristel Acacio, "Managing Labor Migration: Philippine State Policy and International Migration Flows, 1969–2000," *Asian and Pacific Migration Journal* 17, no. 2 (2008): 103–32; and Rhacel Salazar Parreñas, *Servants of Globalization: Women, Migration, and Domestic Work* (Stanford, CA: Stanford University Press, 2001).

2 For examples of cultural studies scholarship that bridge the divide between the colonial and the postcolonial, see Denise Cruz, *Transpacific Femininities: The Making of a Modern Filipina* (Durham, NC: Duke University Press, 2012); and Martin F. Manalansan and Augusto Espiritu, eds., *Filipino Studies: Palimpsests of Nation and Diaspora* (New York: New York University Press, 2016). Studies on Philippine communism or the Hukbalahap Revolution are exceptions to the typical periodization. Examples include the following: Ken Fuller, *Forcing the Pace: The Partido Komunista ng Pilipinas—from Foundation to Armed Struggle* (Quezon City: University of the Philippines Press, 2014); Vina Lanzona, *Amazons of the Huk Rebellion: Gender, Sex, and Revolution in the Philippines* (Madison: University of Wisconsin Press, 2009); Benedict Kerkvliet, *The Huk Rebellion: A Study of Peasant Revolt in the Philippines* (Berkeley: University of California Press, 1997).

3 Colleen Woods, "Building Empire's Archipelago: The Imperial Politics of Filipino Labor in the Pacific," *Labor: Studies of Working-Class History in the Americas* 13, nos. 3–4 (2016): 131–52.

4 On Filipino laborers and Guam, see Alfred PeredoFlores, "'No Walk in the Park': US Empire and the Racialization of Civilian Military Labor in Guam, 1944–1962," *American Quarterly* 67, no. 3 (2015): 813–35.

5 Christopher Capozzola, *Bound by War: How the United States and the Philippines Built America's First Pacific Century* (New York: Basic Books, 2020), 28–9; Brian Linn, *Guardians of Empire: The U.S. Army in the Pacific, 1902–1940* (Chapel Hill: University of North Carolina Press, 1997), 44–5.

6 A notable exception is Flores, "No Walk in the Park," 813–35.

7 Quoted in Howard T. Fry, "The Bacon Bill of 1926: New Light on an Exercise in Divide-and-Rule," *Philippine Studies* 26, no. 3 (1978): 257–73.

8 Harry N. Whitford, "Rubber and the Philippines," *Foreign Affairs* 4, no. 4 (July 1926): 677–9.

9 Fry, "Bacon Bill," 259.

10 Mark R. Finlay, *Growing American Rubber: Strategic Plants and the Politics of National Security* (New Brunswick, NJ: Rutgers University Press, 2009), 62–3.

11 Russell B. Porter, "Thompson Watches Filipinos at Work," *New York Times*, July 19, 1926.

12 Justin F. Jackson, "A Military Necessity Which Must Be Pressed: The U.S. Army and Forced Road Labor in the Early American Colonial Philippines," in *On Coerced Labor: Work and Compulsion after Chattel Slavery*, ed. Marcel M. van der Linden and Magaly Rodríguez García (Leiden: Brill, 2016), 127–58.

13 Greg Bankoff, "Wants, Wages, and Workers: Laboring in the American Philippines, 1899–1908," *Pacific Historical Review* 74, no. 1 (February 2005): 59–86.

14 Editorial, "Our Labor Problem," *American Chamber of Commerce Journal* 3, no. 1 (January 1923): 19.

15 Bankoff, "Wants, Wages, and Workers."

16 Paul Kramer, *The Blood of Government: Race, Empire, the United States, and the Philippines* (Chapel Hill: University of North Carolina Press, 2006), 201–4.

17 Anne L. Foster, *Projections of Power: The United States and Europe in Colonial Southeast Asia, 1919–1941* (Durham, NC: Duke University Press, 2010), 43–4.

18 William Cameron Forbes, *The Philippine Islands*, vol. 1 (Boston: Houghton Mifflin, 1928), 186.

19 Philippines Bureau of Civil Service, *Twenty-Seventh Annual Report of the Director of Civil Service to the Governor-General of the Philippine Islands for the Year Ended December 31, 1926* (Manila: Bureau of Printing, 1927), 35.

20 Colleen Woods, *Freedom Incorporated: Anticommunism and Philippine Independence in the Age of Decolonization* (Ithaca, NY: Cornell University Press, 2020), 31–2.

21 *The Port of Manila: A Year Book 1928* (Manila: Manila Harbor Board), 11.

22 Ibid., 7.
23 Edward Rosenberg, "Filipinos as Workmen," *American Federationist* 10, no. 3 (October 1903): 1021–31.
24 Ibid., 1022.
25 On hiring Chinese laborers, see Rebecca Tinio McKenna, *American Imperial Pastoral: The Architecture of US Colonialism in the Philippines* (Chicago: University of Chicago Press, 2017), 60–3.
26 Rosenberg, "Filipinos as Workmen," 1021.
27 Bankoff, "Wants, Wages, and Workers."
28 On "standard of living" and the American Federation of Labor's anti-Asian politics, see Masayo Umezawa Duus, *The Japanese Conspiracy: The Oahu Sugar Strike* (Berkeley: University of California Press, 1999), 258.
29 *Building the Navy's Bases in World War II: History of Bureau of Yards and Docks and the Civil Engineer Corps, 1940–1946* (Washington, DC: US Government Printing Office, 1947), iii.
30 Irene Murphy to Frank Murphy, February 1, 1946, box 1, "Correspondence," Irene Murphy Papers, Bentley Historical Library, Ann Arbor, MI.
31 Robert A. Taft, "War Damage Insurance Coverage for the Philippine Islands," *Congressional Record*, vol. 91, part 6 (Washington, DC: US Government Printing Office, 1945), 8311–12.
32 Irene Murphy to Frank Murphy, February 1, 1946.
33 Christina Evangelista Torres, *The Americanization of Manila, 1898–1921* (Quezon City: University of the Philippines Press, 2010), 57–64.
34 Irene Murphy to Frank Murphy, February 1, 1946.
35 Quoted in Woods, *Freedom Incorporated*, 60.
36 AmCross Manila to AmCross Washington, March 19, 1946, RG 94, Records of the Foreign Service Posts of the Department of State, Philippine Islands, US Embassy Manila, Classified General Records, 1946–1948, box 10.
37 United Nations Relief and Rehabilitation Administration, *UNRRA in the Philippines, 1946–1947*, Operational Analysis Papers, UNRRA, 1948.
38 Report 209, October 27, 1947, RG 84, Foreign Service Posts of the United States, Manila Embassy, General Records, 1947, 842-850.03, box 26.
39 "Civil Affairs in Manila, a Brief Review of the Period from 3 February 1945 to 30 June 1945," RG 496, Records of the General Headquarters of the Southwest Pacific Area and United States Army Forces, Pacific, Civil Affairs Section, General Correspondence, 1944–1945, box 2281, NARA II.
40 "Labor Dep't Probers Find No Discrimination in Guam," February 3, 1948, *Manila Chronicle*, microfilm. Cleveland, OH: Bell & Howell, Micro Photo Division, Library of Congress, Washington, DC.

41 US Army Forces, *Engineers of the Southwest Pacific, 1941–1945: Reports of Operations [of the] United States Army Forces in the Far East, Southwest Pacific Area, Army Forces, Pacific*, vol. II, 194.
42 Lindesay Parrot, "We Build a Base That Surpasses All Others," *New York Times*, July 22, 1945.
43 Woods, "Building Empire's Archipelago," 141.
44 Bruce Cumings, *Dominion from Sea to Sea: Pacific Ascendancy and American Power* (New Haven, CT: Yale University Press, 2010), 393.
45 CINCFE to MARBO, PHILRYCOM, May 7, 1947, box 103; General Correspondence Files, 1944–1952; GHQ; Records of the General Headquarters, Far East Command, Supreme Commander Allied Powers, and United Nations Command, RG 554, NARA, College Park.
46 For a thorough treatment of the first ten years of the US occupation of Okinawa, see David John Obermiller, "The US Military Occupation of Okinawa: Politicizing and Contesting Okinawan Identity, 1945–1955" (PhD diss., University of Iowa, 2006); and Jonathan Swenson-Wright, *Unequal Allies? United States Security and Alliance Policy towards Japan, 1945–1960* (Stanford, CA: Stanford University Press, 2005).
47 Embassy of the US in Manila to Philippine Acting Secretary of Foreign Affairs, May 13, 1947, file 000006-002; Administrative Files; Labor Department; Records of the US Civil Administration of the Ryuku Islands (hereafter USCAR); Records of the US Occupation Headquarters, WWII, RG 260, Okinawa Prefecture Library, Naha, Okinawa.
48 Embassy of the US in Manila to Philippine Acting Secretary of Foreign Affairs, May 13, 1947. See also Woods, "Building Empire's Archipelago," 144–5.
49 Woods, "Building Empire's Archipelago," 136.
50 Recruitment of Personnel for R and U Activities, August 30, 1947, RG 554, Records of the General Headquarters, Far East Command, Supreme Commander Allied Powers, and United Nations Command, MARBO, Adjutant General Section, Correspondence Files, 1944–1952, box 24.
51 Recruitment of Personnel for R and U Activities, August 30, 1947, RG 554, Records of the General Headquarters, Far East Command, Supreme Commander Allied Powers, and United Nations Command, MARBO, Adjutant General Section, Correspondence Files, 1944–1952, box 24.
52 Seventh and final report of High Commissioner to the Philippines Islands Covering the Period from September 14, 1945, to July 4, 1946, RG 84 Foreign Service Posts of the United States, Manila Embassy, General Records, box 10.
53 On Luzon Stevedore Company, see Woods, "Building Empire's Archipelago," 142–3.
54 Flores, "No Walk in the Park," 820–1.
55 US Embassy to Secretary of State, February 8, 1948, RG 84 Foreign Service Posts of the United States, Manila Embassy, General Records, box 10.

56 Woods, "Building Empire's Archipelago," 148.
57 Oliver Elliot, *The American Press and the Cold War: The Rise of Authoritarianism in South Korea, 1945–1954* (New York: Springer International, 2018), 133–4.
58 Pedro Iacobelli, "The Other Legacy of the Korean War: Okinawa and the Fear of World War III," in *The Korean War in Asia: A Hidden History*, ed. Tessa Morris-Suzuki (Lanham, MD: Rowman and Littlefield, 2018), 123.
59 George Barrett, "Report on Okinawa: A Rampart We Built," September 21, 1952, *New York Times*.
60 Ibid.
61 Ibid.
62 Ibid.
63 See also Johanna O. Zulueta, *Transnational Identities on Okinawa's Military Bases: Invisible Armies for wages in U.S. Dollars* (New York: Palgrave Macmillan, 2020).
64 Comparative wages of different nationalities of Okinawa, Labor Relations Program Files, Records of the Labor Department, Administration Files, 1952–1972, RG 260, Records of US Occupation, USCAR, box 2.
65 Woods, "Building Empire's Archipelago," 137–8. Military officials in Okinawa were informed that the debate over the Fair Labor Standards Act would not include the island and therefore would not apply to either Filipino or Ryukyuan laborers. In fact, the act would not include any of the US bases in the Pacific.
66 United States House Committee on Education and Labor, Minimum Wages in Certain Territories, Possessions, and Overseas Areas of the United States, part one (Washington, DC: US Government Printing Office, 1956), 115.
67 "Philippines Government Negotiations in Relation to 1947 Employment Agreement," box 1, Records of the Assistant Secretary for Manpower Relating to the Alien Labor Policy, Guam, 1947–1971, General Records of the Department of Labor, RG 174, NARA.
68 Army-Air Force Wage Survey, 1955, file 015002-882, Civil Administration of the Ryukyu Islands, Records of USCAR, Records of the US Occupation Headquarters, WWII, RG 260, Okinawa Prefectural Archive, NAHA.
69 Comparative wages of different nationalities of Okinawa, Labor Relations Program Files, Records of the Labor Department, Administration Files, 1952–1972, RG 260, Records of US Occupation, USCAR, box 2.
70 CINCFE to Department of Army, November 19, 1948, RG 554, Records of the General Headquarter, Far East Command, Supreme Commander Allied Powers, and United Nations Command, Engineer Section, General Correspondence, Classified, 1948, box 114.
71 Ibid.
72 Ibid.

73 "Okinawa Lands," October 24 and 25, 1955, Hearings before a Subcommittee of the Committee on Armed Services, House of Representatives, 84th Congress (Washington, DC: Government Printing Office, 1957), 2.
74 Carlton Skinner to Oren Long, October 26, 1949, RG 126, Office of Territories, Classified File, 1907–1951, box 534.
75 Oren Long to James Davis, March 1, 1949, RG 126, Office of Territories, Classified File, 1907–1951, box 534.
76 Carlton Skinner to Oren Long, October 26, 1949.
77 Ingram M. Stainback to James Davis, February 17, 1950, RG 126, Office of Territories, Classified File, 1907–1951, box 534.
78 R. S. Herman to High Commissioner of the Trust Territories of the Pacific, August 22, 1950, RG 126, Office of Territories, Classified File, 1907–1951, box 534.
79 Filipino Allegations of Discrimination by US Agencies in the Ryukyu Islands, RG 260, box 6. Labor Relations Program Files, Records of the Labor Department, Administration Files, 1952–1972, RG 260, Records of US Occupation, NARA.
80 Ibid.
81 US Embassy, Manila, to US Secretary of State, February 7, 1957, file 000006-002; Okinawa Prefectural Library, Naha, Okinawa. See also Woods, "Building Empire's Archipelago," 149.

4

University, Landed Class, and Land Reform: Transwar Origins of Private Universities in South Korea, 1920–1960

Do Young Oh

Introduction

The university in South Korea is often labeled as an "oxbone tower," in contrast to the more popular term "ivory tower."[1] This term derives from the phenomenon of farmers selling their cattle in order to pay their children's tuition, with that money often used to construct new campus buildings. The term first appeared in newspapers in 1969 when national assembly members used it to criticize the private universities' profit-seeking and asset-accumulating behaviors at the time.[2] It is still widely used because the higher education structure has not changed significantly since then. Private universities dominate the higher education system in South Korea, and their operations are primarily funded by tuition fees, meaning that the burden of education has been transferred to households to a great extent. On the other hand, private universities have been considered as assets of their founders like chaebols in South Korea. According to an investigation in 2015, half the private universities were run by families of their founders.[3] Substantial corruption has accompanied this nepotistic system. Until 2019, the government has detected 1,367 cases of misappropriation of funds and accounting fraud by private universities since they were established.[4] Considering there are 293 private universities in South Korea, this equates to an average of 4.7 cases per university. Such investigations show a problematic situation of private universities in South Korea today.

This chapter examines the processes through which the private university was born and its subsequent expansion, focusing on the transwar period between 1920 and 1960. It traces how and why the higher education sector is often considered an unsolved problem in South Korean society. Here, I use a "transwar" frame as a strategy to overcome dichotomic conceptualizations of the colonizer and the colonized in the Korean Peninsula as well as disparate conceptions of colonial and independent Korea. Korean literature studies have already begun to mobilize such a framework, as done by Lin Pei-Yin and Kim Su Yun.[5] Among Korean historians, it is well known that interminable debates have taken place to identify the origins of Korean capitalism.[6] Such a debate focusing on the political economy of colonial society often ended up as an attempt to either justify Japanese imperialism or counteract that view. But these debates often overlooked the discussion of the "gray zone" until the end of the twentieth century among Korean historians. As argued by Yun Hae-Dong, there were complex and diverse interactions between multiple actors under colonial rule, and these interactions and relationships were crucial in the formation of Korean society following liberation from Japan.[7]

Investigating higher education institutions and their relationships with society gives us an effective opportunity to tackle this issue. The institutions were established by different colonial interests and have been operating by interacting with diverse parts of society. Even the Korean War could not stop the operation of private universities. In this regard, an investigation of higher education institutions during the transwar period can be an opportunity to understand the transformations of Korean society as a continuous story. Even though, as Shin Gi-Wook argued, the modern history of South Korea was not linear but uneven and fractured,[8] it can be said that the higher education sector, as a relatively homogeneous group, has been continuously evolving by interacting with other parts of society.

This chapter focuses on the relationship between the university and the landed class throughout the transwar period, which is believed to have formed the historical conditions of higher education institutions today. According to Jones and Sakong's study of the Korean economy in the 1970s, 41.4 percent of university professors and 46.8 percent of businessmen were from landlord families during the colonial era.[9] Such data suggest there is a demonstrable linkage between preindustrial elite groups and higher education elites. Carter Eckert's landmark study on the Kyŏngsŏng Spinning and Weaving Company shows how the landed class transformed itself to become the industrial class under colonial rule and thereby maintained their wealth and power.[10] Yet, while his study provides an in-depth understanding of the transition process to the industry sector, it barely mentions any such similar transition in the context of the higher education sector. Considering the fact that Kim Sŏng-su, the founder of the same company, was also president of Korea University, it is worth investigating how the landed class transformed itself into educational elites and how the higher education institutions were established and developed throughout the transwar period.

The Emergence of the Pro-Japanese Landed Class

When the Korean Peninsula was in turmoil after the first opening of its port to Imperial Japan in 1876, the contradiction of the class system was intensifying and external pressures by the world powers to open its ports were increasing. While there were several attempts to revolutionize the country, the *yangban* class, landed aristocracy of the Joseon Dynasty, wanted to protect their economic footing by maintaining the landlord system.[11] They still needed their lands as the significant source of their income regardless of the fierce battles between different political *yangban* groups such as the pro-Japanese and pro-Russian ones of the time. Subsequent interventions such as Kwangmu Land Reform of 1898, under the newly proclaimed Korean Empire, were also no more than reassurances of the existing rights of the state and the landed class by stipulating their ownership rather than dismantling their powers. This particular reform process was not completed due to the rapidly changing political circumstances but was later conducted by the colonial government more comprehensively under colonial rule from 1910.

The landed aristocracy who were able to adapt themselves to the new system could keep their wealth and power under colonial rule and had the opportunity to continue doing so following the liberation of Korea in 1945. Exploitation in Korea had intensified from 1910 while certain groups of Koreans benefited from it. After 1906, the Japanese were legally permitted to possess land in Korea. Thus, Japanese-owned land, which was purchased through expedient methods,[12] was legalized, and commercialized farming by Japanese was intensified. Even though the colonial state once owned 40 percent of land in Korea in 1930, the existing landed aristocracy was able to maintain and increase its land ownership until 1945.[13] Lee Se-Young's in-depth analysis of agricultural land ownership change in four villages located in the southwest region, between 1910 and 1945, shows that while farmland ownership by the Japanese was increasing, Korean large farmland owners were less affected by the increasing presence of the Japanese.[14] Throughout Japanese colonial rule, the number of Koreans holding 500,000 square meters of farmlands remained above 1,500.[15] This shows that a few Koreans were still able to maintain and accumulate wealth under colonial rule.

These landlords were not a homogeneous group, but those who were not able to adapt to the changing environment and were not supportive of the colonial regime fell behind. For example, in Chŏnbuk Province, the number of large landlords owning more than approximately 1 square kilometer (100 chŏngbo) of land increased from seventy-eight in 1926 to eighty-three in 1938, but of the eighty-three, only twenty-two were previously counted in 1926.[16] Over twelve years, more than 70 percent of Korean landowners in the region lost their status as a large landowner. In this regard, it can be assumed that it was challenging to maintain wealth even for the landed class under colonial rule. Korean historians such as Hong Sung-Chan argued that "dynamic landlords" were able to survive by receiving incentives from the colonial government and adjusting themselves in opposition to "stagnant landlords."[17] A small number of them were known as active supporters of the independence movement such as the Ch'oe family in Kyŏngju, but most of the large landowners were part of a social basis, to varying degrees, in support of colonial rule.[18]

Some large landowners were able to transform themselves as industrialists by utilizing their wealth. The most well-known case is the Kim family from Koch'ang as investigated extensively by Eckert.[19] The family grew their wealth by agricultural land accumulation following the opening of Korean ports. They then established the Kyŏngsŏng Spinning and Weaving Company (later Kyŏngbang) in 1919 thanks to their economic and political opportunism. The organization was considered one of the most successful Korean companies during colonial rule. The story of the Kim family is not a rare case. According to a study by Jones and Sakong on entrepreneurs in South Korea in the 1970s, 46.8 percent of them were from agricultural landowner families.[20] Eckert assumed that the actual portion was likely higher than the statistics, considering other well-known cases such as Kim Chong-han, founder of the Hansŏng Bank.[21] In this regard, there were ample opportunities for the landed aristocrats to diverge their economic bases toward colonial capitalism.

The landed aristocracy was also often involved in establishing schools in Korea. A large number of private schools were already in operation before the 1910 annexation. It is estimated that 1,402 private schools operated as of 1910.[22] While the number of public primary schools increased from 126 in 1910 to 561 in 1920, more than 70 percent of the newly established schools were converted from existing private schools.[23] Kang Myung-Sook argued that the establishment of public schools was often the result of the nexus between the colonial government and local elite groups.²⁴ While the colonial government wanted to expand basic educational opportunities at lower cost, local elites wanted to take the initiative regarding the colonial transformation of their region by establishing and supporting local schools. In this regard, colonial education was a political process and often worked as a means to protect the power of the landed class.

Growth of Higher Education under Colonial Rule

Since the colonial government tended to restrict higher education opportunities in Korea, opportunities to establish and operate higher education institutions were granted only to a few limited groups. Kim Sŏng-su, the founder of the Kyŏngsŏng Spinning and Weaving Company, was the one who took over Posŏng Professional School, which suffered financial difficulties in 1932, and helped in expanding it further. The other influential group was American missionaries: Union Christian College and Severance Union Medical College were established before 1910. Ewha College for Women and Chosen Christian College also began providing higher learning opportunities following the annexation. While the relationship between missionaries and the colonial government was not straightforward, the colonial government offered relatively favorable conditions for missionaries to operate their schools even during the "military rule" period between 1910 and 1919. However, they were unable to acquire full-fledged university status, not least because there was no definition of the university in the first educational ordinance in Korea announced in 1911. The amended ordinance in 1922 permitted the establishment of a university, but the colonial government never allowed additional universities other than Keijō Imperial University in Korea, and so they had to remain as professional schools.²⁵

Another critical pillar of higher education in Korea was formed by governmental institutions, including Keijō Imperial University. The colonial government established several professional schools providing practical training in law, science, engineering, and commerce as of 1916. The Imperial University was then established in 1924 as the first Imperial University outside of Japan following the announcement of the 1922 amended educational ordinance. There were two drivers behind the rationale to establish an Imperial University in Korea. Firstly, there were increasing demands from Korean people, particularly after the People's University Movement starting from 1923, which was the largest Korean social movement after the March First Movement, as well as the emerging presence of mission schools.[26] In this regard, the colonial government dealt with such pressures under its "cultural rule." Secondly, the demand for higher education from the Japanese settlers in Korea also increased. In 1920, the Japanese population in Korea was 347,850, doubling in 10 years while the Korean population grew by 8 percent during the same period.[27] A consequence of this was that education opportunities in government schools were more often granted to the Japanese. At the Imperial University, two-thirds of the enrollment quota was allocated to Japanese students, with similar allocations in professional schools.[28] But Koreans who were able to graduate from these government schools could enjoy both tangible and intangible benefits as colonial elites.

The landed aristocracy was the most substantial group that could access educational opportunities. As of 1944, 78.2 percent of the Korean population had never received any formal education while only 0.1 percent had received higher education.[29] Having access to higher education was associated with relatively higher economic and political status in colonial Korea. For example, when graduating from medical professional school, an empire-wide medical license was granted from 1922 onward.[30] Imperial University graduates were frequently offered a higher position in the colonial government.[31] Fierce competition to enter higher learning institutions thus emerged among those who could afford it. A newspaper article discussing the severe competition for school entrance in 1928 was headlined thus: "Competition for School Entrance Like the Gate of Hell That Doesn't Open Even If You Knock."[32] To increase the likelihood of admission around that time, private academies and supplementary lessons were common to prepare students for school entrance exams.[33] Such investments and opportunity costs were affordable only for the propertied class, combined with the colonial government's strategy to cooperate with them.[34] In this regard, higher education was one of the guaranteed paths for the landed class to continue to reproduce their wealth and power.

The landed aristocracy also had the opportunity to study abroad, particularly in Japan. Until 1920, when the colonial government relaxed its policy to allow students to study abroad, opportunities were mostly restricted to the children of landed aristocrats, colonial capitalists, and bureaucrats.[35] Kim Sŏng-su also benefited from Japanese higher education by studying political science at Waseda University. His younger brother, Kim Yŏn-su, also studied at Kyoto Imperial University. As of 1920, more than one thousand Korean students were at universities in Japan, such as Keio, Waseda, and Meiji.[36] While rarer, there were also Korean students in the United States, with the estimate being more than three hundred students in the United States in the 1920s.³⁷ Not every student studying abroad was pro-Japanese. For instance, in 1919, Korean students in Tokyo organized the February Eighth Movement, inspired by Woodrow Wilson's principle of national self-determination. Nonetheless, those who were educated abroad were typically part of elite groups of society regardless of their position on colonial rule or their political views more generally. Many became leaders of various parts of Korean society during and after the colonial regime.

The reproduction of power also materialized within the higher education sector. In 1939, in Chosen Christian College, there were 21 Korean professors out of the 29 faculty members who held voting rights. Of the total 39 faculty members, 14 held undergraduate degrees from universities in Japan. Some of the key Korean staff included Dr. Yu Ŏk-kyŏm and Dr. Yi Myomuk, and many of them played an important role after liberation under the United States Army Military Government in Korea (USAMGIK). Not everyone is known to be from the landed aristocracy, as in the case of Dr. George L. Paik, who was a farmer's child, but according to a survey of 761 university professors in the 1970s, 41.4 percent were from agricultural landowner families, similar to the entrepreneurs mentioned above, while 18.8 percent were from industrialist families.³⁸ Since opportunities to climb the social ladder from the masses to the elite were minimal, it can be argued that the higher education sector was also the monopoly of the landed class.³⁹ Of course, it does not mean that the landed aristocracy in the Joseon Dynasty was the same as the colonial elite group. Those who failed to adapt to changes of the time or who actively resisted the colonies had no choice but to drop behind. Yet, those who survived had an opportunity to keep their power and wealth after the liberation of Korea in 1945.

From Landlords to Intellectuals

On August 15, 1945, Koreans faced an unexpected liberation due to the surrender of Imperial Japan. While Koreans dreamed of a newly independent state, what they faced was division between North and South Korea along the 38th parallel. For the Soviet Union and the United States, it was not an unexpected division. Both great powers projected their interests in the Korean Peninsula, particularly when the Chinese Civil War peaked after 1947. Korea then became an arena for ideological competition between the Eastern and Western blocs. Even after the end of the Cold War, the division between the two Koreas—an ostensibly temporary arrangement at the time—remains. In the southern part of Korea, from 1945 to the April Revolution in 1960 and the May 16 military coup d'état in 1961, Korean society experienced radical sociopolitical changes through a number of significant events.

While the landlord system was well established at the end of colonial rule, the liberation posed a signification challenge to the system, which had a symbiotic relationship with colonial capitalism. The Communist Party of Korea had already adopted the August Thesis by Pak Hŏn-yŏng in September 1945, which declared the need for radical land reform. The North then took the lead to dismantle the existing landlord system. The Provisional People's Committee of North Korea announced their own land reform on March 5, 1946, and completed the process within a month. The process was based on confiscation without compensation and free distribution. This process led to the growing popularity of the committee among peasants since only 4 percent of farmers possessed 58.2 percent of the entire arable land in the northern half of Korea in 1945.[40] In South Korea, the land ownership situation was considered more problematic. According to a report by the US Department of State, it was estimated that 75 percent of the rice lands in South Korea were cultivated by tenant farmers in 1945.[41] For the USAMGIK and the political leaders of South Korea, it became urgent to counteract the land reform in North Korea as part of their anti-communism strategy.

Despite such pressures, the land reform process in South Korea was not carried out quickly, partly due to the Korea Democratic Party, founded in September 1945, which was known for its favorable attitude toward large landlords.[42] Its founding members included several former pro-Japanese collaborators as well as large landlords such as Kim Sŏng-su and educators such as Dr. Yi Myomuk from Chosen Christian College. The party gained power with the support of the USAMGIK by working as its implementation arm because the military government needed a reliable local partner to pursue its anti-communist strategy.[43] In liberated Korea, Left and Right tended not to be distinguished by political ideologies but by their commitment to the implementation of land reform and elimination of pro-Japanese influences, as argued by Bruce Cumings.[44] In this regard, the party was lukewarm in its motivation to implement the reform while various political parties within South Korea demanded it, since there was a popular support for dissolving the system of semi-feudalism. The USAMGIK drafted the land reform bill and introduced it to the South Korean Interim Legislature in December 1947. Chu Chong-Hwan understands the USAMGIK's action as its decision to protect the capitalist class by sacrificing the landlord class for political and social stability, as had previously taken place in postwar Japan.[45] Nevertheless, the Korea Democratic Party delayed the land reform preparation process. In the end, the bill was eventually rejected due to the "strong influence of landholding interests" in the legislature in January 1948, according to the US Department of State.[46]

The land reform was initiated in South Korea before the outbreak of the Korean War, but the result of land distribution was not as significant as was the case in North Korea. The agricultural land distribution was mentioned in the first constitution in South Korea, enacted in July 1948, and the land reform was initiated again after the establishment of the South Korean government on August 15, 1948. It was agreed that the reform needed to be based on compensated acquisition and charged distribution. Still, the government and the National Assembly had a tug of war over the detailed methods by which to compensate the landlords. In the end, the first land reform bill was proclaimed on June 21, 1949, but amended on March 10, 1950, followed by the ordinance and regulation declared on March 25 and April 29, respectively. The delay meant that the landlords could proactively respond to the proposed reform by disposing of their excessive lands in advance. As a result, as of June 1949, only 29 percent of arable land in South Korea was subjected to the reform.[47] According to Ha and Lee's study on the land reform process in a village in the Kyŏngsang region, landlords sold 61.9 percent of their land prior to the reform, and only 12.7 percent of their land was confiscated.[48] It was only after the Korean War that the landlord class was dissolved since the war destroyed properties and resulted in inflation.

University as Part of the Anti-communist Alliance

Japan's intensifying militarism during the war period could not slow down the growth of higher education in the Korean Peninsula. Students enrolled in the colonial government professional schools had almost doubled from 1,292 in 1937 to 2,421 in 1943.[49] While 75 percent of students in 1943 were Japanese, Koreans benefited from studying in private professional schools such as Chosen Christian College. The number of private professional school students increased from 2,390 in 1937 to 4,025 in 1943 while 81 percent of them were Korean.[50] Union Christian College in Pyongyang decided to close down in 1938 due to the colonial government's enforcement of shrine worship,[51] but most of the other professional colleges were in operation. For example, Chosen Christian College was confiscated by the colonial government in August 1942 due to intensifying hostile relations with the United States. The school was then headed by the

Japanese,[52] but the actual period that the school was not in operation was less than two years, from May 1944 to November 1945.[53] Right after liberation in 1945, the school hired Korean faculty members who used to teach at the school to prepare for its reopening.[54]

Higher education institutions and educators in South Korea after liberation needed to be part of the anti-communist alliance like the landlord class mobilized by the USAMGIK. The USAMGIK had two main principles for the recruitment of Korean officials. First, they were to be highly educated English-speaking people with a pro-American ideology, and second, they were to hold an anti-communist and anti-Soviet stance. According to the figures produced by the South Korea Interim Government established by the USAMGIK in February 1947, out of twenty-five senior officials, twelve had studied in the United States and eleven in Japan.[55] While many of them collaborated with Imperial Japan, their career in the USAMGIK allowed them to continue their career as politicians and bureaucrats following the establishment of the South Korean government. Overall, the administration, legislation, and judicature systems, in addition to the police, were formed based on the Japanese Government-General of Korea, and Koreans who worked for the government were employed again for the USAMGIK's anti-communist agenda. It meant that members of the colonial landed class had the opportunity to reposition themselves as political leaders in South Korea.

The colonial educators also established several new universities by taking advantage of their favorable relationships with the USAMGIK. The military government established the Korean Committee on Education as a core advisory group for educational matters. Of the eleven members of the committee, seven held positions in professional schools as a professor or a director. They could be generally categorized as Christians, educated in Japan or the United States, and members of the Korea Democratic Party.[56] While they were guiding the educational policy of South Korea, they also worked to promote their professional schools as universities. When the USAMGIK allowed private professional schools to take on university status in June 1946, three professional schools, Chosen Christian College, Ewha College for Women, and Posŏng Professional School, became the first private universities in South Korea in August 1946. Kang Myung-Sook considered the rapid promotion of these private schools as being a consequence of their close relationships with the USAMGIK, since the key members of these schools were also members of the Education Committee.[57] She also argued that other universities were established using their favorable relationships with the USAMGIK, and some of them even received vested properties for their operations.⁵⁸ By the end of the USAMGIK rule in 1948 there were forty-two universities in South Korea, showing truly unprecedented growth considering the fact there was only one university in Korea before 1945.⁵⁹

The massive increase in universities continued. As of 1960, there were eighty-one universities and colleges and 107,684 students.⁶⁰ Such an explosion was only possible with strong and widespread demand from the public. As discussed above, while Korean society experienced radical changes, some groups were able to keep their wealth and power through their educational backgrounds. In particular, after liberation, people were reassured that an educational background was a basis for the ladder of success as well as maintenance of power, since they saw that many pro-Japanese figures were appointed again as senior government officials by the USAMGIK and then the independent republic.⁶¹ The universities often recruited more students than their given quotas, and non-permitted universities were also in operation. When the Ministry of Culture and Education initially ordered the universities to reform in December 1956, thirty-two out of fifty-five universities were instructed to stop recruiting students and close their departments.⁶² Some universities nonetheless ignored the government order and continued to accept more students.⁶³ Such tendencies are evidence of lax management of universities based on the popular demand for higher education at the time.

Overall, the landed class and colonial elites were able to mobilize the higher education sector in a way that enabled them to protect their power and wealth. Like most people, they also faced stiff challenges after liberation and throughout the Korean War. While Korean society was in turmoil, universities were considered a haven for landlords and colonial elites as well as students where they could pursue their different material interests. For the government, it was an opportunity to deal with increasing popular demand for higher education by minimizing its spending. The universities established under colonial rule rapidly acquired elite status, followed by the ones founded right after liberation. This structure of higher education has not changed much to this day. As of 2016, 78 percent of the students are educated in private universities.⁶⁴ These private universities are still operating based on student tuitions in much the same way as in the beginning. The share of tuition of the university's operating revenue reached 80 percent in 2007 although this has gradually reduced to 60 percent as of 2016.⁶⁵ Some of them still operate as family businesses like chaebols. For example, the chairman of the educational foundation of Korea University is Kim Sŏng-su's great-grandson, inheriting the position over three generations.⁶⁶ In this regard, the structure formed throughout colonial rule and the early independence period can still be found in the current landscape of the higher education sector in South Korea.

Land Reform and the Explosion of Private Universities

Finally, it is necessary to look at how the land reforms in South Korea contribute to forming this uneven structure. According to a newspaper article in 1955, it was estimated that the tuition fees paid by university students accounted for 5.4 percent of the amount of currency in issue at the time.[67] The article complained that universities were using this money for lending at usury.[68] The popular demand for higher education resulted in private universities engaging in a range of profit-seeking behaviors. Private universities at the time often operated as a means of wealth accumulation. The steep increase in the number of private universities after liberation was made possible by various interests, including those of the landed class, the government, educators, and students. While other factors such as student demands have already been examined, the land reform process was considered an important factor in leading to the increase.

The Farmland Reform Act of 1949 aimed to redistribute excessive farmland owned by large landowners to peasants in order to transform Korean society from semi-feudalism to capitalism.[69] Any piece of land larger than 3 hectares was purchased by the government and sold to peasants in the land reform, but there were special conditions for educational foundations. These exceptions were made possible by campaigns conducted by the universities. Private schools formed the Educational Foundation Association in August 1948 and demanded special compensation as well as their right to invest in state-run corporations to receive a dividend.[70] Eventually their demands were reflected in the Farmland Reform Act of 1949, enforced in June 1949, stipulating that the special regulation would be applied to the educational foundations in Paragraph 6 of Article 6 as follows:

> Article 6. The following farmland will not be purchased by this act.
>
> ...
>
> Para. 4. Farmland that the government determined to be necessary to change the land use for government, public institutions, and educational institutions
>
> Para. 5. Self-cultivating agricultural land owned by recognized schools, religious institutions, or other welfare agencies, but other land owned by educational foundations will be purchased through a separate regulation.

Para. 6. Agricultural land for special purposes such as teaching and research within the limits set by the government.

It took two more years before the Special Compensation Act on Educational Foundations' Farmland was enacted in July 1951. The act includes an article to double the compensation in the case of farmland owned by educational foundations, along with other favorable conditions. It also permits foundations to receive half of the compensation in the form of vested properties by giving them high priority to purchase them.

The ordinance for the special compensation act was enacted only in May 1953, which was almost four years later when the initial land reform act became operational. The ordinance limited compensation to the educational foundations established prior to April 30, 1950. While the government already indicated in January 1949 that private universities would receive favorable treatment, there is a ten-month gap between the reform act and the cutoff point specified by the ordinance.[71] This resulted in a loophole whereby a university established even after the promulgation of the land reform act could benefit through the special compensation act. The favorable conditions for private universities include their right to purchase vested properties. The government granted top priority to any university seeking to purchase such properties. The value of the land owned by the foundations was also fully acknowledged, while others were gradually depreciated when their lands were larger. Overall, the government granted favorable conditions to private universities to protect and accumulate their wealth through the reform. It was also an opportunity for large landlords to protect their wealth by collaborating with private universities.[72]

In 1948, according to the Educational Foundation Association, 122 educational foundations held around 18,850 hectares of farmlands.[73] A total of 775 cases ultimately received double compensation thanks to the Special Compensation Act on Educational Foundations' Farmland, of which 64 percent were educational foundations.[74] Not all of the universities established between 1945 and 1950 had such involvement in the land reform process, but it is frequently argued by several educational historians such as Kim Jeong-In that most private universities established during the period, except those established by religious institutions, were related to large landowners.[75] These developments resulted in making the private university a land-based institution for protecting the wealth of the founders and landlords, rather than for educating students. This is an important factor in explaining the nature of private universities in South Korea. Such a result might not be surprising considering the fact the USAMGIK and Korean politicians were hesitant to conduct the land reform in the beginning since they held close relationships with large landlords.[76]

A few studies have empirically confirmed the relationship between private universities and landlords. Oh Sung-Bae investigated sixteen newly established private universities between 1945 and 1950. According to his study, eight out of the sixteen were established by individuals, and only one was an educator.[77] The remaining seven were bureaucrats, businessmen, and landlords who were known to have a close relationship with the landed class.[78] Newspaper articles at the time as well as other investigations confirm that farmlands were donated to at least seven universities among them and other existing universities.[79] For example, in the case of Konkuk University, more than 20 hectares of farmlands were donated by two people in 1949.[80] Oh Sung-Bae assumes that there were other universities that benefited from the land reform.[81] Kang Myung-Sook also investigated the details of the amount of land given to eight universities under the USAMGIK. Even though she concluded that the land reform was not a major driver resulting in the massive increase in private universities at the time, her study still shows that four of eight universities received farmland donations.[82] While it is unknown how the donors eventually benefited from the universities, their donations were crucial since the universities needed to have assets to gain permission to be established as a university. While the motivations for donation could vary, it is difficult to argue that goodwill of landlords drove this process, especially since ten out of the sixteen universities founded between 1945 and 1950 were established or run by former pro-Japanese figures.[83] The establishment of private universities thus needs to be understood as a collaboration between landlords and former pro-Japanese elites to protect their power and influence in the newly established republic.

The rapid transformations of Korean society, including the Korean War, made it difficult for landlords to protect their wealth, but the education foundations were in a relatively favorable position compared to others. The land reform in South Korea was based on compensated acquisition, and the government aimed to support the landlords to invest in vested properties by using the compensation to purchase the properties so that they could become industrialists. However, priority for disposal of a vested property was given to existing managers and occupiers of those properties. Thus, in reality, it was difficult for landlords to purchase the properties, but as an exception, the education foundations were given the top priority to acquire vested properties. Such a privilege often resulted in conflicts with the existing managers and occupiers. One newspaper article titled "The Age of Privilege for the Educational Foundations" described a place of a bid as follows:

> On the 6th, in the Seoul Government Property Bureau, Tongsŏng Educational Foundation won the bids for three buildings with two to three times larger prices than the estimated values. Before the bid, there was a brawl between the representative of the foundation and the tenants. People who sympathized with the tenants shouted, "kill that guy," and the gang that had been waiting kicked the representative out of the building, then kidnapped the person until the deadline of the bidding.[84]

Such conflicts took place repeatedly as other newspaper articles confirm.[85] In other words, these articles indicate that the universities were able to utilize their privilege to diversify their assets from farmlands despite resistance from tenants. Last, it is important to note that the land reform process indirectly influenced the improvement of education levels by transforming peasants into landowners who gained the ability to provide more stable support for their children's education.[86] Right after liberation in 1945, there were only 7,819 university students, but in 1960, fifteen years later, the number of university students increased by 12.9 times to 101,041.[87] The average household expenditure on education also increased by 6.4–10.9 percent when compared with the period before the land reform.[88] Statistics like these illustrate the origin of the term "oxbone tower." Empowered peasants were also part of this phenomenon. In this regard, the land reform supported the growth of private universities in two ways: by increasing the number of private universities and by supplying students for them by meeting the demands of different class groups.

Epilogue: The Transwar Legacy of Private Universities

As universities grew, they moved away from the status of elitist institutions to reflect a more diverse aspect of society. Such transition seems evident when looking into a series of events in 1960. When Syngman Rhee, the first president of South Korea, amended the constitution in 1954 to enable his third presidential term, his party conducted election fraud during the presidential and vice presidential elections in March 1960. This led to protests against the fraudulent elections by public and middle and high school students in Masan and elsewhere. Students of Korea University then initiated their protest on April 18, 1960, resulting in a nationwide protest on April 19. While 186 people were killed by the police and the military, on April 25 more than 250 university professors announced the declaration of the state of affairs and marched together with students and the public to demand the resignation of Rhee,[89] and one day after this protest, Rhee resigned. Throughout the process of the April Revolution in 1960, many university students and professors were decoupled from the power structure to support the sociopolitical transformation of society.

The events in 1960 did not constitute a sudden transformation following the transwar period but rather the accumulated dynamics of society over time. The repressed demand for higher education under colonial rule was co-opted by the desire of colonial elites and landed class to protect their wealth and power. Thereafter, there were widespread frustrations among graduates and students due to a general lack of job opportunities to satisfy their expectations during the postwar period.[90] Afterward, the university became the field of struggle in which various interests intersected. The June Democratic Uprising in 1987 was a key moment led by university students resulting in the end of the military regime.

Still, private universities also are closely related to political elites. One of the latest events to show such a relationship was the resistance against the revised Private School Act in 2005 led by the Hannara party, which is often argued to be the political offspring of pro-Japanese groups.[91] The Private School Act was revised by the then majority Uri Party in December 2005 to promote more transparent and democratic management of private schools.[92] The revised act included a restriction on the chairman's power to appoint the chairman's family members in the educational foundation committee to no more than one-fourth of the total committee members, reduced from one-third. It also restricted by five years the reappointment of committee members who had been expelled for corruption. This revised act was considered an attack on the properties and rights of the Hannara party. Thus, Park Geun-hye, the leader of the party at the time who also used to be a chairman of Yeungnam University, began a protest by boycotting the National Assembly with the support of the educational foundations. Ultimately, the act was revised again in July 2007, after a year and a half, to the point of losing the entire purpose of reform.[93] Such an event underscores the close relationship between private university owners and politics that exists even today. Investigating the nexus between the landed class and the higher education sector throughout the transwar period provides critical clues to understanding why such a problem remains in Korean society.

Notes

1 This chapter is written based on the author's doctoral thesis submitted to the London School of Economics and Political Science in September 2017. The author wishes to thank Hyun Bang Shin, Kris Olds, Jamie Doucette, Jung Won Sonn, Murray Low, and Tim Bunnell for their support on his doctoral thesis. He also thanks Max Ward, Reto Hofmann, and Dongkyung Shin for their helpful comments and suggestions on an earlier version of this chapter.
2 "Shinhŭngsadaegŏnmurŭn ugolt'ap," *Tonga Ilbo*, January 21, 1969.
3 "Taehak mullyŏ pannŭn 'kŭmsujŏ'tŭl ashinayo," *Han'gyore 21*, July 25, 2016.
4 Chinshik Song, "Sariptae 1kot p'yŏnggyun 4.7kŏn piri, piwi chŏkpal kŭmaek ch'oeso 2624ŏk," *Kyŏng Hyang Sinmun*, June 19, 2019.
5 Pei-Yin Lin and Su-Yun Kim, "Introduction," in *East Asian Transwar Popular Culture: Literature and Film from Taiwan and Korea*, ed. Pei-Yin Lin and Su Yun Kim (Singapore: Palgrave Macmillan, 2019), 1–20.
6 For account of different schools of thought in terms of colonial history of Korea, see Chan-Seung Park, *The Writing of Korean History in the 21st Century* (Seoul: Hanyang University Press, 2019).
7 Hae-Dong Yun, *Shingminjiŭi hoesaekchidae* (Seoul: Yŏksabip'yŏnsa, 2003).
8 Gi-Wook Shin, *Peasant Protest and Social Change in Colonial Korea* (Seattle: University of Washington Press, 2014), 3–8.
9 Leroy P. Jones and Il Sakong, *Government, Business, and Entrepreneurship in Economic Development: The Korean Case* (Cambridge, MA: Harvard University Press, 1980).
10 Carter J. Eckert, *Offspring of Empire: The Koch'ang Kims and the Colonial Origins of Korean Capitalism, 1876–1945* (Seattle: University of Washington Press, 1991).
11 Yong Sop Kim, "Modern Agrarian Reforms Claimed by the Reformist in 1884–94," *Tongbanghakchi* 15 (1974): 126–45.
12 To secure their rights to lands, Japanese settlers lent landowners' names or lent money at usury. For more discussion, see So-Jeong Moon, "Formation of Japanese Landlordism under the Korean Empire," *Han'guksahoesahak'oenonmunjip* 2 (1986): 57–79.
13 Carter J. Eckert, Ki-baik Lee, Young Ick Lew, Michael Robinson, and Edward Willett Wagner, *Korea Old and New: A History* (Cambridge, MA: Harvard Korea Institute, 1990), 266.
14 Se-Young Lee, "The Structural Change of Landownership in Naeseo-myeon Changweon-gun Gyeongsangnam-do from 1910 to 1945," *Journal of Korean History* 21 (2007): 5–73.
15 Si-Won Jang, "Study on the Mode of Existence of the Large Landowners during the Colonial Period in Korea" (PhD diss., Seoul National University, 1989).

16 Hui-Jei Lee, "Capital Accumulation of Korean Landlord in Colonial Period" (MA diss., Yonsei University, 2000).
17 Sung-Chan Hong, "1940nyŏndae chŏnban ilcheŭi han'gungnongŏp chaep'yŏnch'aek," *Kuksagwan nonch'ong* 38 (1992): 205–41.
18 Shin, *Peasant Protest and Social Change in Colonial Korea*.
19 Eckert, *Offspring of Empire*.
20 Jones and Sakong, *Government, Business, and Entrepreneurship in Economic Development*.
21 Eckert, *Offspring of Empire*.
22 Myung-Sook Kang, *Sarip'akkyoŭi kiwŏn* [Origins of private schools] (Seoul: Communication Books, 2015).
23 Myung-Sook Kang, "A Study on the Private Primary School in the 1910s," *Korean Journal of History of Education* 33, no. 2 (2011): 3–6.
24 Kang, *Sarip'akkyoŭi kiwŏn*.
25 Ki-Hoon Lee, "Avison and Higher Education under Japanese Occupation," *Yonsei Journal of Medical History* 13, no. 1 (2010): 15–25.
26 There were several motivations to do so. In the aspect of nationalism, there was a need to strengthen people's capacity by "skill cultivation." For individuals, receiving higher education was a means to climb the social ladder. Confucian ideology stressing governance by men of merit based on talent and virtue was also important. For more discussions, see Eckert et al., *Korea Old and New*, 291; Seong Cheol Oh, *Shingminji ch'odŭnggyoyugŭi hyŏngsŏng* (Seoul: Kyoyukkwahaksa, 2000), 187–202; Michael J. Seth, *Education Fever: Society, Politics, and the Pursuit of Schooling in South Korea* (Honolulu: University of Hawai'i Press, 2002).
27 Keong-Suk Park, "Population Dynamics of Korea during the Colonialization Period (1910–1945)," *Korea Journal of Population Studies* 32, no. 2 (2009): 52; Gyu-Soo Yi, "The Existing Forms and Transition of Japanese Residents in Chosun Seen through the Demography," *Korean History Education Review* 125 (2013): 47.
28 Japanese Government-General of Korea, *Statistical Yearbook 1939* (Seoul: Japanese Government-General of Korea, 1939).
29 Seong Cheol Oh, "Shingminjigiŭi kyoyukchŏk yusan," *History of Education* 8 (1998): 228–31.
30 Eunjin Cho, "The Government Specialized School System Establishment and Management in Korea during 1910s–1920s" (MA diss., Seoul National University, 2015).
31 Shin Jang, "Study of Bureaucracy of the Japanese Colonial Empire," *Kokusai shinpojūmu* 30 (2008): 367–84.
32 "Ttudŭryŏdo anyŏllinŭn ip'angnanŭi chiongmun," *Tonga Ilbo*, March 12, 1928.

33 Dong-Hwan Kim, "A Study on the Entrance-Examination-Oriented Education in Japanese Colonized Period," *Korean Journal of Sociology of Education* 12, no. 3 (2002): 25–53.
34 Ibid.
35 National Institute of Korean History, *New Edition of Koran History 47* (Gwacheon, South Korea: National Institute of Korean History, 2001), 264–9.
36 "Chosŏn'gakchi sunhoegangyŏn," *Chosŏn Ilbo*, June 24, 1920.
37 Sun-Pyo Hong, "Ilcheha migukyuhakyŏn'gu," *Kuksagwan nonch'ong* 96 (2001): 166.
38 Jones and Sakong, *Government, Business, and Entrepreneurship in Economic Development*, 230.
39 Ibid.
40 *History Net*, s.v. "1946nyeon bukan toji gaehyeoge daehan beomnyeong," http://contents.history.go.kr/front/hm/view.do?treeId=020208&tabId=01&levelId=hm_157_0010 (accessed September 1, 2020).
41 US Department of State, Division of Research for Far East, *The Redistribution of Korean-Owned Farm Lands in South Korea*, 1948, OIR Report no. 4863 (preliminary version), http://archive.history.go.kr/image/viewer.do?system_id=000001041487.
42 Inhan Kim, "Land Reform in South Korea under the U.S. Military Occupation, 1945–1948," *Journal of Cold War Studies* 18, no. 2 (2016): 109–11.
43 Korean History Society Modern History Research Unit, *Han'guk'yŏndaesa 1* (Seoul: P'ulbit, 1991), 41.
44 Bruce Cumings, *The Origins of the Korean War: Liberation and the Emergence of Separate Regimes, 1945–1947* (Princeton, NJ: Princeton University Press, 1981), 86.
45 Chong-Hwan Chu, "Ilche chosŏn t'ojijosasaŏbe kwanhan 'shingminjigŭndaehwaron' pip'an," *Critical Review of History* 47 (1999): 198–225.
46 US Department of State, *The Redistribution of Korean-Owned Farm Lands in South Korea*.
47 Miae Jeong, "A Study on the Effect of the Change of Landed Classes by Land Reform after Korean Liberation" (MA diss., Ewha Womans University, 1991), 36.
48 Yu-Sik Ha and Jong-Bong Lee, "A Research on the Fluctuation of Land Ownership before Agricultural Land Reform in Wongchon-myon, Ulsan-gun," *Taegusahak* 123 (2016): 29.
49 Japanese Government-General of Korea, *Statistical Yearbook 1939*; Japanese Government-General of Korea, *Statistical Yearbook 1943* (Seoul: Japanese Government-General of Korea, 1943).
50 Ibid.
51 Do Young Oh, "The University and East Asian Cities: The Variegated Origins of Urban Universities in Colonial Seoul and Singapore," *Journal of Urban History* (advanced online publication), doi:10.1177/0096144220941199.

52 Do-Hyung Kim, "Nationalism of Severance Medical College in Modern Korea," *Yonsei Journal of Medical History* 22 (2019): 7–33.
53 *History Net*, s.v. "Yonhi Professional School," http://contents.history.go.kr/front/tg/view.do?treeId=0202&levelId=tg_004_2270&ganada=&pageUnit=10(accessed September 1, 2020).
54 Jin-A Chung, "The Trends of the Circle of Economics in Korea and Economics Education in the College of Commerce and Economics of Yonsei University during the 20 Years after the Liberation (1945–1965)," *Korean Journal of Economics* 22, no. 3 (2015): 451–95.
55 Man-Gil Kang, *Han'guksa* (Seoul: Han'gilsa, 1994).
56 Suk Joon Kim, *Migunjŏng shidaeŭi kukkawa haengjŏng: Pundan kukkaŭi hyŏngsŏnggwa haengjŏng ch'ejeŭi chŏngbi* (Seoul: Ewha Womans University Press, 1996).
57 Myung-Sook Kang, "Setting of Private College or University and Expansion of Higher Education Opportunity under the USAMGIK," *Asian Journal of Education* 4, no. 1 (2003): 155–79.
58 Ibid.
59 Ibid., 157.
60 Korea Higher Education Research Institute, "Number of Universities in South Korea," *KHEI Statistics*, March 10, 2013, https://khei-khei.tistory.com/579; "Number of University Students in South Korea," *KHEI Statistics*, April 11, 2013, https://khei-khei.tistory.com/585.
61 Ookwhan Oh, *Han'guksahoeŭi kyoyukyŏl: Kiwŏn'gwa shimhwa* (Seoul: Kyoyukkwahaksa, 2000), 224–38.
62 "Taehakŭl chŏngbi: chŏn'guk 55kyo chung 32kyoe tanhaeng," *Tonga Ilbo*, December 21, 1956.
63 "Ilbudaehak kijullyŏngŭl mushi," *Tonga Ilbo*, March 26, 1957, 3.
64 Korea Higher Education Research Institute, "Number of University Students in South Korea," *KHEI Statistics*, September 17, 2018, https://khei-khei.tistory.com/2279.
65 Jhungsoo Park, Heejung Hong, and Hyunjung Lee, *Taehaktŭngnokkŭm munjewa taehakchaejŏngjiwŏnjŏngch'aek kaesŏnbangan* (Seoul: National Assembly Budget Office, 2009).
66 "Taehak mullyŏ pannŭn 'kŭmsujŏ'tŭl ashinayo."
67 "Hagwŏne mollin ton paegŏk: Koridaegŭmsŏre kamshiŭi nun," *Tonga Ilbo*, May 19, 1955.
68 Ibid.
69 Sang-Hwan Jang, "Land Reform and Capitalist Development in Korea," in *Marxist Perspectives on South Korea in the Global Economy*, ed. Martin Hart-Landsberg, Richard Westra, and Seongjin Jeong (Aldershot: Ashgate, 2007), 157–82; Sang-Jin

Jang, "Land Reform," in *Encyclopedia of Korean Culture* (Seongnam, South Korea: Academy of Korean Studies, 1995), http://encykorea.aks.ac.kr/Contents/Index?contents_id=E0059210.

70 "Kyoyukchaedanŭi nongt'o," *Tonga Ilbo*, January 21, 1949; "Nongjigaehyŏk," *Tonga Ilbo*, May 9, 1974; Myungho Park, *Land Reform in Korea* (Sejong, South Korea: Korea Ministry of Strategy and Finance, 2013).

71 Sung-Bae Oh, "Exploration of Private University Expansion Process: Based on Land Reform after the Liberation," *Journal of Korean Education* 31, no. 3 (2004): 53–73.

72 Ibid.; Park, *Land Reform in Korea*.

73 "Kyoyukchaedan paegip'altanch'e," *Chosŏn Ilbo*, August 6, 1948.

74 Oh, "Exploration of Private University Expansion Process."

75 Gwang Ho Lee, "Haebangjik'u kodŭnggyoyukkigwan sŏllip ch'ujinseryŏgŭi sahoejŏk paegyŏng," *Yonsei Review of Education* 5, no. 1 (1992): 63–85; Oh, "Exploration of Private University Expansion Process"; Jeong-In Kim, "Han'guk sahak hyŏngsŏngŭi yŏksawa kujojŏk t'ŭksŏng," in *Sahangmunjeŭi haedabŭl mosaek'anda*, ed. Sahangmunje haegyŏrŭl wihan yŏn'guhoe (Seoul: Shilch'ŏnmunhak, 2012), 29–45; Park, *Land Reform in Korea*.

76 Seongho Kim, Kyungsik Chun, Sang-Hwan Jang, and Sukdoo Park, *Nongjigaehyŏksa yŏn'gu* (Seoul: Korea Rural Economic Institute, 1989).

77 Oh, "Exploration of Private University Expansion Process."

78 Ibid.

79 Kang, "Setting of Private College or University and Expansion of Higher Education Opportunity under the USAMGIK."

80 "Chŏngdaejaedanhwangnip samssioŏgwŏnhŭisaro," *Chosŏn Ilbo*, September 16, 1949.

81 Oh, "Exploration of Private University Expansion Process."

82 Kang, "Setting of Private College or University and Expansion of Higher Education Opportunity under the USAMGIK."

83 Jungseok Park, "'Minjokkyoyukcha'ro pyŏnshinhan ch'inilp'a 87myŏng ... 13kaegyonŭn sesŭp," *Newstapa*, July 25, 2019, https://newstapa.org/article/xTHN6.

84 "Mun'gyojaedanŭi t'ŭkkwŏnshidae," *Kyŏng Hyang Sinmun*, May 8, 1953.

85 "'Usŏn' akyongŭl tansok," *Chosŏn Ilbo*, May 15, 1953; "Sŏurŭn'gangmaeboryu," *Chosŏn Ilbo*, June 8, 1953.

86 Chan Su Seo, "Han'gugŭi injŏkchabonch'ukchŏkkwajŏnggwa kŭ yoin," *Journal of Korean National Economy* 5 (1987): 69–90; Jang, "Land Reform and Capitalist Development in Korea"; Park, *Land Reform in Korea*.

87 Young-Chul Kim, Jeong-Gyu Lee, and Gyu-Tae Kim, *An Analytical Study on Demand for Higher Education* (Seoul: Korea Educational Development Institute, 2000).

88 Robert B. Morrow and Kenneth H. Sherper, *Land Reform in South Korea* (Washington, DC: Agency for International Development, 1970).
89 Korea Democracy Foundation, *Han'gungminjuhwaundongsa 1* (Paju, South Korea: Tolbegae, 2008).
90 Chang Eun Lee, "Socio-political Terms and Micro-Factors as to 'April 18th Nonviolent Direct Actions' Waged by Students at Korea University—Focused on Broad Struggle Frameworks and Active Networks," *Sa-Ch'ong* 71 (2010): 12–13.
91 For example, when the "Special Act on Asset Confiscation for Pro-Japanese and Anti-National Collaborators to the State" was initially voted in in December 2005, the Hannara party was boycotting the National Assembly regarding their opposition to property-related laws. But when the law was revised and voted in in August 2006, nine members from the Hannara party opposed the revision. Similarly, when the Special Act on the Inspection of Collaborations under the Japanese Occupation was revised, 29 percent of the party members voted against the revision as the largest opposition group.
92 Sang-Chul Lee, "The Analysis of Amendment Process and Major Contents of Private School Law," *Journal of Educational Administration* 24, no. 1 (2006): 197–224.
93 "Hannaradangŭn '2005nyŏn sahakpŏp' kiŏk'anŭn'ga," *Ohmynews*, August 5, 2009, http://www.ohmynews.com/NWS_Web/View/at_pg.aspx?CNTN_CD=A0001190266.

Part Two

Ideological Transwar Regimes

5

Resetting China's Conservative Revolution: "People's Livelihood" in 1950s Taiwan

Brian Tsui

As a state, the Republic of China (ROC) is a kind of its own. In its almost eleven decades of existence, it took on many guises: from a warlord-controlled, unstable polity in the 1910s–1920s and a party-state that claimed control over a fragmented continental nation to a Cold War remnant of "Free China" and an electoral democracy governing Taiwan and adjacent islands. In all these stages of the ROC's dramatic transformation, the Guomindang (GMD; also known as the Chinese Nationalist Party or, officially, the Kuomintang) has played a major role. In particular, the party, its leadership, and doctrines were enmeshed in the ROC's tumultuous transition from Nanjing to Taipei through the twentieth century. The relocation of government headquarters from the Chinese mainland to Taiwan was a result of interparty rivalries within China. Yet, the geopolitical configurations that beset Asia and the wider world call attention to the global significance of the Chinese Civil War.

This chapter argues that the ideological legacy of the conservative revolution—a nation-building and modernization project informed by anti-colonialism, anti-communism, and state-managed capitalism—in mainland China was transplanted onto Taiwan in the 1950s and made pliable to US-led geopolitical designs for the Asia-Pacific. It pays attention to both the continuities and ruptures of GMD rule across the Taiwan Strait, focusing on the rearticulation of the party-state's strategies in nation and society building as its president, Chiang Kai-shek, settled into the same office that housed Japanese colonial governors. Instead of examining concrete policies, however, this chapter scrutinizes its ideological texts and meta-texts, in particular senior cadres' diaries. Specifically, it explains why Chiang was compelled to "complete" Sun Yat-sen's (1866–1925) canon in

1953, almost three decades after the *Three People's Principles* was first published, and how his two "supplementary" chapters (*Yu le liangpian bushu*; hereafter "Supplement") signaled a recalibration of China's conservative revolution.

Additions to the *Three People's Principles* impacted heavily on public life in GMD-controlled Taiwan. As the ROC's default ruling party until 1996, when the republic's presidential election was first contested by opposition politicians, Sun Yat-sen's political philosophy and its paraphernalia undergirded the state's doctrine, if not always devoutly. Along with the posthumous personality cult built around Sun, the late revolutionary leader's eponymous *Three People's Principles* held exalted status in GMD-governed areas.[1] The *Three People's Principles* was the staple of political indoctrination in Nationalist China since 1928, when Chiang Kai-shek nominally unified the country under a government the party led. Taught under the guise of party theory (*dangyi*) or civics (*gongmin*), catechism on Sun Yat-sen thought was an integral part of the schooling process, so much so that it was part of Taiwan's college entrance examinations until 1998.[2] The *Three People's Principles* was originally a collection of sixteen lectures on the principles of *minzu* (nationalism), *minquan* (democracy), and *minsheng* (people's livelihood) Sun gave in Guangzhou, where the Nationalist government was headquartered in 1924.[3] Of the three principles, *minsheng* was the most controversial, since it was entangled with socialism, communism, and Marxism. The fact that the speeches were delivered at the height of the First United Front, an alliance the GMD forged with the communists against the warlord-controlled regime governing from Beijing in exchange for Comintern aids, introduced nuances to Sun's attitude toward communism. His ambiguity contrasted sharply with the virulent hostility against Chinese communism held by Chiang and his government. Chiang's additions to the canon represented an attempt to adapt the GMD's ideological inheritance, shaped during the interwar era, to Cold War geopolitical realities.

My inquiry into Supplement challenges two approaches to the history of Taiwan and/or the ROC that downplay transwar—the Chinese Civil War that began in 1927 and its intersections with a regional order, the domineering power of which changed from Japan to the United States—vicissitudes. Views aligned with the GMD, particularly when Chiang and his son Ching-kuo were in power, consider socioeconomic developments in Taiwan as the culmination of the revered revolutionary Sun Yat-sen's vision for China. The ROC's achievements in its "model province" (*mofan sheng*) would have been more widespread on the mainland if the GMD had prevailed over the Chinese communists. Contrary to this interpretation is one that sees the GMD state's loss of mainland China as a decided break in its history. Calling it "Taiwanization" (*Taiwan-ka*), Wakabayashi Masahiro charts the reduction of the ROC from a continental state to an island one, as a tumultuous process which saw an authoritarian "settler state" (*sensensha kokka*) dominated by mainland Chinese elite eventually took on liberal democratic and Taiwanese guises.[4] This Taiwan-centrism gains traction as the island's population increasingly questioned their Chinese identity.

Both viewpoints, diametrically opposed as they are, downplay the complex connections between the party-state headquartered in Taipei, the revolutionary project that formed the ROC in the first place, and how Cold War geopolitics made the GMD rework its nation- and social-building strategies. During its stint in mainland China, the regime's appeal to nationalism and a corporatist alternative to the capitalist order both domestically and internationally belied a state and a movement that harbored world-historical ambitions, setting itself as an example for other societies at the receiving end of capitalist imperialism, particularly those in Asia, to follow. Reduced in its territorial reach to the island of Taiwan and a few archipelagos off Fujian Province and hinged on US military protection, the GMD state's desire to overcome global modernity was no longer tenable. The "updated" canon reflected the circumstances the GMD confronted and the party's reduced ambitions in the 1950s. While continuing to celebrate its Chinese nationalist credentials, the regime's claim to a distinct solution to achieving national independence and taming capitalism while leveraging the latter for economic development rang hollow. Instead, Chiang's additions to the principle of people's livelihood (*minsheng*) in the *Three People's Principles* projected a developmentalist, welfarist vision that sought to legitimate the postwar consensus in the "free world." Yet, the revised canon, published in 1953, was amorphous enough that it allowed for interpretations that stressed continuity between Sun's original ideals and those that were attributed to his successor at the helm of the party-state. It provided critical ideological glue between interwar and wartime China, on one hand, and postwar Taiwan, on the other.

Resetting the Conservative Revolution

The early 1950s was a period of tremendous flux; the United States had replaced Japan as the regional hegemon, leading a global crusade against communism. The Korean War prompted Washington to provide military protection to Chiang's regime and turn Taiwan into one of its unsinkable aircraft carriers. The GMD party-state, once abandoned by its American sponsors, gained a new lease of life and vowed to reclaim (*guangfu*) the Chinese mainland from its communist nemesis. "Free China" rested its legitimacy on Sun Yat-sen's revolutionary enterprise, which was putatively derailed by Beijing. As I argue elsewhere, the GMD initiated a conservative revolution—a project promoting state-directed capitalist development while suppressing its attendant sociopolitical chaos—since the party's break with its one-time communist allies.[5] The party's governing premise was the transformation of China, with Taiwan as its experimental site, into a modern, sovereign industrial power that commanded leadership over an Asia freed from Western colonial dominance. Exercising effective control over only the lower Yangzi region of China even during its heyday before the formal onset of the Second Sino-Japanese War, the body politic the party-state claimed to govern was tentative and fragmented. Exiled to Taiwan, the GMD had a chance to relaunch its conservative revolution, albeit in a highly modified form.

Shortly after moving to Taiwan, the GMD reignited the conservative revolution that imploded in mainland China. Social and cultural movements, the methods of which stemmed from the party-state's mobilization experience on the mainland, were launched. While Japan and, by extension, the Axis powers were the evil empires against which the Chinese nation was kept "free," the socialist bloc and the government headed by Mao Zedong and Zhu De in Beijing became China's existential threats in the 1950s. To be sure, state-led campaigns began in earnest once the ROC took over the island from Japan, with a focus on imparting Chinese culture and Mandarin on a population who mostly did not partake in China's revolutionary experiences. While sinicization, often couched in terms of cultivating the voluntaristic "national spirit," continued to be key, "anticommunism and resistance against Russia" became the leitmotif of mass movements. Animosity against Japan, Washington's other unsinkable aircraft carrier in Asia, was downplayed.[6] In April 1950, the GMD established the Chinese Youth Anti-Communist and Resist Russia League (*Zhongguo qingnian fangong kang-E lianhehui*). Led by Chiang Kai-shek's son Ching-kuo and National Taiwan University president Fu Sinian, the league resembled GMD-led youth organizations on the mainland. League propaganda slogan alluded to Sparta and Prussia, focusing on their putative austere martial. Members, most of them university students and recent high school graduates, patrolled the streets, dissuading diners, moviegoers, and drivers from indulging in frivolities and consuming scarce resources, reminiscent of the New Life Movement Chiang launched in 1934. The league was subsequently absorbed by the China Youth Anti-Communist Corps (*Zhongguo qingnian fan'gong tuan*) in March 1952.[7] The corps also founded the Chinese Youth Writing Association (*Zhongguo qingnian xiezuo xiehui*). Together with the Chinese Literary Association (*Zhongguo wenyi xiehui*), founded in May 1950, the organization was the vehicle through which the GMD produced anti-communist and Chinese nationalist literary materials for popular consumption.[8] In terms of aesthetics, modes of organization, and its exaltation of the nation against all other forms of politics, the GMD transplanted the paraphernalia of China's conservation revolution onto the territories it still governed.

Yet, GMD rule was not a replica of its reign in mainland China. The regime proved much more effective in introducing socioeconomic changes to Taiwan. Shredded of debilitating factional strife as party elders either passed away or were sidelined, more capable cadres took over. Official such as Premier Chen Cheng (1897–1965) were efficient state builders. A trusted subordinate of Chiang, Chen was tasked with spearheading economic development in Taiwan and reforming the battered party. His job was made much easier by the fact that defense was outsourced to the United States, relieving the regime of substantial military expenses that had drained the state's coffers on the mainland. Thus, while the party's agrarian programs on mainland China quickly grounded to a halt during the Nanjing Decade (1927–1937), the GMD succeeded in bringing about sweeping campaigns in rural Taiwan. Land reform in the Taiwanese countryside, as economist Chu Wan-Wen observed, was nothing less than "social change of a revolutionary nature." As a class, the landlord was obliterated by a series of measures the party-state imposed from 1949 to 1953 under Chen's supervision. The government stressed the gradualist and incremental nature of its agrarian project—from rent reduction and sale of public land through reregistration of the cadastre and the Land to the Tiller program. The GMD's ability to carry through agrarian programs without appealing to class struggle and revolutionary violence created an alternative, albeit on a scale much smaller than mainland China, to land reform pursued by the Chinese Communist Party (CCP).[9] It echoed strongly Sun Yat-sen's concern for the land problem in his lectures on *minsheng*. Sun's second lecture on people's livelihood, in which the revered revolutionary sought to relate to the social goals of his communist allies while distinguishing them from those he urged GMD cadres to take up, highlighted land ownership as the cardinal problem that plagued modern societies. He saw his own country as virgin territory insofar as industrial capitalism was concerned, at one point comparing the country to Australia, a settler colony of which the population was a lot smaller than China's. The crux of the *minsheng* principle was to avoid the accumulation of land among a few hands before "industry and commerce [were] fully developed." The GMD's method, however, was different from that of the communists as the former recognized private ownership of land, just not how landlords could profit excessively from it at the expense of those who labored.[10] In subsequent years, activists from across the political spectrum fought vigorously on how the *minsheng* principle could be interpreted and implemented, causing ruptures within the GMD. Among the party's left-wingers, debates continued even after the collapse of the United Front as to whether the GMD should be a vehicle for a social revolution favoring peasants and the much smaller working class or concentrate on bringing about equality between classes through economic development.[11] With the onset of the Cold War, land reform was a centerpiece of the rivalry between the GMD and its communist nemesis, which both ran largely agrarian societies, along with the visions they embodied.

The land reforms Chen introduced in Taiwan renewed scrutiny within the GMD on the principle of *minsheng*. As Chiang conceded in his early June 1952 entries in his yet-unpublished diary, the president "spent rather much thought (*po fei xinli*)" revising his "Essentials of State-Owned Land" (*Tudi guoyou de yaoyi*) speech delivered on April 21 for publication. The aspect that most warranted Chiang's attention was some of Sun's remarks, for example, "The Principle of Livelihood is socialism, it is communism, it is Utopianism."[12] Such a statement was so incendiary that some readers, since Sun's demise in 1925, were shocked into believing that it was forgery and demanded that public security authorities censor it.[13] Chiang stressed that "communism aimed for the complete destruction of the system of private property. The *minsheng* principle not only protected private property but also rewarded legitimate (*heli de*) private enterprises. Communist bandits, on the other hand, not only confiscated private capital but also completely destroyed it."[14] The Generalissmo, therefore, echoed the thrust of Sun's 1920s prognosis, which envisioned, if counterintuitively, a noncapitalistic economy in which private property thrived. Of course, the revered late revolutionary's social ideal belied an "ahistorical and timelessly transhistorical pro-statist principle," an appeal to an exalted order free from imperialism, capitalist modernization, and class struggle.[15] For Cui Shuqin, a Harvard-educated intellectual dedicated to Sun's political philosophy, the *minsheng* principle was a superior form of socialism, facilitating the people's sustainment and flourishing (*yangmin*). To be specific, *minsheng* sought to accord private capital to all, while communism as pioneered in Soviet Russia aimed to strip everyone of property so that everyone joined the proletariat.[16] Following Cui's train of thought, land reform in "Free China" was the state's empowering citizens with value-producing land while land reform in communist-run mainland was expropriation of people's wealth by malevolent cadres.

Cui's interpretation of *minsheng* symptomized the difficult transwar legacy the GMD state inherited from Sun, whose openness to communism proved to be an embarrassment in a fervently anti-communist Taiwan. The statement in Sun's own *minsheng* lectures, which suggested that pre-empting capitalist features in society—"check[ing] the growth of large private capital and prevent[ing] the disease of extreme inequality between the rich and the poor"—was his priority, was downplayed.[17] Ideological warfare against Soviet Russia and communist China became cardinal as, Cui suggested, any overlapping between Sun's thoughts and communism was to be disavowed.[18] Prior ruminations in Republican China on the compatibility between *minsheng* and communism, even non-Marxist ones, were repudiated. Cui's argument was echoed enthusiastically by the Nationalist leadership. At the party's national congress in October 1952, the first one held in Taiwan, Chiang presented a lengthy report, which he began by differentiating between *minsheng* and communism. "One only needed to read carefully lectures on the *minsheng* principle to see how the Premier (i.e., Sun) fully refuted all core elements of Marxism such as historical materialism, surplus value and class struggle." The party chief bemoaned how cadres became "lost (*miwang*)" and used Marxist concepts such as dialectical materialism to understand the Three People's Principles. Some even "distorted the Three People's Principles in order to pander (*kaolong*) to communist bandits." But Sun's purportedly ideological ecumenism vis-à-vis communism had been linked to the revolutionary's policy, hammered out in 1923, to ally with Soviet Russia and cooperate with the Chinese communists. Chiang sought to stress that Sun's position was borne out of expediency and "the neglect of the China question in U.S. diplomacy" in the early twentieth century.[19] To put it even more bluntly, as Cui did, Sun's apparent reconciliation with communism was nothing but a tactical ploy to rally Chinese communists behind the Nationalist banner in the 1920s.[20] Far from a meeting of minds, Sun's tolerance of Soviet Russia and Chinese communists was no more than a strategy to advance China's own interests as the GMD defined them. Ideological concessions to communism as espoused by the Russians or the Chinese communists were out of the question.

Chiang's attempt to rationalize, or explain away, Sun's embrace of Soviet assistance and Chinese communists on strategic grounds was one means by which the GMD head sought to draw the line. The other prong of this endeavor to end ideological confusion or, indeed, debates was to rearticulate and renew the canon. As Chiang remarked in the conclusion of his report, cadres "must cleanse thoughts within the party, return to teachings bequeathed by the Premier, in particular the understanding that the Three People's Principles were rooted in

[China's] national spirit and culture."[21] Land reform, as *minsheng* principle in action, compelled Chiang and other senior cadres to revisit the entanglement between Sun's thoughts and various forms of socialism. GMD's discourse on land reform hinged on the recognition and protection of private property. Taipei's land policy, Chiang explained, was to allow for "the reasonable existence of private property (including land ownership) system under the principle of land nationalization." This is because it was a defining principle in Sun's thinking that he was not against capital but only the concentration of it in a few private hands. Land reform pursued by the GMD, hence, could not be compared to what the communists were carrying out on the mainland. Turning Marxian class analysis on its head, Chiang accused "cunning bandits Mao [Zedong] and Zhu [De]" of "exploiting, incessantly and by layers, the proletariat." While the GMD, as "a party representing all people," empowered the citizenry, the communists stripped people of their land and enriched themselves. This, Chiang charged, was nothing less than dictatorship (*zhuanzheng*) of the ruling class which Mao and Zhu represented.[22] Mass dispossession, Stalinist terror, and concentration of wealth in the hands of the communist elite were far from what the *minsheng* principle envisioned.

The stark contrast Chiang set up between land reform on Taiwan and land reform on the mainland became the foundational narrative of the GMD's self-image as the legitimate Chinese government, temporarily exiled onto the subtropical former Japanese colony. Chen Cheng, Chiang's right-hand man, reproduced this narrative in a celebratory mood for an international readership who might "want to carry out similar projects" in 1961. His book, translated as *Land Reform in Taiwan* in English in the same year the original Chinese version was published, came out in Spanish and French in 1964 and 1966, respectively, making it comprehensible to political elites in newly independent countries across Asia, Africa, and the Americas. The introductory chapter of Chen's book traced the genealogy of China's "land problem" to Dong Zhongshu (179–104 BCE), a Han Dynasty scholar who was credited with making Confucianism into a state ideology. After describing briefly how rulers and officials in the Han and Song Dynasties dealt with the land issue, Chen turned abruptly to Taiwan, "as the Chinese mainland is presently under Communist occupation." He marshaled figures showing that prior to initiatives implemented by the GMD, "maladjustment in land distribution and land utilization" in Taiwan was dire and called for state interventions. Turning to Sun Yat-sen as the theoretical basis for lands reform, Chen stressed that the late revolutionary, while advocating land nationalization, would "let private individuals have land ownership …

because private individuals are by no means entirely free but are bound by the laws and regulations of the country." Compared with the benign measures rolled out in Taiwan, land nationalization in mainland China was "expropriation of all property," a "reign of terror," and peasants reduced to "serfs."[23] The superiority of the *minsheng* principle over Marxism was, for Chen, obvious.

Cleansing Thoughts

There is an unmistakable sense of déjà vu in Chiang and Chen's readings of *minsheng*, which aimed, among other things, to disabuse the Chinese citizenry and foreign observers of the compatibility between Sun's national revolution and the political designs of its erstwhile partner-turned-enemy. Chiang himself lamented in the party congress report that his exegesis of *minsheng* came too late as cadres' thoughts and beliefs had been contaminated by communism since Sun's death, a reason which the party chief cited for China's crisis. Yet, the GMD cannot be faulted for not trying to clean the air or, less generously, suppress dissent. In the mid-1920s, even before the United Front forged by Sun collapsed, ideologue Dai Jitao (1891–1949) took pains to establish *minsheng* as an ideology that facilitated a unique form of revolutionary politics. As I argue elsewhere, it promised drastic social change but excluded class struggle as a strategy, favoring a depoliticized approach whereby a technocratic vanguard served as mobilizers and coordinators of capital and labor.[24] Corporatism was the core of the national revolution, the legacy of which the GMD must defend from Marxist critiques.

To differentiate *minsheng* further from Marxist historical materialism, Dai made the bold claim that Sun's talks on clothing (*yi*), food (*shi*), housing (*zhu*), and transportation (*xing*)—material necessities of the people—did not complete the revolutionary's lectures on *minsheng*. Dai claimed to have seen written notes held by Sun's widow indicating that two topics—sustaining the living (*yangsheng*) and disposal of the dead (*songsi*)—were to be discussed by the revered leader if he had lived beyond March 1925. From these notes, Dai extrapolated that the two unspoken themes that Sun took to his grave were *yu* and *le*, both contributing to the citizenry's "beautiful and elegant enjoyment" (*youmei gaoshang de xiangle*).[25] He also argued, therefore, that *minsheng* was in its philosophical fundamentals distinct from communism. The latter, Dai explained,

> was very naïve, taking as its theoretical basis Marx's historical materialism. *Minsheng*, on the other hand, was based on thoughts derived from China's

primordial ethical and political philosophy. Therefore, the purview [of these two ideologies] was very different. The problems that communism wanted to solve was confined to those of economic life. *Minsheng*, in embodying *yu* and *le*, went beyond economic life.²⁶

On one hand, Dai was intent on elevating *minsheng* into a philosophy grounded in nebulous, Confucian-sounding dictums such as benevolence (*ren'ai*) and the doctrine of the mean (*zhongyong*).²⁷ On the other hand, he agreed with commentators that *minsheng* was no more than a social policy, a strategy of development for a late industrializing country. The ideologue endowed the creed with utopian aspirations, alluding to the timeless Confucian ideal of great harmony (*datong*). However, *minsheng* philosophy promised an end to the ills of capitalism and liberation of oppressed nations around the world. Dai's reading of *minsheng*, with its eclectic mix of registers, allusions, and vocabularies, exacerbated what historian Marie-Claire Bergère calls the "intellectual confusion" whereby the three meanings of *minsheng*—philosophical, normative, and programmatic—were entangled and not carefully parsed through in Sun's own lectures.²⁸ Sun's energetic speeches, if effective for rallying the committed, did not form a coherent philosophical program. This aporia between the ahistorical, nativist framing of *minsheng* and *minsheng* as an alternative strategy of dealing with imperialist capitalism, both locally inflected and as a global problematic, was left unaddressed until 1953.

Updating the Canon for Cold War Taiwan

Of course, adding Supplement to a long-cherished canon was not just about bridging an epistemological gap. Such an act also betrayed the changing political conditions which underscored the discrepancies between what *minsheng* meant when the GMD was paramount in China and when the party-state's survival was at the mercy of US protection. A close reading of the Supplement, in comparison with earlier texts produced before the end of China's anti-Japanese resistance war, attests how *minsheng* was (1) reshaped to legitimize the developmentalist, welfarist focus of the GMD state as it settled onto Taiwan; and (2) cleansed of its global and potentially more radical ambitions.

Just a decade before the Supplement was published, Chiang wrote *China's Destiny*. Published at the tail end of the Second Sino-Japanese War, *China's Destiny*, written in response to the abolition of treaties imposed by the United

States and Britain since the Opium War, offered a grand narrative of modern China's submission to Western imperialism and its rebirth as a major nation-state. As the famed writer Lin Yutang (1895–1976) introduced it to an American readership, the book was nothing less than a statement of "China's responsibilities growing out of her great heritage and her new status as an independent nation." It outlined Chiang's "philosophy of revolution and cultural and moral reconstruction."[29] The American journalist Philip Jaffe (1895–1980) hyperbolically named it "the *Mein Kampf* of China," claiming that the "antidemocratic views and opposition to all concepts of Western liberalism" the book expressed were sources of embarrassment for the pro-GMD government in Washington.[30] Indeed, the penultimate chapter of *China's Destiny* described China's resurgence as an event of world-historical significance. It chastised the West for creating a global order which saw "capitalism and imperialism reinforcing each other," resulting in constant international and domestic strife. The independence of China represented not just the ascendency of a new power, much less a new hegemon in the mode of Japan in Asia or Germany in Europe. It represented the triumph of Chinese political philosophy represented by the likes of Mencius and Laozi, under which "Asiatic people" coexisted peacefully before the onslaught of Euro-American imperialism. The same philosophy and morality, with China's independence, would bring Asia freedom and lasting peace.[31] Chiang's triumphalism was echoed in state-sanctioned materials intended for students. A companion to the *Three People's Principles*, published in 1943 with the blessing of the Ministry of Education, claimed that Sun's creeds overcame (*kefu*) the three malicious systems of thought prevailing over the world: capitalism, imperialism, and communism.[32] China was uniquely placed to bring about global unity because of its population size, large territory, long history, wealth of resources, and moral attraction to other "weaker" (*ruoxiao*) nations across the world. The catechism went on to forecast blithely that China would spearhead the formation of a world government—with singular executive, legislative, and judiciary branches—which would be set up under the guidance of the Three People's Principles. China's kingly way (*wangdao*) would pave the way for an order under which "national borders were abolished, peoples lived in harmony, economic cooperation reigned and cultures converged."[33] Such gestures against capitalist imperialism and the nation-state system in the language of Pan-Asianist unity, even if rhetorical, became hollow if not downright ludicrous with "Free China" reduced to running Taiwan and a few archipelagos off the coast of communist-controlled Fujian province.

"Supplement," on the other hand, was a very different text. To begin with, its tone was much somber, a shift that was no doubt overdetermined by the GMD's existential crisis. While *China's Destiny* ruminates on the "lasting peace and the emancipation of mankind [sic]" and the "sufferings and tribulations" China had gone through since the nineteenth century, "Supplement" outlined specific plans and policies.³⁴ *China's Destiny* offered broad strokes of modern history, but "Supplement" was detailed and was almost one-third as long as the abridged version of Sun's sixteen lectures that the GMD produced for public consumption. In this sense, "Supplement" was very different from Sun's own *Three People's Principles*, which as a propaganda tool was a product of "fiery oral rhetoric" and "forceful, simple formulations."³⁵ These intertextual differences are attributable to the individuals who created the documents. While Chiang claimed ownership over both *China's Destiny* and "Supplement" as his own works, neither was the product of one man alone. The latter, moreover, could not be more remote from Sun's style. Both texts included the input of Tao Xisheng (1899–1988), a historian whom Arif Dirlik labels a GMD Marxist—someone who rejected class struggle but retained Marxist frameworks under which he diagnosed society.³⁶ Associated with the GMD "left," the figurehead of which was Wang Jingwei (1883–1944), Tao, like many Marxists, was a contributor to a major debate on Chinese social history in the late 1920s and 1930s, in which not only the country's past but more importantly its revolutionary future were at stake. China, Tao argued, had been stuck between feudalism and capitalism for two millennia since the Warring States period (475–221 BCE). The GMD's task, therefore, was to deliver the nation from this conundrum so that it evolved into a capitalist society and followed a putatively universal mode of development. Instead of a social revolution, which Tao was vehemently against, he advocated a *political* one which would allow the state to spearhead industrialization and eliminate residual feudal forces in society. As a historical materialist, Tao was therefore also different from Dai Jitao, who first highlighted *yu* and *le* as Sun's legacy to be fleshed out by his followers. While conversant in Marxism, Dai was more invested in claiming for Sunist thoughts nationalist and pan-Asian credentials by appealing to Confucian vocabularies. Indeed, Dai's interpretation of *minsheng* put stress on its alleged nonmaterialistic, spiritualist elements. Tao's contributions to "Supplement" were tantamount to a reinterpretation of Dai, whose demise in 1949 ended the elder's hold on what *minsheng* meant.

The pronounced differences between *China's Destiny* and "Supplement," meanwhile, can partly be explained by Tao's varying degree of involvement in their respective production processes. Tao reportedly claimed that his contributions to Chiang's major treatises—including the two titles under discussion and the 1956 *Soviet Russia in China* (*Su-E zai Zhongguo*)—were no more than that of a "typewriter that put on record the thoughts of its owner."[37] However, his other accounts contradicted this claim and show that his contributions to Chiang's ideological state apparatus were uneven. A 1964 collection of Tao's essays insisted that the sexagenarian played a mere editorial role in the creation of *China's Destiny*, a claim Dirlik finds plausible given that the story of China's decline in Chiang's book was out of tune with his Marxist historical framework.[38] In contrast, Tao's recently published personal diary, compiled by his son, shows that the then chief lecturer (*zong jiangzu*) at his party's think tank Research Institute of Revolutionary Praxis (*Geming shijian yanjiusu*) was the main force behind "Supplement." Tao started writing "Supplement" on January 10, 1953, and delivered the manuscript to the publisher on November 13 in the same year. During this period, the diary mentions the drafting, revising, and printing of "Supplement" at least seven times. After "Supplement" was made available to the public, Tao wrote newspaper articles explaining the chapters and gave multiple lectures on them for audiences ranging from members of the GMD-led youth movement and rank-and-file cadres to officers in the air force and government officials.[39] On his part, Chiang commissioned Tao to write "Supplement" on November 12, 1952, and commented on drafts, requesting revisions throughout the process.[40] Thus, despite his disclaimer and self-effacement, Tao's fingerprints were all over "Supplement."

"Supplement" and Reorientation of the Conservative Revolution

Tao's central role in putting together such canonical texts as "Supplement," in addition to numerous speeches and exhortations attributed to Chiang, indicates that he became the GMD's core postwar ideologue as the party considered how it should govern Taiwan, with a view to eventually reconquering mainland China. While Taiwan's economic growth was promoted as vindication for the efficacy of free enterprise, the island actually witnessed, from the 1950s until at least the 1960s, what much of East and Southeast Asian societies experienced, that is, state-led industrialization under which private capital played a subordinate and collaborative role in an export-oriented economy. Main drivers of Taiwan's development under the GMD such as Chen Cheng and engineer Yin Zhongrong (1903–1963) cited the British Labour Party and the Meiji government in Japan, respectively, as inspirations for the policies they formulated for Taiwan. They subscribed to the standard *minsheng* position that the state, not private capital, should perform a domineering and paternalistic function in the economy. It goes without saying that this position was incompatible with free-market propaganda served by both Washington and Taipei.[41] Instead, it bore strong resonances with the corporatist approach to industrialization championed by Wang Jingwei and the "left" GMD in the 1930s, a strategy that drew on Sun's emphasis on managing private capital and was pitched as an alternative to liberal capitalism and communism. It also represented a shift in Chiang's vision—salient during the GMD's reign in mainland China but no longer applicable in Taiwan as military defense was provided by the United States—which privileged military industries in the nation-building process.[42] Seen under this light, Tao's growing prominence in the GMD's ideological state apparatus on Taiwan was unsurprising.

Unlike *China's Destiny*, therefore, "Supplement" showed clear signs of Tao's ruminations on China that were carried over from his time on the mainland. It reflected Tao's Marxian belief in one universal mode of development to which China, like Euro-America before it, must conform. "The basic aim," the Supplement stated in its beginning section, "of the *minsheng* principle is industrial development."[43] Industrialization meant that the bulk of Taiwan's— and eventually mainland China's—population would be displaced from the countryside and relocated to cities. It also created incredible unevenness in society, whereby structures, norms, and relations inherited from the past were upended while modern equivalents had yet to coalesce into a coherent, even whole. As "Supplement" puts it, "the main tendencies of Chinese society which have developed in the course of the last three decades are two: gradual decay in agriculture without the compensatory advantage of industrial development; disintegration of the old social organization without the emergence of a new one to take its place." What unfolded in twentieth-century Taiwan/China was made to vindicate what Sun had described as the cause of revolutionary upheaval in nineteenth-century Euro-America, that is; the benefits mechanization brought about were negated by social displacement. Not properly managed, capitalist social change threatened to derail the national revolution. Such ruminations were not merely academic, as "Supplement" lamented that social disintegration ended up benefitting the Chinese communists and their Russian sponsors, who exploited it to their advantage.[44] Instead, they set the stage for the general tone the "Supplement" adopted in its proposal for China's future.

Yu and *le*, like the four elements of *minsheng* that Sun covered three decades ago, served to manage the transition from agrarian to industrial society and absorb the resultant blow on the nation's fabric. Refuting the option to give free rein to centrifugal forces in society, "Supplement" cited Sun's definition of socialism to justify "planned social reform" and "methodical planning." This strain of thought found strong echoes in Dai's valorization of a strong state, which would use the tool of a vanguard revolutionary party to magnify the benefits of industrialization while thwarting class tensions, imperialist encroachment, and sociocultural disorientation that global capitalism brought about. It, however, also gave ideological voice for the GMD's new developmentalist focus on producing labor-intensive goods for export instead of developing a military-industrial complex. This is obvious from the opening section of the *yu* chapter, which debunked Malthusianism by citing Sun's concern that China's population was too small compared to that of other powers. Yet, while Sun alluded to fear of hostile states colonizing China's frontier regions, "Supplement" saw increasing the population as a way to expand the pool of industrial labor. To encourage population growth and improve the quality of the workforce, "Supplement" envisioned a paternalistic welfare state. The rest of the *yu* chapter was devoted to education and welfare provisions for children, the disabled, the divorced and the widowed, and the elderly (both sustenance and disposal after death). The narrative was similar for each aspect the chapter covered: disintegration of old social structures, demands of modernity, Chinese communist mischief, and constructive work to be undertaken by the state in Taiwan and eventually the mainland. Take, for example, the issue of elderly care. "Supplement" cited the loosening of "patriarchal family system," the rise of the nuclear family—which put less emphasis on the roles of grandparents—and widespread unemployment of older people in the machine age as causes for the plight of the elderly. To make matters worse, the communists allegedly promoted patricide and forced family members to struggle against one another, thus widening further the gap between the elderly and their technically adept, urbanized offspring. The GMD's task was to rekindle "the Chinese people's innate love for their family." Having stressed the GMD's role as the custodian of China's Confucian tradition, the "Supplement" turned abruptly to pensions and aged care homes. It envisioned broad provisions of pensions for workers in both the public and private sectors and aged care facilities for the homeless in every county and city.[45] Taken together, the first of the two supplementary chapters read like a blueprint of a welfare state for an industrializing society, with ample, colorful dose of anti-communist rhetoric and perfunctory nods to Confucianism.

This medley of distinct philosophical and political traditions suggests that the text was a result of composite authorship, although it leaves little to no doubt that Tao was responsible for execution. Tao, unlike the likes of Dai Jitao, had little investment in Confucianism and Chinese traditions. His bookshelf in the 1950s featured works of US-based sociologists such as Karl Mannheim and Pitirim Sorokin. As a Protestant Christian, Tao also read theologian Louis Berkhof. Confucian classics were conspicuous by their absence.[46] This indifference toward China's putative national essence diverged from the GMD's position, embraced by Chiang, that Sun was the intellectual inheritor of China's heritage that began with Confucius and Mencius. While Chiang Kai-shek was also a Christian, the generalissimo had always accorded a strong Confucian tinge to the state he led and, more remarkably, did not share Tao's materialist epistemology. This tension between Tao's own intellectual disposition and the party-state's apparent Confucian obsession was apparent in Chiang's comments on his subordinate's drafts. Having read the first draft of "Supplement," Chiang requested major revisions. "The chapter on *le* was very weak," Chiang bemoaned in his diary. Given Tao's materialist outlook, it is not surprising that he was not conversant in what Dai cryptically called "beautiful enjoyment." Chiang instructed Tao to expand the *le* chapter with a focus on the humanistic and martial arts (*wen, wuyi*). Under both categories, discussion was to begin with the Six Arts (*liuyi*)—Confucian education for men in imperial China—and move on to modern art forms. Humanistic arts, thus, encompassed not only poetry and *go*, a refined chess-like strategy board game, but also film and radio. As for sustainment of the living and disposal of the dead, Chiang continued, discussion should reference "ancient system" (*gushi zhidu*).[47] Tao paid little more than lip service to Chiang's exhortation. The *le* chapter in the "Supplement" followed the pattern in the *yu* chapter. It, too, put emphasis on concrete steps the regime would take to address challenges brought about by industrial capitalism. Water conservation, forestry, and urban parks were identified as critical to a "healthy and happy environment," even though they had at best a tenuous connection to the humanistic arts or Confucian values Chiang championed. Rivers, lakes, and woods, while lauded for contributing to the nation's beauty purportedly cherished through generations, were prized as much for the very concrete goals such as ensuring soil conservation and supply of clean drinking water as their contribution to enjoyment and spiritual well-being. The rationale for the building of urban parks was Sun Yat-sen's land equalization principle, rather than anything particularly Confucian or ancient. Private ownership of urban spaces should be put under check and parks built, along with children's playgrounds and sports fields, for public enjoyment. Even discussion of literature and music, supposedly spiritual components of *minsheng*, followed the pattern described above. Modern cultural industry, Tao had Chiang remark, meant commercialization of literature and music. Against "yellowbacks"—profitable reading materials and equivalents in music and film—the communists proffered "Red propaganda" through the very means that the Nationalist state counted upon to edify the masses and reignite in them, however fleetingly, China's glorious literary and musical memories. It became imperative for the state to make these arts widely and affordably available to citizens, with infrastructure such as theaters and opera houses in major cities.[48]

This remarkably measure-driven approach to promoting "health and happiness," as the official English translation of the text rendered *le*, found echoes in exegeses on the renewed canon. Such observation was reinforced in a catechism written for high-school students. The author Cheng Jingfu, a literary editor and writer, committed his career to vanquishing "Red" literature and promoting "liberal democratic" ones. He cited *La Marseillaise* at the French Revolution as a fine example of how the people could be inspired to fight an enemy without swords and other weaponry.[49] Yet, when explaining the *le* principle to young readers, Cheng followed Tao's discussion of building public facilities—woods and rivers, sports fields, children playgrounds. He privileged, like Tao, provisions to urban dwellers (*shimin*) and facilities agreeable to children's bodies and hearts (*yishen yixin*).[50] The message had consistently been that outlets for relieving the urban population of stress from factory or office discipline were vital measures to fulfill the goals of *minsheng*, at least insofar as furthering citizens' happiness was concerned. Simply put, the two chapters of "Supplement" constituted a blueprint for building a robust welfare state to soften the blow of capitalist urbanization. It laid out measures that, along with land reform and other initiatives undertaken by Nationalist technocrats, were symptomatic of what Bruce Cumings identifies as East Asian developmental state, with its emphasis on mass education and state-coordinated industrialization and appeal to the nation's cultural essence.[51]

Conclusion

As a text produced in the aftermath of the Korean War, thanks to which the GMD could expect US guarantee of its military hold on Taiwan, "Supplement" displayed remarkable continuities and permutations in the party-state's self-identity. A corporatist approach to industrialization, animosity against class struggle, and primacy of a state staffed by technocrats remained at the core of the GMD's vision for nation building and its claim to offer an alternative to both liberal capitalism and revolutionary socialism. At the same time, the party's diminished and precarious geopolitical existence as a virtual protectorate of Washington allowed, if not compelled, Chiang to shift his government's military focus to one that privileged industrial development and the construction of a welfare state. This subtle but significant change was underscored by the materialist turn of *minsheng*. Instead of emphasizing the incendiary and idealist urges in Sun's ideology, "Supplement" "completed" *minsheng* by listing a set of initiatives that complemented and rationalized Taiwan's anticipated urbanization. Instead of providing a superior alternative to capitalist modernity, the ultimate goal of the conservative revolution promised concrete benefits such as jobs, pensions, compulsory education, childcare, and care for the elderly. That this shift paralleled much of East Asia and Europe was unsurprising given larger Cold War rivalries between the "free world" and the socialist bloc.

This chapter traces the transwar legacy the GMD state carried from mainland China to Taiwan. While its primary focus is on the Chinese Civil War, trends that solidified in the 1950s were transnational as the United States and Britain designed arrangements after the Pacific War, with American military hegemony in the Asia-Pacific region as their cardinal goal. Chiang reconciled himself to the "Cold War reconfiguration," as Wang Hui calls it, at the 1943 Cairo Conference.[52] His deference to the United States set the tone of *minsheng* and of Taiwan's developments in the 1950s and beyond. Indeed, the few years from the end of the Second World War in 1945 until the incremental hardening of Cold War dichotomies in the 1950s saw the conservative revolution that informed the party-state being reduced from overseeing a continental-size country to perching on Taiwan and a few small archipelagoes thanks to US military and economic might. This dramatic decline in the GMD's fortunes resulted in a change not just of scale but of the nature of the nationalist revolution (*guomin geming*) the party led. Just as the GMD ideological commitments changed under the Cold War order, so did the nature of the arguably unfinished Chinese Civil War, as revolutionary mobilization increasingly gave way to competing modes of state-driven economic development. With Chiang Kai-shek's demise, military "recovery" of mainland China faded from the GMD agenda. As ROC president, Chiang Ching-kuo oversaw a détente between the two rival Chinese governments, pitching Taiwan—under the banner of the Three People's Principles—as a successful model of industrial modernization against mainland China, which was recovering from the chaos of the Cultural Revolution. Taiwan was presented as a land of material abundance and an economy well connected with those of Japan, North America, and Europe, qualities which the Chinese communists under Deng Xiaoping (1904–1997) were themselves pursuing. The Three People's Principles gave thin cover to the capitalist, urban modernity the GMD celebrated in the late twentieth century, despite Sun's rejection of capitalism in his *minsheng* speeches. As the GMD's influence on Taiwan politics waxed and waned since the 1990s, the Three People's Principles, along with the intellectual labor invested into *minsheng*, gradually faded from public memory. While the party itself remains a political force to this day, the GMD has all but abandoned any pretense to offer a mode of social formation different from the one that has prevailed with the end of the Cold War.

Notes

1 Chen Yunqian, *Chongbai yu jiyi: Sun Zhongshan fuhao de jian'gou yu chuanbo* (Nanjing: Nanjing daxue chuabshe, 2009).
2 Perri Johanna Strawn, "Teaching Nationalism in the Crucible: Changing Identities in Taiwan High Schools after Martial Law" (PhD diss., Yale University, 1999), 241.
3 The Guomindang produced official English translation of its core texts. The translator of *Three People's Principles* was the Presbyterian missionary Frank W. Price, who also translated many of Chiang's speeches during the war of resistance against Japan and assisted in jurist Wang Chonghui's translation of *China's Destiny*. Unless otherwise stated, this chapter cites official translations, with minor stylistic changes, where they are available.
4 Wakabayashi Masahiro, *Taiwan no seiji: Chūka Minkoku Taiwan-ka no sengoshi* (Tokyo: Tōkyō daigaku shuppankai, 2008). A Chinese translation came out in Taiwan in 2014.
5 Brian Tsui, *China's Conservative Revolution: The Quest for a New Order* (Cambridge: Cambridge University Press, 2018).
6 Tehyun Ma, "Making Taiwan Chinese, 1945–60," in *Routledge Handbook of Revolutionary China*, ed. Alan Baumler (London: Routledge, 2019), 204–9.
7 Jennifer Liu, "Indoctrinating the Youth: Guomindang Policy on Secondary Education in Wartime China and Postwar Taiwan, 1937–1960" (PhD diss., University of California, Irvine, 2010), 114–23.
8 Feng-Huang Ying, "Reassessing Taiwan's Literary Field of the 1950s" (PhD diss., University of Texas at Austin, 2000), 26–9.
9 Qu Wanwen, *Taiwan zhanhou jingji fazhan de yuanqi: houjin fazhan de weihe yu ruhe* (Taipei: Lianjing, 2017), 87–8; Julia C. Strauss, "Campaigns of

Redistribution: Land Reform and State Building in China and Taiwan, 1950–1953," in *States in the Developing World*, ed. Miguel A. Centeno, Atul Kohli, and Deborah J. Yashar (Cambridge: Cambridge University Press, 2017), 335–54.
10 Sun Yat-sen, *San Min Chu I: The Three Principles of the People* (Chungking: Ministry of Information of the Republic of China, 1943), 419–31.
11 Margherita Zanasi, *Saving the Nation: Economic Modernity in Republican China* (Chicago: University of Chicago Press, 2006); Brenda Sansom, "'Minsheng' and National Liberation: Socialist Theory in the Guomindang, 1919–1931" (PhD diss., University of Wisconsin–Madison, 1988).
12 Sun, *San Min Chu I*, 364.
13 Cui Shuqin, *Sanmin zhuyi xinlun* (Taipei: Taiwan shangwu yinshuguan, 1987), 255. This book was first published in January 1945, before Japan surrendered to the Allies, when full-fledged hostilities between the GMD and the Chinese Communist Party were supposed to be manageable for national unity's sake.
14 Lü Fangshang, *Jiang Zhongzheng xiansheng nianpu changbian*, vol. 10 (Taipei: Guoshiguan, Guoli Zhongzheng jiniantang guanlichu and Caituan faren Zhongzheng wenjiao jijin hui, 2015), 61–2.
15 Rebecca E. Karl, "'Serve the People': An Exemplary Chinese Socialist Text of 1944," in *Reading the Postwar Future: Textual Turning Points from 1944*, ed. Kirrily Freeman and John Munro (London: Bloomsbury, 2019), 221.
16 Cui, *Sanmin zhuyi xinlun*, 272–3.
17 Sun, *San Min Chu I*, 441.
18 Cui, *Sanmin zhuyi xinlun*, 258.
19 Chiang Kai-shek, *Zongtong Jianggong sixiang yanlun zongji*, vol. 25, 113–14, http://www.ccfd.org.tw/ccef001/index.php?option=com_content&view=categories&id=103&Itemid=256 (accessed April 15, 2020).
20 Cui, *Sanmin zhuyi xinlun*, 262.
21 Chiang, *Zongtong Jianggong sixiang yanlun zongji*, vol. 25, 143.
22 Ibid., vol. 5, 47–9.
23 Chen Cheng, *Land Reform in Taiwan* (Taipei: China Publishing, 1961), xiii, 1–17.
24 Tsui, *China's Conservative Revolution*, 37–9.
25 Ibid., 42. Official English translation of "Supplement" rendered *yu* and *le* as "national fecundity, social welfare and education" and "health and happiness," respectively. The translator opted not to decide on individual English words to encapsulate the meaning of the two Chinese characters but simply list items discussed under the two categories, belying the myriad meanings of *yu* and *le*. Underscoring the ambiguity of the two terms, this chapter adopts pinyin transliteration throughout.
26 Dai Jitao, *Sun Wen zhuyi zhi zhexue de jichu* (1925; reprint, Taipei: Zhongyang gaizao weiyuanhui wenwu gongying chu, 1951), 15.

27 Ibid., 21, 54.
28 Marie-Claire Bergère, *Sun Yat-sen* (Stanford, CA: Stanford University Press, 1998), 381–2.
29 Lin Yutang, "Introduction," in Chiang Kai-shek, *China's Destiny*, trans. Wang Chung-hui (New York: Macmillan, 1947), viii–x.
30 Philip Jaffe, "The Secret of *China's Destiny*," in *China's Destiny and Chinese Economic Theory* (New York: Roy, 1947), 19.
31 Chiang Kai-shek, *China's Destiny*, trans. Wang Chung-hui (New York: Macmillan, 1947), 228–34.
32 Liu Xiuru, *Sanmin zhuyi jiaocheng* (Chongqing: Zhengzhong shuju, 1943), 301.
33 Ibid., 301–4.
34 Chiang, *China's Destiny*, 235; Chiang, *San Min Chu I*, 215.
35 Bergère, *Sun Yat-sen*, 353.
36 Arif Dirlik, *Culture and History in Postrevolutionary China: The Perspective of Global Modernity* (Hong Kong: Chinese University Press, 2011), 69; "T'ao Hsi-sheng: The Social Limits of Change," in *The Limits of Change: Essays on Conservative Alternatives in Republican China*, ed. Charlotte Furth (Cambridge, MA: Harvard University Press, 1976), 305–31.
37 Tao Tailai and Tao Jinsheng, *Tao Xisheng nianbiao* (Taipei: Lianjing, 2017), 293.
38 Tao Xisheng, *Chaoliu yu diandi* (Taipei: Zhuanji wenxue chubanshe, 1964), 204; Dirlik, "T'ao Hsi-sheng," 305n1.
39 Tao Jinsheng, *Tao Xisheng riji: Zhongguo minguo lizu Tai, Peng, Jin, Ma de lishi jianzheng*, vol. 2 (Taipei: Lianjing, 2014).
40 Lü, *Jiang Zhongzheng xiansheng nianpu changbian*, 120–220.
41 Nick Cullather, "'Fuel for the Good Dragon': The United States and Industrial Policy in Taiwan, 1950–1965," *Diplomatic History* 20 (1996): 1–8. Tao himself was also reportedly interested in referencing postwar experiments undertaken in Western countries in his formulation of *minsheng*, with a view to finding a "third way" (Tao and Tao, *Tao Xisheng nianbiao*, 292).
42 Zanasi, *Saving the Nation*.
43 Chiang, *San Min Chu I*, 216.
44 Ibid., 218–19.
45 Ibid., 250–4.
46 Dirlik, "T'ao Hsi-sheng," 325; Tao, *Tao Xisheng riji*, 606, 612.
47 Lü, *Jiang Zhongzheng xiansheng nianpu changbian*, 196.
48 Chiang, *San Min Chu I*, 294–306.
49 Ying Fenghuang, *Wuling niandai wenxue chuban xianying* (Taipei County: Taibei xian wenhua ju, 2006), 3–4.
50 Cheng Jingfu, *Sanmin zhuyi zhi lilun ji shiti jieda* (Taipei: Banyue wenyi she, 1957), 69.

51 Bruce Cumings, *Parallax Visions: Making Sense of American-East Asian Relations at the End of the Century* (Durham, NC: Duke University Press, 1999), 88–92.
52 Wang Hui, *The Politics of Imagining Asia* (Cambridge, MA: Harvard University Press, 2011), 243–60. Wang pivots his discussion on Okinawa or the Ryukyus but makes a much more significant argument on the Cairo Conference as an "omen" of the Cold War.

6

"*Volksgeist*-ism": Ideational Flows between Europe, Japan, and Indonesia, 1920s–1960s

David Bourchier

Introduction

In 1935, Indonesian nationalist Subardjo Djoyoadisuryo, a graduate of Leiden University's law school, paid a visit to the Tokyo home of Professor Ōgushi Toyoo, one of the authors of the ultranationalist textbook *Kokutai no Hongi*. Speaking in German, they found themselves in furious agreement about the need to reject enlightenment era theories of law derived from the West and replace them with indigenous, historically evolved principles rooted in the spirit of the nation, the *Volksgeist*.[1] The episode highlights the transnational appeal of what I have called *Volksgeist*-ism, the theory that a country's legal and political institutions must express the unique character of its people.

This chapter explores ideational flows among Europe, Japan, and Indonesia between the 1920s and the 1960s. It focuses on continuities between the orthodoxies of the "Leiden School" in the 1920s, Japanese cultural nationalism in the 1930s and 1940s, and Indonesian political thinking in the Cold War period. The common element illuminated here is the romantic era concept that legal and political legitimacy derives not from adherence to a set of universal principles but from the organic and deep-rooted spirit of the people. After tracking the instrumentalization of *Volksgeist*-ism in Europe and Japan, and during the Japanese occupation of Indonesia, the chapter traces its reception and subsequent deployment in Indonesia. It describes how early nationalists were drawn to the idea after being exposed to the body of Dutch scholarship extolling the virtues of Indonesian customary law and the legal theory that underpinned it. It goes on to explore how the conviction that Indonesia should look to its own philosophies of governance was reinforced by contacts with like-minded Japanese nationalist intellectuals both before and during the occupation.

Special attention is paid to the role played by the Indonesian jurist Supomo in the constitutional debates of 1945, first because of his close links to both Dutch and Japanese streams of *Volksgeist*-ism and second because the "integralist" vision he articulated was to become a key reference point in Indonesian constitutional thought. To demonstrate how *Volksgeist*-ism has been deployed in the service of political interests, the chapter will examine how, after a period of revolution and progressive reform, conservative elements associated with the administrative elite helped revive *Volksgeist* arguments in the early 1950s and how these were developed by elements of the military opposed to parliamentary democracy. It describes how a common dislike of the multiparty system saw Sukarno first collaborate with the military to revive the 1945 Constitution and then deploy a left-populist variant of *Volksgeist*-ism to legitimize his Guided Democracy. The last section tells the story of Soeharto's right-wing military takeover in 1965 and how his ideologues sought to redefine Indonesian culture as static, conservative, and hierarchical in support of his policies to centralize power and suppress oppositional activity in Indonesia.

Adopting a transwar approach disrupts the standard periodization of Indonesian history into colonial, wartime, and postindependence eras established as a result of academic convention, access to sources, and sympathy with the nationalist project. To the extent that historians have examined legacies of Dutch and Japanese colonial rule in Indonesia, they have tended to focus on structural inheritances, including the bureaucracy, the legal system, and the military. Less attention has been given to ideational continuities, again, perhaps, in deference to nationalist sensibilities but also, in the case of *Volksgeist*-ism, because they appear in the political realm as a vernacular idiom, using the vocabulary of idealized village tradition. It is only when we examine the writings of some of the key ideologues behind both Presidents Sukarno and Suharto in the first two decades after independence that the genealogy of their indigenist ideologies becomes apparent.

Lineages of *Volksgeist*-ism

Volksgeist-ism is best understood as the marriage of two ideas, both dating from the period of romantic German nationalism in the late eighteenth and early nineteenth centuries. The first is Johann Gottfried Herder's notion that people are what they are not by virtue of their common membership of humanity, as the enlightenment philosophers claimed, but because they were raised within the matrix of a particular culture with its own unique, historically evolved language, customs, and collective memory.[2] Each culture, he argued, was the manifestation of a distinctive spirit, which he called, without any hint of chauvinism, the *Volksgeist*. This idea proved extremely influential, providing an easily accessible intellectual foundation for nationalist sentiment not only in the German-speaking territories under Napoleonic occupation but, ultimately, for nationalist movements around the globe. The second idea was formulated by the jurist Friedrich Karl von Savigny and his student Georg Puchta, who founded what came to be known as the Historical School of Law (*Historische Rechtsschule*) in 1815. Proponents of this school held that law, like language and custom, was valid only if it was the product of slow, unconscious distillation of the historical and living traditions of particular nations (i.e., the *Volksgeist*). Law could not be created by legislators or transplanted from one context to another as was advocated by proponents of a German Civil Code based on the Napoleonic Code. Rather, it had to be discovered by painstaking research into the legal norms living in particular societies. Even though the Historical School lost the argument in Germany, it flourished for several decades and influenced legal and political philosophy from Norway to Japan.[3]

To understand how *Volksgeist*-ism made its way to Indonesia, it is necessary to turn our attention to the lesser-known world of Dutch legal anthropology. The discipline of ethnological jurisprudence (*Völkerkunde*) arose in Germany as a direct product of the Historical School.[4] Otto von Gierke, Jakob Grimm, and their colleagues devoted themselves to delving deep into German history and culture to discover legal principles that could contribute to the building of an historically authentic legal system. German legal scholarship had a major influence in the Netherlands, and Historical School thinking also found devotees among legal scholars there. Foremost among them was Cornelis van Vollenhoven, who served as professor of the *Adat* Law of the Netherlands East Indies at Leiden University from 1901 until 1933. *Adat* is the Indonesian word for "custom." *Adatrecht*, or customary law, was the primary subject of interest for legal anthropologists associated with what became known as the Leiden School.

The often-passionate debates over the proper place of *adat* in the complex legal regime of the Netherlands East Indies have been dealt with in detail elsewhere.[5] Suffice it to say here that this issue assumed great importance in Dutch colonial policy in the first quarter of the twentieth century thanks to the public efforts of Van Vollenhoven and his Leiden School colleagues in advocating for the recognition of *adatrecht*. Surprising as it may seem in retrospect, his argument that the recognition of *adat* was necessary to shield traditional societies in Indonesia from the corrosive influence of foreign capital and alien Western legal systems succeeded in preserving a plural system of law in which myriad *adat* jurisdictions were protected by the colonial state.

From 1902, Leiden University had the monopoly for the training of future Dutch civil servants for the East Indies administration,[6] and Van Vollenhoven himself supervised a generation of lawyers and administrators. Most significant for current purposes, the Leiden School also attracted a small but highly influential cohort of postgraduate students from its sprawling Southeast Asian colony. Van Vollenhoven's purported discovery of a coherent indigenous legal system in the Indies characterized by reciprocity, harmony, and communalism made a tremendous impression on these young students, awakening in them a deep pride and furnishing them with a basis for imagining Indonesia as a single nation. In 1922, Indonesian students based in the Netherlands changed the name of their organization from Indies Association to the Indonesian Association (*Indonesische Vereeniging*), making it the first organization to use the term "Indonesia." It is difficult to overestimate the significance of this moment because as well as making Indonesia conceivable for the first time, it also cemented in place the linkage between the idea of Indonesia and its "national personality" as harmonious and communalistic. The embrace of this representation of Indonesian-ness promoted by the Leiden School privileged a static, agrarian, and inward-looking model of Indonesian culture over other possible models, including, most notably, one based on the cosmopolitan Islamic cultures that had taken root across the archipelago in the preceding centuries.

It was not only Van Vollenhoven's idyllic depiction of *adat* that his Indonesian students took to heart but also the theoretical underpinnings of his approach. So pervasive was this view that writer and novelist Takdir Alisjahbana would later lament that "a whole generation of Indonesian jurists" had grown up "willing to accept Van Vollenhoven's ideas as essentially the most satisfactory basis for a national legal system."[7] The influence of *Volksgeist*-ism reached well beyond students of *adat* law. Subardjo Djoyoadisuryo, a key figure in the early nationalist movement and Indonesia's first foreign minister, wrote admiringly of Savigny and Jhering and of being struck by the parallel between their accounts of the imposition of Roman law on Germany and the situation in Indonesia. On his return from Berlin in 1927, Subardjo wrote that he had been impressed by von Savigny's concept that unless law was rooted in the culture and history of a people, it would undermine the state. This was a clear sign for me that the system of Dutch law in my country had obstructed the natural growth of Indonesian *adat* law. Von Savigny's famous phrase "*Das Recht ist und wird mit dem Volke*" ("law exists and evolves with the people") reinforced my view that our struggle for independence must look for its strength in our nation's identity to oppose powerful alien influences.[8]

Thanks to the close institutional links between Leiden and the Law School in Jakarta, the basic premises and assumptions of the Historical School of Law entered the canon of legal education in Indonesia. From its foundation in 1924 the Law School employed several former students of Van Vollenhoven, including leading exponents of legal anthropology F. D. Holleman and Bernard ter Haar. In 1941, Raden Supomo was the first Indonesian to be appointed as a professor in the Law School. Supomo had studied under Van Vollenhoven and following his graduation from Leiden in 1924 had built a reputation as Indonesia's foremost expert in *adat*. Upon taking up his position in Jakarta Supomo gave a speech in which he argued that critics of Europe's overly individualistic legal order would do well to look to Indonesian *adat*, which already had a long tradition of solving conflict through conciliation and communal mindedness. In doing so he was reprising a familiar distinction between the "litigious, materialistic, selfish" West and the "harmony seeking, spiritual and communalistic" East which, while redolent of European orientalism, also underlined the distinctiveness, if not the moral superiority, of Indonesia in a way that resonated strongly with elements of the mainstream nationalist movement.

Savigny in Japan

Arguments between universalist and particularistic conceptions of law in the first half of the twentieth century were taking place simultaneously across multiple countries. This debate was particularly pronounced in Japan. Following the Meiji Restoration of 1868, the government implemented sweeping administrative, military, and legal reforms with the twin imperative of centralizing power and revising the unequal treaties with Western nations. Priority was given to establishing a unified legal code which would replace Japan's patchwork of feudal laws and provide a basis for dealing with the West. As with the other Meiji reforms, Japan's jurists looked to European models. Meiji-era intellectuals had an intense interest in the philosophical rivalries raging in Europe, and there was a high level of engagement with British, French, and German legal thinkers in particular.[9] Arguments over the drafting of a Japanese Civil Code in the 1890s closely mirrored those in Germany, with proponents of a French-inspired code in Japan pitted against those who held that such a code would impose alien values and corrode the time-honored conventions of filial piety and household organization that were integral to Japanese social cohesion and identity. The most prominent opponents of the draft code were the brothers Hozumi Nobushige and Hozumi Yatsuka, both of whom had studied in Germany in the 1880s before being appointed as law professors at Tokyo University. Both were strong admirers of Savigny, and Nobushige became known as the founder of Japanese historical jurisprudence.[10] Even though a version of the code was eventually passed in 1898, Yatsuka's radical opposition did much to lay the foundations of cultural nationalism in Japan. In his view the national essence (*kokutai*) of Japan was based on an affinity between the family and the divinely ordained imperial state. Japan's national character "was not only unique but was also irreconcilable with either the Christian customs or the liberal thoughts of French Revolutionists."[11] By 1900, buoyed by Japan's military victories over China, Meiji ideologues increasingly described the *kokutai* as superior to the essences of other nations—as Carol Gluck explains "'more' unique ... ageless, continuous, and secure in its ancestral tradition."[12]

The first two decades of the twentieth century saw a significant rise in cultural nationalism in reaction to the socially disruptive industrialization programs of the Meiji state and what right-wing intellectuals saw as the "decadent Westernism" of the liberal Taishō era (1912–1926). The shift toward a more militant and chauvinistic mood was encouraged by the government's sharp shift to the right in the early 1930s in reaction to intensifying class and ideological conflict. In many cases, this concern with asserting national distinctiveness was viewed not simply in terms of Japan but of Asia as a whole, with writers such as the folklorist Yanagita Kunio condemning Western capitalism as a threat to the "Asian *gemeinschaft*" based on agrarian communalism.[13]

Viewed from Indonesia, Japan presented an attractive model. Not only had it resisted colonization, it had succeeded in defeating a European power in the Japan-Russian War of 1905 and was, from the 1930s onward, working hard to promote itself as an ally in the struggle against European colonialism in Asia. In a 1936 letter to his wife, the leading socialist intellectual Sutan Sjahrir noted that the Japanese had been "so successful in winning over our common people, as well as the middle groups and civil servants ... All over Indonesia, and all the way down to the *kampungs* [poor neighborhoods] in the most remote areas, people have faith in Japan's might, against which the Dutch are powerless."[14] With one eye fixed firmly on the archipelago's abundant natural resources, the Japanese government also actively courted Indonesia's nationalist elite, sponsoring many budding politicians, journalists, and intellectuals to visit Japan. Such visitors from Indonesia and other Southeast Asian countries received considerable attention from Pan-Asianist and ultranationalist groups in Japan, as well as from leading cultural nationalists. Mohammad Hatta, for instance, who was to become Indonesia's first vice president, was looked after in grand style on a visit to Japan by Iwata Takeo, a representative of the militarist Greater Asia Association, and feted in the press as the "Gandhi of Java."[15]

As alluded to in the opening vignette of this chapter, there was a surprising meeting of minds between some Indonesian graduates of the Leiden School and prominent Japanese cultural nationalist intellectuals. Even in his memoirs published in 1978, Subardjo Djoyoadisuryo, who served as Indonesia's first foreign minister, recounts with some glee how impressed he was with how the nationalist scholars he spoke to during his time in Japan in the mid-1930s thought about state and society, including their thoughts on the *kokutai*.[16] What they shared was not fascism but a deep intellectual debt to the theoretical world of German romantic nationalism, especially the Historical School of Law. For all their differences, they both viewed the Western-dominated world order based on capitalism and enlightenment-inspired legal regimes as in urgent need of replacement, in Asia at least, by new legal and political systems that reflected the unique character of individual nations.

Of course for all the rhetoric of Pan-Asianism and "Asia for the Asians," the Japanese government was interested in Southeast Asia not because of any philosophical imperatives but because of its ample reserves of rubber, tin, timber, and oil. During the 1930s, the Japanese government had done meticulous research on the geography, demography, culture, administration, politics, and natural resources of the region.[17] By the time they invaded Indonesia in March 1942 they were able—to the wonder of many Indonesians—to completely displace the Dutch and take over the reins of the colonial administration in a matter of weeks. Respected nationalist leaders, including Sukarno and Hatta, were released from internal exile and elevated to key positions in the new administration, lending it the legitimacy it needed in the early phase of the occupation.

Aware that they could not afford to antagonize the local population as they had done in China and Korea, the Japanese authorities made considerable efforts to persuade Indonesians to get behind the war and the benefits of the Greater

East Asia Co-Prosperity Sphere. In accordance with the guidelines of a 1941 Army handbook titled *Ideological War in the Southern Area*, the occupation government gave attention not only to instilling respect for the emperor and the importance of the "Japanese spirit" but also to urging Indonesians to rediscover and revive their indigenous values in order to boost national pride and reveal, beneath the corrupting patina of Western influence, basic similarities between Indonesian and Japanese culture.[18] To this end, the Japanese military administration gave prominent cultural and political figures a platform. In 1942, novelist Sanoesi Pane was put in charge of the journal *Keboedajaan Timoer* (Eastern Culture) which ran numerous articles condemning individualism and rationalism and highlighting the similarities between Japanese and Indonesian culture, especially with the pre-Islamic court culture of Java. Later the same year the occupation government established an advisory body called the Research Council on Adat and Past State Organization and appointed to it the highest-ranking nationalist leaders, including Sukarno, Hatta, as well as Supomo and several other Leiden law graduates.[19]

Supomo and Future Indonesian State

As the Allies closed in on Japan's Pacific strongholds, it became increasingly necessary to make concessions to the Indonesians to win their backing for what was expected to be a protracted battle. In late 1944, the Japanese government lifted a ban on flying the red-and-white Indonesian flag and singing the national anthem, and in March 1945, it announced the establishment of a Committee for the Study of Preparations for Independence. The task of this body, consisting of sixty-two older generation nationalist politicians and bureaucrats appointed by the occupation administration, was to draft a constitution for an independent Indonesia. The first order of business in the committee was to decide on a philosophical foundation (*Staatside*) for a future Indonesian state which would decide the character and contours of the constitution. Supomo, who is recognized as the primary author of the constitution, gave an influential speech to the committee on May 31, 1945, spelling out his vision.

Supomo started by endorsing the advice of Major-General Nishimura, the chief of the general affairs department, that the delegates should bear in mind that nations were living beings and that any future system of government should be tailored to the specific character of the nation.[20] "A state's internal organization," said Supomo, recalling a key axiom of the Historical School, "is intimately related to its legal genealogy (*Rechtsgeschichte*) and its social structure."[21] Surveying the ideological landscape of the times, Supomo rejected liberalism and Marxism. Liberalism emerged in the individualistic societies of Western Europe and the United States and was based on the idea of a social contract, which ended up dividing people from one another. Individualism on a national level, he asserted, always gave rise to greed, exploitation, and imperialism. Marxism was also dismissed on the grounds that it was rooted in antagonism between groups, and while a dictatorship of the proletariat may suit the Russians, it was incompatible with Indonesia's traditional social character. The tradition of political thought most in tune with Indonesia's patterns of organization, Supomo argued, was "integralism" which he linked with the work of Spinoza, the German romantic political theorist Adam Müller and Hegel. In this theory, Supomo said, the state encompassed "the social order as a whole," in which all groups, all parts, and all members are bound tightly to one another to form an organic unity.[22] In a nod to his Japanese masters, Supomo used Imperial Japan and the recently defeated Third Reich as examples of integralism, stating that "the principles inherent in the national socialist approach of unity between the leaders and the people and of unity within the state as a whole, fit together well with the eastern way of thought."[23] Imperial Japan's emphasis on the oneness of the state and the people, and on the "family principle" (*kekeluargaan* in Indonesian), was likewise "very compatible" with traditional patterns of social organization in Indonesia.

Drawing on his authority as Indonesia's foremost *adat* law scholar, Supomo summarized what he saw as the key features of Indonesian culture. Referencing Javanese court traditions, Supomo described a belief in the mystical unity of servant and lord (*kawulo dan gusti*) and between the people and their rulers. Evidence of this harmony, Supomo said, could be found in Indonesian village life, where village heads "always consulted with their people" to "preserve the spiritual bonds between the leaders and the people as a whole." In this atmosphere of unity, "all groups in society are encompassed by the spirit of *gotong royong* (mutual assistance) and the family principle." On this basis, Supomo concluded that if the future state was to reflect Indonesia's character and social structure, it must be based on the integralist state concept.[24]

In the integralist state that Supomo advocated, there would be no distinction between state and society, and therefore no need for any constitutional checks and balances or provisions against the abuse of state power, including human rights. It would be led by a figure akin to a messianic Just King (*Ratu Adil*) who would be to the nation what a village head was to a traditional village, interpreting the popular will and giving shape to peoples' sense of justice.[25] While it is easy to discern fascist themes in Supomo's vision, there is no evidence to suggest he envisaged the establishment of a Japanese-style militarist state in Indonesia. His position is better understood as a statement of deference to the government he served and as a conservative response on behalf of the administrative class which had occupied a privileged position under both the Dutch and Japanese regimes to the threat of radical nationalism and Islamism from within Indonesian society. Fortunately for Indonesia, there were more democratically minded delegates in the constitutional debates, including Hatta and Mohammad Yamin who rejected the integralist concept and succeeded in incorporating limited democratic safeguards into the constitution, such as the separation of powers and an article, albeit vaguely worded, providing for the right to organize and the right to free speech. So while the constitution did not realize Supomo's vision of an integralist state, it still bore his imprint, providing for a powerful executive presidency and stressing the importance of *musyawarah* (traditional-style deliberation) over voting, *kekeluargaan* over individualism, and *semangat* (spirit) over written regulations. Supomo had translated *Volksgeist*-ism into an Indonesian idiom and strongly reinforced the idea that the legal and political order in Indonesia should reflect Indonesia's culture or, more accurately, his conservative and aristocratic view of what constituted Indonesian culture, with an accent on hierarchy, order, and harmony. In doing so, he played a vital part in conveying into the postwar period a set of ideas used by conservative cultural nationalists in prewar Europe and Japan.

Pancasila and the Postwar Contestation of *Volksgeist*-ism

On June 1, 1945, the day after Supomo delivered this speech, the preeminent nationalist leader Sukarno formulated a set of guiding principles for the nascent state that he called Pancasila, or "five principles." Widely considered a historic compromise between Islamic and non-Islamic aspirations by emphasizing "belief in a singular divinity," Pancasila also stipulated, in its original iteration, a commitment to democracy based on *musyawarah* and *mufakat* (consensus), two concepts that Sukarno linked clearly to Indonesia's culture. Incorporated into the preamble of the constitution, Pancasila was to assume enormous importance in postindependence Indonesia as a symbolic resource wielded by proponents of rival visions of politics, law, and national identity. As we will see below, however, Sukarno's view of Indonesian culture was more egalitarian than that of Supomo, indicating that harnessing tradition to politics is not always motivated by a hankering for a feudal past.

The Allied victory in the Pacific war in August 1945 changed the domestic political dynamics in Indonesia in a way that saw the 1945 Constitution, written under the auspices of the Japanese, effectively cast aside. Only three months after Sukarno and Hatta proclaimed Indonesia's independence under the protection of the Japanese, Sutan Sjahrir, one of the few prominent nationalists who had refused to collaborate with the occupation government, became prime minister, and Indonesia embarked on a four-year diplomatic and military struggle to gain recognition from the US-dominated West as an independent state. During this period of upheaval, Indonesia attempted to represent itself internationally as a deserving young democracy fighting off colonialism. On the domestic front there was little public sympathy for the concerns of the administrative elite to preserve established structures of privilege and social order.

Between the end of 1945 and the mid-1950s then, *Volksgeist*-ism fell decidedly out of fashion. Following its formal independence in 1949, Indonesia adopted first a federal and then a unitary interim constitution, both of which overtly embraced liberal democratic norms and values. Indonesia during this period was a fully fledged parliamentary democracy with a broad array of political parties, including the Indonesian Communist Party (PKI), competing freely for the support of the population.

Multiparty democracy, however, did not sit well with certain elite interests, and it was not long before *Volksgeist*-ism was recast as an oppositional discourse. As analyzed in detail elsewhere, there were two initial nodes of resistance to parliamentary democracy.[26] The first was the class of territorial administrators who strongly resented the way in which interparty competition had eroded their prestige and upset what they saw as the "tranquility and order" in their domains. The clearest statement of this sentiment came in a 1953 book titled *The Village* by senior civil servant and member of the colonial era legislature Soetardjo Kartohadikoesoemo. In it he condemned the way in which Indonesians had been "drugged" by "individualistic" Western democracy and lamented the erosion of the spiritual bond between rulers and their subjects. Like Supomo, he drew heavily on the writings of the Leiden scholars to argue that a return to the institutions and procedures of *adat*, which he equated with "indigenous Indonesian democracy," could transcend the divisiveness wrought by party politics.[27] The main political vehicle for this group was the Greater Indonesia Unity Party (PIR) which stood for the "restoration of rural stability on a traditional basis."[28] Thanks to the relatively high representation of politicians from an administrative elite background, PIR was the third largest party in parliament before Indonesia's first democratic election in 1955 and controlled several ministerial portfolios.[29]

The second and more significant locus of opposition to the democratic system was a group of senior military officers, politicians, and intellectuals who coalesced around Abdul Haris Nasution, the army chief of staff sacked in 1952 after masterminding a coup attempt. Nasution married into a top-tier family of administrators and shared their disdain for political parties. In 1954, he and his supporters, many of them from PIR, formed the League of Supporters of Indonesian Independence (IPKI), a party devoted to ending the party system. Its manifesto spoke of Indonesian society as a "harmonious unity" that had been undermined by parliamentary democracy and was the first to advocate for a return to the 1945 Constitution.[30] Nasution's closest advisor on constitutional issues was Djokosutono, a Dutch-educated jurist and colleague of Supomo with an encyclopedic knowledge of both European legal philosophy and *adat* law. Djokosutono wrote little, but one consistent theme attributed to him by his contemporaries was his view that Indonesia's legal structures should more faithfully reflect the country's cultural patterns, which he spoke about in terms strongly redolent of Leiden scholars, including Van Vollenhoven, Ter Haar, and Haga.

The parliamentary strength of both groups was dealt a severe blow by their poor showing in the 1955 elections. This electoral rout, combined with the high vote for their arch enemies, the PKI, only sharpened their opposition to the system of parliamentary democracy. Nasution's rehabilitation and reappointment as army chief of staff in 1955 saw him assume a higher profile, and, with Djokosutono's help, he emerged as the leading advocate for military participation in government and a return to the authoritarian 1945 Constitution.

By 1956, President Sukarno too had grown increasingly frustrated with his figurehead status under the democratic constitution and at what he saw as the endless bickering among political party leaders and the country's lack of direction. Bending Historical School premises to his own purposes, Sukarno began speaking more frequently about the cultural inappropriateness of the parliamentary system, contrasting "individualistic" Western democracy, in which "50 per cent plus one are always right" with "Indonesian democracy," based on leadership, social solidarity, and *gotong royong*.[31] After a complex series of crises, including another coup attempt, a number of CIA-backed regional rebellions, and the declaration of martial law in 1957, political power shifted from the cabinet to the army and Sukarno. In February 1957 Sukarno, with the support of Nasution's army, effectively ended parliamentary democracy with his creation of a broad spectrum "*gotong-royong*" cabinet and an appointed National Council. On the advice of Djokosutono, who also helped defend the new arrangements publicly, the National Council was constituted along corporatist lines to include "functional" elements of Indonesian society, including the military. Both bodies would be chaired by the president and run according to the principles of *musyawarah* and *mufakat* (deliberation and consensus) rather than voting.

Sukarno's demolition of parliamentary democracy and the establishment of what would be called—after his 1959 decree resurrecting the 1945 Constitution—Guided Democracy was justified in the name of Indonesianizing the political system. But it was also a way of appealing to his base among radical nationalist groups and communists who had seen themselves as disadvantaged by the previous political dispensation. In a 1959 speech, for instance, he called for a "return to the rails of the revolution," attempting to revive the sense of national purpose and solidarity he recalled from the days of the struggle against the Dutch.[32] So while there is certainly some overlap in his use of indigenous imagery and rhetoric with Supomo and the feudal fringe groups mentioned above, Sukarno's *Volksgeist*-ism differed in some important ways. His view of everyday Indonesian culture was more robust and progressive. Even in 1945 Sukarno had made a point of rejecting Supomo's *kekeluargaan* as "a static concept." *Gotong royong*, he said, was "a dynamic concept ... denoting a strenuous effort, sweating together ... for our common happiness."[33] In calling for a more Indonesian system, Sukarno was also appealing to those on the left who saw Western-derived law, with its concern for procedure and precedent, as standing in the way of popular justice.

Volksgeist-ism, then, is not always conservative. While it draws on constructions of the past, those constructions themselves are contested. With the ultimate defeat of Sukarno and the decimation of the left wing of Indonesian politics in the mid-1960s, the static and hierarchical vision of traditional Indonesian culture cultivated in the prewar period returned to the mainstream. The story of how this happened helps to bring to light not only the ideational continuities between the prewar colonial era and the military-led reaction against leftism in the 1960s but also the institutional bases which help perpetuate them. Particularly important in this regard was the role played by civilian and military lawyers.

Conservative *Volksgeist*-ism Returns

The last years of Sukarno's rule were characterized by a sharp polarization between left and right. As the president relied increasingly on the massive PKI and their allies, the army assumed de facto leadership of the coalition of anti-communist forces. When Lieutenant-General Soeharto seized control of Jakarta on October 1, 1965, and embarked on the physical elimination of the communists, he was lionized by the coalition of students, professionals, Muslim and Christian parties, and others who opposed Sukarno. But it was to be some years before his "New Order" regime worked out a political format and settled on an ideological formula. Soeharto was compelled to promise his urban constituency rule of law and democracy while building a centralized developmental state determined to maintain political stability. At the same time, it faced the challenge of how to establish legitimacy among the population at large for whom Sukarno and his anti-imperialist nationalism were closely tied to their sense of Indonesian identity. How could a pro-Western, pro-capitalist regime legitimate itself as historically authentic?

What emerged was a salad of developmentalism, constitutionalism, and nativism, with phrases such as "accelerated modernization" being used at the same time the government was representing itself as a champion of "indigenous values," committed to a uniquely Indonesian approach to authority and decision-making. Soeharto welcomed foreign aid and employed a large cohort of US-trained technocrats to reconstruct the economy but was himself much more attached to traditional Javanese culture and religion than to the cocktail circuit. In his rare unscripted speeches, he expressed a deep aversion to "imported" ideologies, preferring to promote Javanese maxims and his brand of orderly traditionalism.[34] So it is hardly surprising that he sought out advisors who advocated a return to traditional values. In the Indonesian context, these people were to be found primarily in law schools, where the legacy of Historical School thinking was still strong. Some of the most influential contributors to the ideology of the early New Order were military lawyers as well as some older-generation *adat* lawyers. Almost all were linked to the coalition of conservative anti-party forces in the 1950s discussed earlier and most had close ties with the Military Law Academy.

One of the problems that Soeharto's ideologues faced in staking a claim to the cultural and historical legitimacy of the regime was that Sukarno owned that space. It was Sukarno who had introduced Pancasila and who had claimed to have forged an authentically "Indonesian" alternative to liberal democracy. The response of Soeharto's ideologues was to attempt to prize Pancasila from its author and redefine it to suit the new regime's political ends. Military lawyer Colonel Sutjipto, who had previously been a key advisor to Nasution, identified the problem as stemming from "ideological deviation, that is, betrayal of Pancasila."[35] Sutjipto accused Sukarno of distorting Pancasila to accommodate the "atheistic" PKI, claiming that the New Order forces were better able to guard the integrity of the state philosophy.

Central to the task of recasting Pancasila was an attempt to redefine Indonesia's culture itself. Sukarno had linked Pancasila to the collectivistic, dynamic, and populist elements of village culture. The "indigenous values" promoted by pro-Soeharto ideologues were those valorized by Supomo and the conservative anti-party forces of the 1940s and 1950s: hierarchy, harmony, and order. Sutjipto wrote that the principle of *kerakyatan* in the Pancasila, which had strong overtones of leftist populism, should be interpreted as deriving from "Indonesia's view of life as manifest in the centuries old sayings and lore of Indonesian *adat* preserved and bequeathed to us from our ancestors."[36] Soediman Kartohadiprodjo, professor of law at the University of Indonesia and one of the most influential professors at the Military Law Academy, also called for Pancasila to be reinfused with the authentic Indonesian spirit of *adat*, praising, ironically, the past success of "Dutch heroes" such as Van Vollenhoven, Ter Haar, and J. F. Holleman in protecting *adat* against the impact of Western ideas. The "determined struggle" of these *adat* scholars, he argued, had made Indonesia the only newly independent nation in Asia to have a law system of its own (i.e., *adat*), which is in accordance with its personality. This achievement, he wrote, had been tragically undermined by "Indonesians swallowed up by Western thinking."[37] Soediman's ire was clearly directed at Sukarno, who he condemned for having got it wrong in 1945 as well by including the word "democracy" in the Pancasila at all.

In the early years of Soeharto's anti-communist regime then, Pancasila was drained of its leftist and Sukarnoist resonances and infused with an archaized version of traditional culture, one in which conflict was avoided, leaders were respected, and people accepted their place in an unequal social order. Its status was also expanded. While under Sukarno it was only one of several talismanic devices, in the hands of Soeharto's ideologues it came to be defined as embodying the essential and eternal character of the Indonesian people, making it directly analogous to the prewar Japanese notion of *kokutai*. And like *kokutai*, it was enshrined as the supreme legal norm of the state, with a whole edifice of laws introduced to preserve it and punish those who challenged it. In this way, by defining Indonesia's *Volksgeist* in a specific way, anchoring Pancasila in this purported national spirit, and elevating Pancasila to become the "source of all sources of law," the Soeharto regime was able to justify virtually anything the government did. As one senior general expressed it, "any political action based on the norms of Pancasila ideology is in accordance with the law and legitimate."[38]

In Soeharto's "Pancasila Democracy," then, the few checks and balances provided for in the 1945 Constitution could be overridden, or at least delegitimized, in the name of the national personality. This included the practice of voting in the national legislature, the doctrine of the separation of powers, human rights, political rights, and the notion of opposition itself.[39] All were claimed to have arisen from a fundamentally different cultural setting in the West and therefore did not apply in Indonesia. The argument that traditional Indonesian culture always prioritized the organic unity of the community was also useful to the government as it dismantled the surviving political parties in the early 1970s and corralled most social and political organizations, including trade unions, into state-licensed "functional groups" claiming to represent the interests of society as a whole.[40]

Once Soeharto had hammered out an institutional format for his New Order regime using a combination of repression, law, and patronage, he became increasingly fixated on ideological indoctrination. Teams of ideologues, again with military lawyers well represented, were tasked with transforming Pancasila into an all-embracing moral code which would be taught first in schools and then, at great expense, extended to the broader population. The central message of "Pancasila Moral Education" was that Indonesians were, by their nature, harmonious, cooperative, and obedient. They abided by traditional values of *musyawarah*, *mufakat*, and *kekeluargaan*, resolving differences through consensus and always putting the interests of the group before their own. These values applied equally at the level of the family, the village, and the state, with the national legislature often being likened to a village assembly and the president to a wise and benevolent father.

There has been much written about why Soeharto's administration invested so heavily in this program, which after 1978 was known as P4.[41] There seems little doubt that it was directed in part against political Islam. Soeharto is known to have been deeply suspicious of Islamic political activism, and even though Muslim political parties helped bring him to power, he was frequently frustrated by their resistance to his policies. There is indeed a long history of *Volksgeist* arguments being deployed to delegitimize political expressions of Islam. Most of the Leiden School scholars including Van Vollenhoven were disparaging of Islam, depicting it as of secondary importance to Indonesian culture and siding with the colonial regime's often violent suppression of attempts to organize under its banner. While the Japanese were more much conciliatory toward Islam during their occupation, they nevertheless showed a preference for secular nationalists within the occupation administration and encouraged, as we have seen, the study of *adat* and indigenous models of state organization. Supomo, steeped in Javanese court culture and with his background as a Leiden-trained *adat* law expert, showed little inclination to incorporate Islamic law either into his scholarship or his recommendations. Sukarno too had little sympathy for advocates of an Islamic state, a position that was only reinforced by the Darul Islam uprising against the young republic between 1949 and 1962 and the efforts of Muslim politicians to have Islamic law incorporated into the constitution in the mid-1950s. His appeals to indigenous tradition were not framed in Islamic discourse and were clearly not designed to advance the prospects of Muslim parties.

Soeharto's ambitions though were more far reaching. It is clear from his extemporaneous speeches that he aspired to rid Indonesia of *all* ideologies he considered incompatible with his vision of Indonesian culture. In a 1980 speech to military commanders in Sumatra, he condemned "Marxism, Leninism, communism, socialism, Marhaenism, nationalism [and] religion" for having "submerged" Pancasila and having inspired "unending rebellions."[42] He told a youth group at his home two years later that Pancasila derived from the "pearls of wisdom from our ancestors" and that Indonesia had no need for "modern ideologies," including socialism and liberalism, which had caused only suffering, division, and catastrophes. He recounted how he had strived since the founding of the New Order to have all groups accept Pancasila as the "only ideology."[43] When he finally passed a law mandating Pancasila as the sole ideology for all social and political groups in Indonesia in 1985, he regarded it as his government's "most important and fundamental national decision."[44] A further insight was provided by Soeharto's information minister who in a confidential briefing to his officials said that the purpose of Pancasila education was to root out engrained leftist ideas from the national culture and thereby "make Indonesians truly Indonesian. You have not become a complete citizen until you have mastered P4."[45]

This example illustrates both the instrumental and the constitutive potential of *Volksgeist*-ism. Once the principle is accepted that a country's law and politics should reflect the cultural essence of the nation, it becomes possible for a regime to impose its own reading of traditional culture and to hold its citizens to this standard. In the case of Soeharto's Indonesia, this proved a useful and frequently employed device to silence opponents. If critics violated Pancasila values by protesting and using disrespectful language, were they really Indonesians at all?

I have explored elsewhere the ongoing appeal of *Volksgeist*-ism among Indonesia's political class and in its legal culture.[46] Writing in 1961, Takdir Alisjahbana noted the powerful influence of Van Vollenhoven and the Historical School of Law among Indonesia's first generation of lawyers.[47] Six decades later, under a democratic dispensation, Savigny's ideas are still routinely studied and cited with approval. Indonesian legal journals, one of which bears the title *Volksgeist*, commonly carry articles describing Pancasila as the nation's *Volksgeist* and, more significantly, advocating for Indonesia's laws to more faithfully reflect the *Volksgeist*. This has become especially pronounced in the debates surrounding the revision of the colonial-era criminal code, which is frequently attacked for perpetuating liberal legal norms derived from Europe.

Conclusion

The chapter has attempted to demonstrate the ways in which the premises of Savigny's Historical School informed legal and political thinking in the Netherlands, Japan, and Indonesia between the 1920s and 1960s. It is testament both to the durability and pliability of *Volksgeist*-ism that it could appeal to political actors with as little in common as Dutch scholar-bureaucrats, Japanese right-wingers, and Indonesian nationalists. The main focus of this chapter has been to show how these ideational flows occurred and how they influenced the first generation of Indonesian nationalists and through them, Indonesia's purported national character. The notion that Indonesia's identity is rooted in customary law concepts, and that these concepts have a legitimate role in guiding law and politics, in other words, did not appear out of thin air. It emerged in active dialogue with European and Japanese scholars steeped in romantic Historical School ideas, starting in the early 1920s. While it is important to stress that *Volksgeist*-ism is only one of several strands within Indonesian nationalist thought, and one that was always contested, it nevertheless played a significant role at key historical junctures: the constitutional debates of 1945, the demolition of parliamentary democracy in 1957–1959, and the rise of Soeharto's New Order dictatorship in 1966. In all cases political leaders appealed to notions of authentic Indonesian tradition to steer Indonesia away from Western models of liberal democracy. Viewed in this light, one of the key legacies of the Historical School has been to furnish political contestants with an archive, a discrete vocabulary, to counter the liberal tradition. Reinforcing the instrumentalist perspective is the point that exponents of *Volksgeist*-ism define tradition to suit their purposes. For Supomo and many of the conservatives of the 1950s and 1960s, the image of tradition they drew on was the static and harmonious portrait painted by the followers of the Leiden School. Sukarno meanwhile utilized a more dynamic and communalistic image of village culture to mobilize the people behind his brand of authoritarian populism.

Adopting a transwar perspective has brought to light ideational linkages between the 1920s and the Cold War period that would otherwise have been obscured. Following Carol Gluck's observation that ideologies have "dates, names and faces,"[48] certain key individuals were highlighted in this account of what I have called *Volksgeist*-ism: Subardjo, Supomo, Nasution, Sukarno, and Soeharto. All were profoundly shaped by their experiences before the war, during the war, and especially over the four tumultuous years of revolution that followed the Japanese surrender in 1945. Understanding the changing circumstances in which they lived, both in Indonesia and abroad, is crucial to understanding their thinking and the material circumstances, including their class interests, which influenced them to take particular positions. The personal connections they made with individuals in Europe, Japan, and beyond, explored largely through biographies and memoirs, were likewise crucial for the ideas they sparked. Taking a longer view is also crucial for understanding institutional continuity across many domains. It was due to the close institutional links between Leiden and the Jakarta law school, for instance, that the basic premises and assumptions of the Historical School of Law found their way into the legal education system of Indonesia, and from there into the political sphere. Adopting a transwar and transnational perspective to the transmission and evolution of other ideas, including liberalism, Islamism, and socialism, would likely reveal a wider pattern of ideological confluence across spatial, temporal, and cultural distances.

Notes

1 Subardjo Djoyoadisuryo, *Kesadaran Nasional: Otobiografi* (Jakarta: Gunung Agung, 1978), 198.

2 F. M. Barnard, "National Culture and Political Legitimacy: Herder and Rousseau," *Journal of the History of Ideas* 44, no. 2 (1983): 231–53.

3   Kosaku Yoshino, *Cultural Nationalism in Contemporary Japan: A Sociological Enquiry* (London: Routledge, 1992), 56–9.
4   Robert Gordon, "The White Man's Burden: Ersatz Customary Law and Internal Pacification in South Africa," *Journal of Historical Sociology* 2, no. 1 (1989): 44.
5   Peter Burns, *The Leiden Legacy: Concepts of Law in Indonesia* (Leiden: KITLV, 2004); Daniel Lev, "Colonial Law and the Genesis of the Indonesian State," *Indonesia* 40 (1985): 57–74.
6   Cees Fasseur, "Colonial Dilemma," in *The Revival of Tradition in Indonesian Politics: The Deployment of Adat from Colonialism to Indigenism*, ed. Jamie Davidson and David Henley (London: Routledge, 2007), 51.
7   Takdir Alisjahbana, *Indonesia: Social and Cultural Revolution* (Kuala Lumpur: Oxford University Press, 1975), 71.
8   Djoyoadisuryo, *Kesadaran Nasional*, 135.
9   Peter Dale, *The Myth of Japanese Uniqueness* (London: Routledge, 1990).
10 Yun-Ru Chen and Yun-Ru, "Family Law as a Repository of *Volksgeist*: The Germany-Japan Genealogy," *Comparative Law Review* 4, no. 2 (2013): 22.
11 Ibid., 24.
12 Carol Gluck, *Japan's Modern Myths: Ideology in the Late Meiji Period* (Princeton, NJ: Princeton University Press, 1985), 145–6.
13 Tetsuo Najita and H. Harootunian, "Japanese Revolt against the West: Political and Cultural Criticism in the Twentieth Century," in *The Cambridge History of Japan*, vol. 6, ed. Peter Duus (Cambridge: Cambridge University Press, 1989), 750–4.
14 Sutan Sjahrir, *Indonesische Overpeinzingen* (written under the pseudonym Sjahrazad) (Amsterdam: De Bezige Bij, 1948), 100–1, 160–1.
15 Mavis Rose, *Indonesia Free: A Political Biography of Mohammad Hatta*, Cornell Modern Indonesia Project Monograph Series 67 (Ithaca, NY: Cornell University Press, 1987), 69; I. N. Soebagijo, ed., *Mr. Sudjono, Mendarat dengan Pasukan Jepang di Banten 1942* (Jakarta: Gunung Agung, 1983), 148.
16 Djoyoadisuryo, *Kesadaran Nasional*, 198.
17 Ken'ichi Goto, *"Returning to Asia": Japan-Indonesia Relations, 1930s–1942* (Tokyo: Ryūkei shosha, 1997).
18 Aiko Kurasawa, "Marilah Kita Bersatu! Japanese Propaganda in Java, 1942–45," in *Asian Panorama: Essays in Asian History, Past and Present*, ed. K. M. de Silva Sirima Kiribamune and C. R. de Silva (New Delhi: Executive Committee, 11th Conference of the International Association of Historians, 1990), 487.
19 Gunseikanboe, *Orang Indonesia jang terkemoeka di Djawa* (Jakarta: Gunseikanboe, 1944), 17, 293, 453.
20 This section draws on chapter 4 of David Bourchier, *Illiberal Democracy in Indonesia: The Ideology of the Family State* (London: Routledge, 2015).

21 A. B. Kusuma, ed., *Lahirnya Undang-Undang Dasar 1945: Memuat Salinan Dokumen Otentik Badan Oentoek Menyelidiki Oesaha-2 Persiapan Kemerdekaan* (Jakarta: Badan Penerbit Fakultas Hukum Universitas Indonesia, 2004), 125.
22 Ibid., 124–5.
23 Ibid., 126.
24 Ibid., 127.
25 Ibid., 132.
26 Bourchier, *Illiberal Democracy*, 98–106.
27 Soetardjo Kartohadikoesoemo, *Desa* (Bandung: Sumur Bandung, 1965 [1953]), 126–34, 165.
28 Herbert Feith, *The Decline of Constitutional Democracy in Indonesia* (Ithaca, NY: Cornell University Press, 1962), 144.
29 Ibid., 381.
30 David Jenkins, *Suharto and His Generals: Indonesian Military Politics, 1975–1983* (Ithaca, NY: Cornell University Press, 1984), 229.
31 Feith, *The Decline of Constitutional Democracy*, 515.
32 Herbert Feith and Lance Castles, eds., *Indonesian Political Thinking, 1945–1965* (Ithaca, NY: Cornell University Press, 1970), 99–109.
33 Kusuma, *Lahirnya Undang-Undang Dasar*, 165; Adnan Buyung Nasution, *The Aspiration for Constitutional Government in Indonesia: A Socio-legal Study of the Indonesian Konstituante, 1956–1959* (Jakarta: Pustaka Sinar Harapan, 1992), 98–9.
34 Ken Ward, "Soeharto's Javanese Pancasila," in *Soeharto's New Order and Its Legacy: Essays in Honour of Harold Crouch*, ed. Edward Aspinall and Greg Fealy, Asian Studies Monograph 2 (Canberra: ANU E-Press, 2010).
35 Sutjipto, *Tumbuhnya Tunas Baru diatas Humus dari Daun Tua-Kering jang Berguguran: Sebuah Capita Selecta* (Jakarta: Penerbit Fakta, 1967), 1.
36 Ibid., 10–11.
37 Soediman Kartohadiprodjo, *Beberapa pikiran sekitar Pantja Sila* (Bandung: Alumni, 1970), 102.
38 Yoga Soegomo, *Perbandingan antara Demokrasi Eropa dan Demokrasi Pancasila di Indonesia sebagai Subyek Penelitian Demokrasi* (Jakarta: Pustaka Kartini/PT Sarana Bakti Semesta, 1986), 16.
39 Edward Aspinall, *Opposing Suharto: Compromise, Resistance, and Regime Change in Indonesia* (Stanford, CA: Stanford University Press, 2005), xi.
40 David Reeve, *Golkar of Indonesia: An Alternative to the Party System* (Singapore: Oxford University Press, 1985), 324–59.
41 See, for example, Michael Morfit, "Pancasila: The Indonesian State Ideology According to the New Order Government," *Asian Survey* 21 no. 8 (1981): 838–51; and Seun-Won Song, *Back to Basics in Indonesia? Reassessing the Pancasila and*

    Pancasila State and Society, 1945–2007 (PhD diss., Athens, College of Arts and Sciences, Ohio University, 2008).
42 *Kompas*, April 8, 1980.
43 David Bourchier and Vedi Hadiz, eds., *Indonesian Politics and Society: A Reader* (London: RoutledgeCurzon, 2003), 99–109.
44 Soeharto, *Soeharto: Pikiran, Ucapan dan Tindakan Saya*, autobiography as told to G. Dwipayana and K. H. Ramandan (Jakarta: PT Citra Lantoro Gung Persada, 1988), 382.
45 Departeman Penerangan, *Peningkatan Penerangan yang Berwibawa, Himpunan Pidato Menteri Penerangan RI 1978–82* (Jakarta: Departemen Penerangan, 1983), 209.
46 David Bourchier, "The Romance of Adat in the Indonesian Political Imagination and the Current Revival," in *The Revival of Tradition in Indonesian Politics: The Deployment of Adat from Colonialism to Indigenism*, ed. Jamie Davidson and David Henley (London: Routledge, 2007), 113–29.
47 Alisjahbana, *Indonesia*, 71.
48 Gluck, *Japan's Modern Myths*, 8.

7

Reproducing the "Emperor System Within": Transwar Criminal Rehabilitation and Imperial Benevolence in Japan, 1920–1960

Max Ward

Introduction

This chapter explores the development of the criminal reform system in Japan between the 1920s and 1960s, focusing on transwar institutional developments as well as the continuing symbolic association of criminal reform with the emperor system (*tennōsei*) and its ideology of imperial benevolence (*jikeishugi*).[1] In so doing, I seek to challenge a conventional approach to Japanese history in which Japan's military defeat in 1945 demarcates both a historical rupture between Japan's prewar empire and postwar nation formation as well as a clear political demarcation between interwar militarism/fascism and postwar liberal democracy. Such an approach overlooks the complex processes through which some ideas, practices, institutions, and/or policies that had been developed in the prewar period and which assumed new functions during wartime mobilization were then recalibrated to function in the postwar order. It also evades the more difficult question of what it means that institutions central to the consolidation of militarism and fascism in the 1930s were touted as examples of Japan's democratic reform in the late-1940s and beyond.

Such evasions can be found in conventional histories of the development of criminal reform policies in Japan. For example, it is often claimed that Japan's criminal rehabilitation system was not fully implemented until after the war, when earlier ad-hoc reform experiments were systemized and implemented in its early postwar criminal justice system as part of the broader liberalization and democratization of Japan during and after the Allied Occupation (1945–1952).[2] In one official history, prewar reform developments are relegated to the "prehistory" (*zenshi*) of criminal rehabilitation, obscuring the fact that the postwar criminal reform system inherited a wide array of legal, institutional, and discursive precedents that had been developed in the 1920s and which were consolidated in the late 1930s.[3] In the secondary literature, the extent to which criminal rehabilitation was institutionalized in the postwar period is lauded as an example of Japan's postwar liberal approach to criminal justice.[4]

As David Garland has noted, rehabilitation informed criminal justice systems in many postwar welfare states, whether Keynesian, social democratic, or, in our case, the "Japanese-style welfare state."[5] He calls these postwar systems as comprising a "penal welfare complex" in which welfare services were combined with "distinctive correctionalist motifs," including rehabilitation, indeterminate sentences, and "the specialized arrangements that supported them," such as "probation, parole, juvenile courts, treatment programmes, etc."[6] This took place also in Japan. And although Western scholars often celebrate the unique "benevolent paternalism of Japan's [postwar] criminal justice system," we need to remember that this was part of wider, international trend of postwar welfare state formation.[7]

When we expand the historical scope, however, we find that Japan's institutionalization of rehabilitation began much earlier, starting with experiments by a new cadre of justice officials in the 1920s who were inspired by ideals of criminal reform under the rubric of "rehabilitation" (*hogo*). This paralleled the development of Japan's similarly overlooked welfare experiments dating back to the 1920s, as outlined by Gregory Kasza.[8] Along with welfare policies, early experiments in criminal reform were consolidated in the late 1930s, part of a wider campaign following Japan's invasion of China in July 1937 to revise laws and regulations governing such things as public health, national health insurance, and, in this case, overseeing ex-offenders and youth delinquents.[9] The transwar history I outline in this chapter reveals that postwar Japan's particular "penal welfare complex" was formed in the crucible of war mobilization in the late 1930s, when earlier ad-hoc criminal reform experiments were brought together within a wider welfare campaign. Scholar Takahashi Mutsuko calls this campaign "welfare for warfare" and points to how welfare work (*kōsei jigyō*) was linked specifically to the emperor and the war campaign that was being carried out in his name.[10]

Indeed, the first time that "rehabilitation" was codified for adult offenders was in a 1936 law targeting political criminals who, having renounced political positions that threatened the imperial sovereign, were placed within programs to ideologically convert them as loyal imperial subjects.[11] This history is rarely included in studies of Japan's criminal justice system. Further complicating the conventional scholarship are the transwar ideological associations of criminal reform with the imperial household, even as the status of the emperor shifted from divine sovereign to, as the 1947 constitution designates, "the symbol of the State and of the unity of the People, deriving his position from the will of the people with whom resides sovereign power."[12] English-language studies of the postwar system largely overlook this symbolic association, although the official literature on ex-offender support is adorned with photographs of the imperial family and reprint imperial rescripts and speeches given at conferences for criminal reform.

I begin this chapter by reviewing how "relief" (*jukkyū*, *kyūgo*) policies were imbricated with the formation of the new imperial state after 1868, and central to what Yasumaru Yoshio has called the "formation of the image of the modern emperor" in the latter half of the nineteenth century.[13] This continued into the twentieth century, as the government attempted to manage the socioeconomic dislocations during Japan's particularly condensed capitalist development.[14] Then, when official criminal reform policies were consolidated in the 1920s and 1930s, they were also brought under the sign of imperial benevolence (*jikei*) and associated with reform and welfare. And as I will show in the second half of this chapter, although the postwar Japanese state reestablished criminal reform policies under a broader campaign for public welfare, such reform policies continued to be associated with the benevolence of the now "symbolic" (*shōchō*) emperor, most explicitly through publicized imperial donations or imperial visits to events commemorating relief and criminal reform. It was precisely in this new "symbolic" status that the imperial household functioned to create what Okudaira Yasuhiro has called the "emperor system within" (*uchi naru tennōsei*), in which a cultural and emotional affinity for the emperor was internalized, becoming a mechanism for self-control in postwar liberal society.[15] I contend that the transwar history of criminal rehabilitation provides a particularly illuminating example of how these kinds of affective associations were both reproduced and transformed across the transwar period in Japan, reproducing the "emperor system within" up to today.

Early Precedents: State Relief, Pardons, and the Ideology of Imperial Benevolence

The association between criminal rehabilitation and imperial benevolence in Japan dates back to the Meiji period (1868–1912) when imperial pardons for prisoners were issued to commemorate important milestones in imperial state formation. Imperial pardons were part of the new Meiji state's wider effort to associate the imperial household with acts of state benevolence, a strategy that Ikeda Yoshimasa and Endō Kōichi have argued reinforced the new state's ideological claim that imperial "benevolent rule" (*jinsei*) had been restored after centuries of samurai-military government.[16] This included early relief policies enacted as early as 1874, which, as Takahashi Mutsuko reminds us, were to "be understood as a manifestation[s] of the mercy of [the] *tennō* (emperor) to his subjects."[17] Toward this end, the new imperial state created a system to manage relief efforts (*kyūsai seido*) in times of natural disasters and other emergencies, which would soon include direct donations from the imperial family that were accompanied by imperial rescripts informing the populace of the emperor's enduring love and concern for their well-being.[18] These kinds of imperial donations and rescripts served to convey the "ideology of benevolence" (*jikeishugi*) that many scholars see as central to the function of the modern emperor-system.[19] This continued as the imperial state sought to manage the socioeconomic dislocations that attended the rapid but uneven development of capitalism at the turn of the twentieth century.[20] In this context, imperial donations continued into the 1910s and 1920s, even as relief policies transformed in response to changing socioeconomic conditions, including broader national coordination among private and local charity and reformatory services.[21]

Parallel with these relief efforts, imperial pardons were increasingly issued to prisoners in the Meiji period and were often explicitly political in nature. For example, on the day that the Meiji Constitution was promulgated in 1889—a constitution that not only located sovereignty in the "line of Emperors unbroken for ages eternal" (Article 1) but also invested the emperor with powers of "pardon, commutation of punishments and rehabilitation" (Article 16)— 454 individuals charged with lèse-majesté (*fukeizai*) or plotting insurrection (*nairan inbō zai*) were granted imperial pardons.[22] In addition to these official commemorations, imperial pardons also became linked to events in the imperial family, such as births, deaths, or marriages. When the Meiji emperor passed away in 1912, over twenty-five thousand convicts and ex-convicts were either released from jail, had their records expunged, or sentences reduced.²³ Imperial pardons continued thereafter, and as an official history summarizes, "imperial pardons" both "celebrating and bereaving events in the imperial household" were "closely related to the development of criminal reform work during this period."²⁴ Although such pardons were implemented through a modern legal and penal system, carried out as acts of sovereignty, and commemorated the events in the formation of the new imperial state, officials portrayed them as continuing ancient imperial rituals dating back to the fifth century (if not earlier), a narrative that the secondary scholarship on Japan's criminal justice system often reproduces.²⁵

Complementing these periodic imperial pardons, ex-offender support was first developed by private (*minkan*) welfare organizations that were sustained by donations from local businesses, prefectural governments, and, periodically, the imperial house. This includes the first youth reformatory, the Ikegami Reformatory (Ikegami kankain), established in Osaka in 1883 and the Shizuoka Prefectural Ex-Prisoners Rehabilitation Corporation (Shizuokaken shutsugokunin hogo kaisha) for released adults established in 1888.²⁶ Soon thereafter, dozens of other private youth and parolee reformatories were established in prefectures throughout Japan.²⁷ Circulating among these private institutions were a variety of new publications specializing in what was being called reform (*hogo*) and societal reintegration efforts.²⁸

As part of an effort to oversee the new process of criminal rehabilitation, the Prison Bureau (Kangoku kyoku) was moved from the Home Ministry to the Justice Ministry in 1900, which established a licensing system stipulating new regulations for private organizations working with adult ex-prisoners. At the same time, a Home Ministry bill was passed by the Imperial Diet in 1900—the Reformatory Law (Kanka-hō, No. 37)—that established prefectural reformatories (*kankain*) throughout Japan primarily for youth, bringing private (*minkan*) reformatories already in existence into this system through a new designation as "substitute" (*daiyō*) reformatories.²⁹ In other words, a division of labor emerged at this time between the Home and Justice Ministries, as the former assumed responsibility for juvenile services, while the latter focused on adult ex-offenders.³⁰ This institutional complexity was compounded when the Home Ministry began to establish state-run reformatories (in addition to supervising private and prefectural reformatories) in 1918, while the Justice Ministry continued to oversee parolee services through private institutions.³¹ As Takahashi Mutsuko notes, reformatories not only constituted a particular mode of welfare through a reformatory system—what Japanese scholars have called "reformatory relief" (*kanka kyūsai*)—but such welfare had the "aim of securing the social order" as well as guiding its recipients "to become good citizens contributing to the development of the state."[32]

The Emergence of Criminal Rehabilitation in the 1920s

With the socioeconomic dislocations following the First World War, Japan's "reformatory welfare" system came under stress.[33] And with fears of anti-colonial activism and the Bolshevik Revolution in mind, state officials sought to respond to these changing socioeconomic conditions in order to stave off their potential political repercussions. Such welfare efforts continued to be linked to the imperial household. For example, as Michael Lewis has noted, during the nationwide rice riots in the summer of 1918, the government distributed bags of imperially donated rice (*onshi mai*) as well as coupons to the poor that "carried a message explaining that the holder was a recipient of imperial benevolence and should be grateful for the emperor's concern."[34]

At this time we can locate a shift in emphasis from early "charity" (*jizen*) work targeting the poor and their moral reform, to a concern over general social conditions—including that of the urban working class, tenant farmers, women working in lite-industry, and other social classes—which generated a new conception of "social work" (*shakai jigyō*) that such conditions require.[35] In 1922, the Home Ministry consolidated its Local Affairs Bureau (which included a local relief section) into a Social Bureau (Shakai-kyoku) to coordinate new efforts in managing welfare services in Tokyo and other urban areas.[36] Soon thereafter, prefectural governments and Japan's colonial government-generals followed suit.[37] The creation of the Social Bureau was one facet of a more interventionist approach witnessed in multiple government agencies in the 1920s, including the Justice Ministry's increasing efforts to provide more services to adult ex-offenders to prevent criminal recidivism.[38] It is from these efforts that Japan's transwar criminal rehabilitation system really began to take shape in the 1920s.

In October 1920, a "Rehabilitation Section" (Hogo-ka) was created in the justice minister's secretariat in order to, as one official history summarizes, "conduct research on planning and administering rehabilitation service," first to juveniles, and then to explore extending such services to adult offenders.[39] Recall that up to this point the Home Ministry was responsible for juveniles, and thus the Justice Ministry's plan entailed encroaching into the Home Ministry's jurisdiction. Carrying out this research was a new cadre of reform-minded justice officials that emphasized "rehabilitation" (*hogo*) over the earlier moral "reform" (*kanka*) and "charity" approaches reviewed above. And although what was increasingly being called "rehabilitation work" (*hogo jigyō*) had been carried out up to this point by private organizations licensed through the Justice Ministry, these reform-minded justice officials envisioned closer state oversight and the expansion of such services. Criminal rehabilitation was to be systematic, individualized to each offender's particular needs, and extended over a longer period of time in order to guarantee social integration. In May 1922, the Prison Bureau transferred responsibility to oversee aid for paroled adult offenders to the Rehabilitation Section, which quickly reviewed reform policies and proposed reforms to streamline rehabilitation services.[40]

In addition to the creation of the Rehabilitation Bureau, there were two more important milestones in the development of criminal rehabilitation procedures in the 1920s. The first was the passage of the 1922 Juvenile Law (Shōnen hō, to take effect in 1923), which not only shifted oversight for youth delinquents from the Home Ministry to the Justice Ministry but also overhauled the entire juvenile justice system, bringing a variety of institutions and private groups under the direction of the Justice Ministry.[41] This law outlined procedures for, among other things, establishing juvenile courts in Tokyo and Osaka and guidelines for adjudicating juvenile cases and, most importantly, providing indeterminate sentencing to allow courts to coordinate welfare services for petty juvenile criminals who were released before being officially indicted or sentenced.[42] Although indeterminate sentencing had been practiced before, it was not until the 1920s that it was implemented on a wide scale.[43] Indeed, the Juvenile Law provided for the first systematic experimentation with indeterminate sentencing, giving juvenile courts the discretion to assess if a youth, before being prosecuted, had the potential to be reformed under the supervision of a guardian (*hogosha*) and/or placed within a private reform group (*hogo dantai*) that worked in coordination with the Justice Ministry. As David Ambaras explains, such policies "reflected the consensus among key elements of the state and middle-class reform lobby ... on the need for new agencies of intervention into the lives of delinquent adolescents."[44] Justice officials did not desire such interventions to be limited to just youth delinquency cases, for in the same year of the Juvenile Law, a new Code of Criminal Procedure was promulgated (to go into effect in 1924) that extended "suspension of indictment" to adult offenders as well.[45]

In addition to the passage of the Juvenile Law and the extension of some of its reform policies to adults, the second milestone in the development of Japan's transwar criminal rehabilitation system was the formation of a semiofficial criminal reform group for adult offenders in indeterminate sentence programs, called the Imperial Renovation Society (Teikoku kōshin kai). Established in the first year of the Shōwa Emperor's reign (1926), the society was established in part with a donation from the Imperial Household Agency. The Imperial Renovation Society was the first reform group that dealt specifically with adult detainees who had been released through two indeterminate sentence programs: "Suspended Indictment" (*kiso yūyo*) or "Suspended Sentence" (*shikkō yūyo*). When activated, detainees would be released to guarantors (*mimoto hikiuke*)—often family members, but this could also be a representative from groups such as the Imperial Renovation Society or a Buddhist temple—who would monitor their activities and work with procurators in order to assess the degree to which a suspect was reforming. Monthly reports would be collected on the detainee's progress, and after an average of six months the procurator would determine whether or not to release the detainee from their indictment or sentence.

By 1927, there were around eight hundred private (*minkan*) organizations that provided services to discharged adult prisoners and protection and rehabilitation services to juvenile offenders.[46] Two days celebrated and informed the wider community of criminal reform initiatives: "Reform Day" (Hogo dē, officially named Shihō hogo kinen bi), first celebrated on September 13, 1925, to commemorate the efforts of paroled adult ex-offenders; and "Juvenile Protection Day" (Shōnen hogo dē), first established on April 17, 1927.[47] And parallel with such initiatives, officials also passed revisions to prison guidelines, the most important being the 1933 Progressive State System for the Treatment of Prisoners (Gyōkei ruishin shogū rei), which provided a four-tiered classification system that was to cultivate a prisoner's sense of "repentance" (*kaishun*) with the goal of their "reformation and resocialization" as they served their sentences.[48] This law is presented in the official history as "the first clear step toward [the] humanitarian treatment of prisoners," which entailed bringing in outside "specialists" to assess and make treatment recommendations.[49]

Parallel with these criminal justice reforms, other initiatives linked to welfare and imperial benevolence were underway in the late 1920s and early 1930s. In regards to welfare, the most notable reform was the passage of the 1929 Relief Law (Kyūgo-hō), which replaced the earlier 1874 Relief Ordinance in response to the economic turbulence of the 1920s and codified the more interventionist relief experiments of the 1920s.[50] Similarly, imperial pardons continued to be issued, for example, in January 1924 to commemorate the wedding of Crown Prince Hirohito, and then in February 1927 to celebrate the ascension of Hirohito to the throne, which included the release, reduction of sentence, or return of rights to over 170,000 individuals across the empire, including in Taiwan, Korea, and the Kwantung Leased Territory.[51] Thus, even as social relief and criminal reform practices went through many changes in the 1920s, their association with the ideology of imperial benevolence continued and was in fact amplified by the expansion of such practices. By the early 1930s, many publications—both official and scholarly—reinforced the connection between relief, clemency, and the imperial household, arguing that such practices expressed imperial benevolence that went back to the period of the Taika reforms (645–650) and beyond.[52]

Imperial Benevolence, Welfare, and Criminal Reform in the 1930s

If the symbolic relation between adult criminal rehabilitation and imperial benevolence was initially implied in the name and early work of the Imperial Renovation Society, it became explicit as procurators started to apply suspension policies to political criminals in the early 1930s. As I have explored elsewhere, thousands of suspected communists and others were arrested in the late 1920s and early 1930s under a new antiradical law called the Peace Preservation Law (Chianijihō).[53] Passed in 1925, the law was used to arrest suspected communists in the Japanese metropole and anti-colonial activists in colonial Korea, both of whom were charged with the crime of joining or forming an organization that threatened imperial sovereignty, defined as having the objective to "alter the *kokutai*."[54] Once suspects were apprehended, the task then became to understand the motivations or beliefs that inspired someone to join a group with such objectives, which coalesced into an official discourse of so-called thought crime (*shisō hanzai*). Then, in 1928–1929, thousands of suspected communists were arrested in an empire-wide coordinated campaign, and in 1928, the government pushed through a revision of the Peace Preservation Law in which the *kokutai* infringement became punishable by death, and a clause was added criminalizing anyone suspected of having committed acts "in order to further the aims" (*mokuteki suikō*) of such organizations, thereby expanding the law's purview.[55]

With the burgeoning number of detained "thought criminals" (*shisō hannin*) in the early 1930s, procurators began to experiment with inducing "repentance" (*kaishun*), resulting in a few defections from the Japanese Communist Party (JCP).[56] Between 1931 and 1932, these experiments coalesced into procuracy guidelines to apply "Charges Withheld" (Ryūho shobun) to thought criminals expressing some sign of remorse and/or reformability.[57] At this time, the Imperial Renovation Society started to take on cases of thought criminals released through Charges Withheld, acting as their guarantor and establishing protocols to assess the degree to which a thought criminal was reforming.[58] By the mid-1930s, such protocols coalesced into the infamous policy of *tenkō*—or "ideological conversion"—in which chaplains, prison officials, family members, and others collaborated to guide thought criminals toward reidentifying as subjects of the emperor.[59]

Consequently, if earlier imperial pardons and donations to criminal reform organizations were presented as *formal* expressions of the emperor's benevolence toward his wayward subjects, the "ideological conversion" policy translated the *content* of imperial ideology directly into the practice of rehabilitation, as detainees were assessed to the degree they reidentified as imperial subjects. However, rehabilitating thought criminals produced new administrative challenges. In particular, some officials became concerned about how to measure the degree to which a political criminal had "converted" as well as the possibility of their ideological "recidivism" (*saihan*) after they were discharged from state supervision.[60] Thus, in 1934 and 1935, justice officials started efforts to streamline the administration of rehabilitation for thought criminals and institutionalize *tenkō* on a wider basis, while at the same time starting to present their success with rehabilitating political criminals as a model for all adult offenders.[61]

Wartime Consolidation of Criminal Rehabilitation

To streamline the process for administering the vast array of thought criminals at some stage of so-called conversion, the Justice Ministry passed the 1936 Thought Criminals Protection and Supervision Law (Shisōhan hogo kansatsu hō), which codified "ideological conversion" as the central policy for administering Peace Preservation Law cases and also marked the first time that "rehabilitation" (*hogo*) was legally codified for adult offenders.[62] This 1936 Law established twenty-two thought protection and supervision centers in Japan and seven in colonial Korea which would assess the degree to which a thought criminal had reformed while in a Suspended Indictment program.[63] In order to streamline the assessment of "ideological conversion," *tenkō* was redefined, in which a full conversion entailed when a detainee "recognize[d] and grasp[ed] the Japanese Spirit" and "actively put it into practice" in their daily lives.[64] Following Japan's invasion of

China in July 1937, many converts (*tenkōsha*) represented their conversions as at the forefront of wider national process in which the general population were to mobilize their spirits for what was being called "national thought defense" (*shisō kokubō*).[65] It was exactly at this time that the Japanese state recalibrated its myriad social welfare efforts to secure resources—material, human, and now spiritual—for the war effort, including the creation of the Ministry of Health and Welfare (Kōsei-shō) in 1937.[66] As Takahashi Mutsuko reminds us, not only did such initiatives "ultimate[ly] aim to secure human resources for continuing wars rather than for genuinely improving the well-being of the people" but, as such, all welfare initiatives at this time placed distinctive "emphasis on [the] *tennō* (Japanese emperor)."[67]

At this time, justice officials pointed to the success of the thought criminal reform experiments as they campaigned to extend such policies to all criminals— not just political—who displayed signs of reformability. For example, in 1936, the soon-to-be director of the Tokyo Thought Criminal Protection and Supervision center, Hirata Isao, argued that the new centers served as the model to establish a new "state system for general parolee reform services" that would extend to all detainees or criminal offenders released through indeterminate sentencing, early release, or parole.[68] Hirata believed that the rehabilitation of political criminals provided the model par excellence for all criminal reform, and envisioned an empire-wide reform system similarly informed by the imperial spirit.[69] This history is almost completely overlooked in the literature on postwar criminal reform in Japan.

As Hirata and others had hoped, a sweeping Judicial Rehabilitation Services Law (Shihō hogo jigyō hō, Law No. 42) was passed in 1939, which established an extensive criminal reform apparatus, including both official and private reform groups overseen by a new foundation called the Judicial Rehabilitation Association, Incorporated (Zaidan-hōjin Shihō-hogo Kyōkai).[70] This association was the precursor to the postwar Japan Rehabilitation Association (Nihon kōsei hogo kyōkai), which continues to operate today. The thousand or so reform groups providing services to youth, adults, and so-called thought criminals were consolidated into 692 groups. Groups were managed through a licensing system, and in locations where private (*minkan*) parolee support groups did not exist, the state mandated that one be created. This law streamlined all earlier experiments in juvenile reform and adult offender rehabilitation and brought all criminal reform groups under the purview of the Judicial Rehabilitation Association.[71] At the same time, volunteer rehabilitation workers were mobilized to assist in such efforts, a precursor to the much celebrated postwar system of "Volunteer

Probation Officers" (VPO, *hogoshi*).⁷² In 1939, fourteen thousand persons were appointed volunteer judicial rehabilitation officers, which increased to thirty-five thousand in 1944.⁷³ Offices were opened in 1940 in seven locations in the Japanese metropole that had jurisdiction over all organizations and individuals providing protective services within a certain region. Thereafter, services provided to adolescents under the 1923 Juvenile Law were incrementally integrated into the new protective services system by 1942.

Thus, by the 1940s, we find a robust criminal rehabilitation system operating in Japan inspired by both principles of reform that had been circulating since the 1920s and the more immediate aim to consolidate penal and welfare policies during wartime. When officials sought to rebuild a criminal justice system in the aftermath of war and defeat in 1945, they drew directly upon this system and translated policies that had been originally coded as ideological conversion and mobilizing the imperial spirit for the war into the postwar idioms of liberalism and democratic reform.

The Recalibration of Criminal Reform after 1945

Following Japan's acceptance of the terms of the Potsdam Declaration in August 1945 and the arrival of occupation forces in early September, the Allied Occupation repealed various laws that were seen as suppressing political opposition and thus contributing to the rise of fascism in the 1930s. Toward this end, on October 4, 1945, General Headquarters (GHQ) issued the Removal of Restrictions on Political, Civil, and Religious Liberties directive (SCAPIN-93)—what is known as the Human Rights Directive. This directive ordered the Japanese government to disband any organs that restricted, censored, or oversaw religious belief, thought, speech, published materials, and so on, including the Special Higher Police (Tokubetsu kōtō keisatsu).⁷⁴ On October 15, the Peace Preservation Law, Thought Criminal Protection and Supervision Law and other related measures for political criminals were repealed.⁷⁵

The Home Ministry was dissolved in 1947, disaggregating Japan's police force into a prefectural system with a National Police Agency located in Tokyo. Compared to the Home Ministry, the Justice Ministry, which as we noted earlier oversaw the prison and criminal rehabilitation systems, escaped largely unscathed, except for an internal purge of high-profile personal connected to the interwar system of policing politics.⁷⁶ And although many of the special laws and institutions that comprised the prewar criminal justice system were abolished, procurators and other justice officials worked quickly to restore and build upon earlier efforts to integrate criminal rehabilitation services into a new criminal justice system under the new principles of "democratization" and "human rights." One of the earliest examples of this trend was a 1946 Justice Ministry directive outlining the implementation of a new Prison Law which read: "As prisoners do not lose their proper rights concerning life, person and property although they are deprived of their liberty, it is required to respect their rights without prejudice and without neglecting care."[77] At the same time, new prison guidelines were issued along with a revision of the Penal Code that, it was argued, aligned "with the spirit of the new Constitution" which went into effect in 1947.[78]

Justice officials saw these reforms as critically important to manage a crime wave in the desperate socioeconomic conditions of post-surrender Japan, peaking in the years 1948–1950 and resulting in overcrowded prisons.[79] Officials were hoping to quickly process, assess, and, when possible, discharge petty criminals, many of them juveniles, back into society. Toward this end, the Justice Ministry reestablished juvenile protection services in 1946, and the government passed a new Juvenile Law in July 1948 (Shōnenhō, No. 168, which took effect January 1, 1949).[80] Indeed, the first session of the Diet under the new constitution in August 1947 was dominated by discussions of revising criminal and administrative laws—not just for juveniles—under these new conditions.[81] Soon thereafter officials extended protection and reform to adult parolees and suspects in either the Suspended Indictment or Suspended Sentence programs, replicating the prewar process in which juvenile reform was extended to adult suspects in the 1920s and 1930s as noted earlier. These latter efforts were formalized through a series of laws in the late 1940s and early 1950s, including the sweeping Offenders Prevention and Rehabilitation Act (Hanzaisha yobō kōsei hō, No. 142) and the Suspended Sentence Protection and Supervision Law (Shikkō yūyosha hogokansatsu hō, No. 58), both passed in 1949. Then, in 1950, the Rehabilitation and Emergency Protection Law (Kōsei kinkyū hogo hō, No. 203) was passed for ex-offenders who were in need of special services, as well as the much-celebrated Volunteer Probation Officers Act (Hogoshi hō, No. 204) which, building from the precedent set earlier in the prewar Judicial Protection Services Law of 1939, established a cadre of volunteer probation officers (VPOs) that would work under the guidance of the local parole board and/or the director of the local parole office.[82] The VPO system was conceptualized, much like the guarantor system for rehabilitating political criminals in the 1930s, as embedded within the national community.[83] And by the time sovereignty returned to Japan in 1952, probationary duties for both youths and adults in the new Judicial Protection System were combined and organized under the local parole office system. Thereafter, subsidiary laws continued to be issued in the 1950s to calibrate the various components of this emerging criminal rehabilitation system, including the Suspended Sentence Protection and Supervision Law (Shikkō yūyo hogo kansatsu hō: 1954, No. 58) which built upon the prewar precedents to extend protection and supervision services to all those with suspended sentences.[84] Then when prostitution was outlawed in April 1958, new protection divisions were instituted to oversee the rehabilitation of women arrested for prostitution.[85]

These criminal reform laws were passed at the same time that Japan's postwar social welfare system was created.[86] Thus, by the end of the 1950s, an extensive criminal rehabilitation apparatus along with a social welfare system had been established, constituting Japan's version of the "penal welfare complex," which, as mentioned earlier, David Garland has identified as one of the main pillars of the welfare state in many postwar countries.[87] The criminal reform complex in Japan is often lauded as an institutional example of Japan's postwar liberalization and democratization, as well as the degree to which rehabilitation both overshadowed a punitive approach to corrections and was based in the community. At the time various campaigns worked to enlighten the public about criminal reform efforts and the role that the wider community plays in such initiatives, including continuing the tradition of commemorating adult and juvenile criminal reform, by this time combined in "Criminal Reform Memorial Day" (Kōsei hogo kinenbi, November 27) and the crime prevention campaign known as "Making Society Brighter Movement" (Shakai o akaruku suru undō).[88] Along with the efforts of almost fifty thousand VPOs working throughout the country and Big Brother and Sister (BBS) volunteers working with youth, criminal and juvenile reform became woven into the fabric of everyday life in postwar Japan.

Ideological Transposition: Imperial Benevolence and the Symbolic Emperor System

From the very first efforts to rebuild this criminal justice system in the late 1940s, criminal reform was, once again, closely associated with the emperor and thus helped to transpose what Endō Kōichi calls the "emperor-system ideology of benevolence" (*tennōsei jikeishugi*) into the postwar period.[89] Emperor Hirohito had renounced his divinity in his so-called Declaration of Humanity (Ningen sengen) on New Year's Day, 1946.[90] Soon thereafter, the new constitution went into effect in May 1947 which declared that the emperor was no longer sovereign but "the symbol of the State and of the unity of the people, deriving his position from the will of the people with whom resides sovereign power."[91] Interestingly, although no longer sovereign, Emperor Hirohito performatively delivered the new constitution by standing before the Diet and asking legislators to "sanction and promulgate" it.[92] As William Marotti argues, such ceremonial performances "marked new authority with old, in a double association with Meiji constitutional authority," since Emperor Hirohito would present the new constitution with the authority given to him by the Meiji Constitution.[93] Such ceremonial performances thus transposed imperial authority into the postwar political settlement.

Much scholarship has focused on how the Allied Occupation refashioned Emperor Hirohito from a sovereign who inherited his legitimacy from his divine ancestors into the postwar "symbol" of the Japanese people and state.[94] Some scholars have gone so far as to call Hirohito the "people's emperor" in the postwar period.[95] However, as Kan Takayuki, Harry Harootunian, and others have persuasively argued, the reconfigured postwar emperor system continued to function as a symbol of an "idealized communal order" that smoothed over the social dislocations and class divisions of capitalism, constituting what Harootunian calls "*gemeinschaft* capitalism."[96] If in the prewar period the emperor functioned as the transcendent sovereign of the imperial *kokutai*, in the postwar he became, Harootunian explains, "a mediator of cultural wholeness" for the postwar national community.[97] In other words, *kokutai* ideology was transposed into the realm of national culture, and one of the threads of this transposition was the reformulation of imperial benevolence through relief, welfare, and criminal reform. This complicates the postwar "people's emperor" thesis mentioned earlier, which posits that the imperial house survived because of the Japanese people's continuing identification with the institution.[98] Rather, such identifications should be understood as produced through modes of affective associations in which the emperor system was refigured in postwar ceremonies and mass media for emotional and cultural identification.[99]

Although Article 25 of the new constitution states in part that "in all spheres of life, the State shall use its endeavors for the promotion and extension of social welfare and security, and of public health,"[100] William Marotti points out that early postwar welfare policies, such as the 1946 Daily Life Security Law (Seikatsu hogo hō, 1946), "reasserted the old relationships of paternal protection" by the state in which "daily life ... was to be constituted as a zone for paternalistic control, sanctioned by an unequal relationship undergirded by imperial authority."[101] And here the benevolence expressed by the newly "symbolic" emperor was of prime importance, for the imperial household not only continued to provide donations for public relief, but also now visited areas devastated by the war or natural disaster, as well as "attending" (*gyōkōkei*) social welfare gatherings, including those of criminal rehabilitation groups.[102] Indeed, it was, paradoxically, in this new "symbolic" function that the emperor and the imperial family began to physically attend such meetings, bequeathing donations and representing imperial benevolence by their presence, unlike they had in the prewar welfare and criminal reform systems. Thus, as Marotti argues in regards to the political function of imperial symbolization, if on the one hand Hirohito's demotion from political sovereign to national symbol "suggests a dematerialization of Hirohito's position," on the other hand, "it was the very materiality of the emperor as symbol that made this role powerful."[103] This dematerialization also worked to transpose the prewar version of the ideology of imperial benevolence into the new postwar political and cultural imaginary, effectively creating what Okudaira Yasuhiro calls the postwar "emperor system within" based on empathy and affection.

The Symbolic Emperor and Postwar Criminal Reform

Such a double association was operative in the realm of criminal reform, transposing the earlier ideology of imperial mercy and benevolence into the postwar symbolizations of imperial empathy and national community. For example, postwar political landmarks such as the promulgation of the new constitution were marked by criminal pardons, which partially explains why justice officials were hurrying to restore the prewar protection and supervision system in order to administer those released. Even before this, criminal pardons continued to be issued as imperial pardons, such as one issued on October 17, 1945, to mark the conclusion of the war.[104] As Endō Kōichi has pointed out, Allied Occupation authorities attempted to discern the relationship between such acts of "benevolent rule" (*jinsei*) and the prewar political system, or if such benevolence had a "separate character and function" from militarism and/or feudalism.[105] Extending Endō's observation, we might interpret these early imperial pardons as refiguring the emperor system to the then emerging postwar order, if not also as explicit strategies to (re-)dress the emperor in the clothes of benevolence in the eyes of Allied Occupation.

According to the new constitution, although criminal pardons were no longer expressions of the will of the sovereign emperor—but rather legal acts of the civilian government—one of the few "acts in matters of state on behalf of the people" granted to the postwar emperor was, "with the advice and approval of the Cabinet," to attest to (*ninshō suru*) "special amnesty, commutation of punishment, reprieve, and restoration of rights."[106] The last instance of the emperor granting amnesty, commutation, and restoration of rights to convicts and ex-offenders was a massive imperial pardon in November 1946—affecting over three hundred thousand convicts and ex-convicts—issued to celebrate the promulgation of the new constitution.[107] Thereafter, he would "attest" to such acts of government, performing the ambiguous "double association" (Marotti) at work in his symbolization whereby he legitimated the acts of the state to which he attested.[108] In March 1947 the Criminal Pardons Law (Onsha hō) was issued that recalibrated the procedures for criminal pardons to the emperor's symbolic role in which the Cabinet would decide upon large-scale pardons for the emperor to "attest to."[109]

It was exactly in this new symbolic capacity that the imperial family started to make appearances at annual gatherings of criminal reform volunteers, which they continue to do today. For example, in November 1952, the emperor and empress convened the first National Gathering of Criminal Reform (Zenkoku kōsei hogo taikai), which gathered over 2,400 people involved in criminal rehabilitation.[110] This event's purpose was not only to gather individuals working in criminal reform work but also to publicize the importance of ex-offender and juvenile reform to the wider community. Thereafter, the emperor and empress as well as other imperial family members continued to grace such gatherings with their "attendance" (*go-rinseki*), thus imparting the symbolic authority of communal empathy and wholeness to criminal protection services, a tradition that continues today.[111] Similarly, the imperial household resumed making donations to support public welfare and criminal reform efforts. For example, the emperor made a donation in April of 1947 in order to promote the efforts of justice reform work to apply across the country. The symbolism of such gestures was formalized in 1949 into an imperial donation every year on the emperor's birthday (April 29) for criminal reform efforts, distributed to various groups throughout Japan.[112]

Crown Prince Akihito is often remembered as symbolizing the emerging postwar consumer culture in the 1950s and 1960s, with his televised marriage to Shōda Michiko in 1959 inspiring a boom in television sales, or in representing postwar middle-class life with photographs of the crown prince and princess visiting the Hibarigaoka apartment complexes (*danchi*), among other media events. However, during this time, the crown prince and princess were also imparting the power of imperial symbolization to the system of postwar youth reform by attending meetings of Japan's Big Brothers and Sisters Movement (BBS undō) that continued the tradition of prewar volunteer efforts for delinquent youth.[113] BBS emerged out of youth protection volunteer efforts in Kyoto in the late 1940s and was soon expanded nationally, becoming formally associated with the international BBS movement in the early 1950s. Attending early gatherings of national BBS groups as well as BBS anniversaries, Crown Prince Akihito and Princess Michiko analogically performed the symbolic function of national unity for youth as Akihito's parents did for adult offenders.[114] Later, Crown Prince Hiro-no-miya took over this symbolic function.[115] Similar to symbolizing youth initiatives, gatherings of the Association for Women Protective Services (Kōsei hogo fujinkai) were also graced periodically with the presence of women from the imperial family.[116] In this way, the division of labor for reforming youth, adult, and female offenders was performed by the imperial family, simultaneously transposing the prewar ideology of imperial benevolence into postwar national culture.[117]

Epilogue: The "Emperor System Within" in the Twenty-First Century

Here I have argued that a transwar approach reveals the complex institutional developments of criminal rehabilitation in Japan, as well as the continuing association of the emperor system and criminal reform across this transwar continuum, both of which are largely glossed over in the existing literature. If in the interwar period imperial benevolence came to be associated with the newly devised criminal rehabilitation efforts so that offenders were reformed as productive and loyal subjects of the imperial sovereign, in the postwar period the imperial family symbolized the national community into which juvenile and adult offenders were being reintegrated, and which provided the tens of thousands of volunteers a cultural value through which criminal corrections and the community were linked. In this way, the "symbolic emperor system" functioned as a medium in the early postwar period for masking the class inequalities during high economic growth, while rehabilitation polices reproduced the affective identifications central to what Okudaira has called the postwar "emperor system within."

In the 1990s, the "emperor system within" was perfected by the Heisei Emperor, who not only continued the tradition of attending criminal reform gatherings and making annual donations to criminal reform groups on his birthday (December 23) but largely defined his thirty years on the throne (1989–2019) by continuously visiting with victims of natural disasters in order to emphasize principles of national unity and imperial empathy during times of hardship.[118] The Heisei Emperor continued to make such visits up through the last months of his reign, and his successor, Naruhito the Reiwa Emperor, is poised to continue this tradition.[119] However, unlike the criminal pardons that were issued when Akihito assumed the throne following his father's death in 1989, the plan to issue a pardon on Akihito's abdication in 2019 was controversial, as public opinion since the early 2000s has increasingly taken a retributive stance toward criminal offenders, thereby challenging Japan's long and celebrated commitment to the rehabilitative ideal in the postwar period.[120] But postwar criminal reform practices and other efforts associated with the imperial house did such an effective job of transposing the ideology of imperial benevolence into the postwar settlement that despite this kind of divergence from public opinion, the continuing affective identification with the imperial family has guaranteed that "emperor system within" will continue into the twenty-first century.

Notes

1 This chapter pursues a question I asked in the epilogue to Max Ward, *Thought Crime: Ideology and State Power in Interwar Japan* (Durham, NC: Duke University Press, 2019), 179–84.

2 See Rehabilitation Bureau, *Non-institutional Treatment of Offenders in Japan* (Tokyo: Ministry of Justice Rehabilitation Bureau, 1974), i.

3 See Kōsei hogo gojūnen shi henshū iinkai, ed., *Kōsei hogo gojūnen shi, Dai ichi hen: Chiiki shakai to tomo ni ayumu kōsei hogo* (Tokyo: Zenkoku hogoshi renmei, 2000), 139–65 (hereafter *KHGS*, vol. 1).

4 See, for example, Elmer H. Johnson, *Japanese Corrections: Managing Convicted Offenders in an Orderly Society* (Carbondale: Southern Illinois University Press, 1996).

5 Roger Goodman, "The 'Japanese-Style Welfare State' and the Delivery of Personal Social Services," in *The East Asian Welfare Model: Welfare Orientalism and the State*, ed. Roger Goodman, Huck-ju Kwon, and Gordon White (London: Routledge, 1998), 139–58.

6 David Garland, *The Culture of Control: Crime and Social Order in Contemporary Society* (Chicago: University of Chicago Press, 2001), 33–4.
7 On "benevolent paternalism," see Daniel H. Foote, "The Benevolent Paternalism of Japanese Criminal Justice," *California Law Review* 80, no. 2 (March 1992): 317–90.
8 See Gregory Kasza, *One World of Welfare: Japan in Comparative Perspective* (Ithaca, NY: Cornell University Press, 2006).
9 For an overview of welfare services during wartime, see Yoshida Kyūichi, *Nihon shakai jigyō no rekishi*, new ed. (Tokyo: Keisō shobō, 1989), 195–217.
10 Takahashi Mutsuko, *The Emergence of Welfare Society in Japan* (Aldershot: Avebury, 1997), 42–6. See Gregory Kasza, "War and Welfare Policy in Japan," *Journal of Asian Studies* 61, no. 2 (May 2002): 417–35.
11 Ward, *Thought Crime*, 138–42.
12 Chapter 1, Article 1, the Constitution of Japan: https://japan.kantei.go.jp/constitution_and_government_of_japan/constitution_e.html (accessed August 15, 2019).
13 Yasumaru Yoshio, *Kindai tennō-zō no keisei*, new ed. (Tokyo: Iwanami, 2017).
14 Takahashi, *Emergence*, 34–8; Ikeda Yoshimasa, *Nihon ni okeru shakai fukushi no ayumi* (Kyoto: Hōken ritsu bunkasha, 1994), 70–2.
15 Okudaira Yasuhiro, "Nihonkoku kempō to 'uchi naru tennōsei,'" *Sekai*, no. 523 (January 1989): 111–30.
16 Endō Kōichi, *Tennōsei jikeishugi no seiritsu* (Tokyo: Gakubunsha, 2010), 1–5; Ikeda Yoshimasa, *Nihon no shakai fukushi shi* (Kyoto: Hōritsu bunka sha, 1986), 163–8.
17 Takahashi, *Emergence*, 34–5. On early state relief efforts, see Ikeda, *Nihon no shakai fukushi shi*, 190–9.
18 Such efforts were designed to undercut critiques of the deficiencies of the new Meiji state. See Ikeda, *Nihon no shakai fukushi shi*, 169–74 and 179–90.
19 Endō, *Tennōsei jikeishugi no seiritsu*, 96; Ikeda, *Nihon shakai fukushi shi*, 379.
20 Yoshida, *Nihon shakai jigyō no rekishi*, in particular 99–128. One example is the establishment of the imperial welfare organization Saiseikai in 1911, which continues operations even today. See Saiseikai, ed., *Onshi zaidan saiseikai shi* (Tokyo: Saiseikai, 1937), https://www.saiseikai.or.jp/about/en/ (accessed August 6, 2019).
21 Takahashi, *Emergence*, 39–42; Yoshida, *Nihon shakai jigyō no rekishi*, 145–69; Ikeda, *Nihon no fukushi shi*, 518–24. From a comparative perspective, see Kasza, *One World of Welfare*, 10–30.
22 *KHGS*, vol. 1, 150.
23 Ibid., 146, 148.
24 Ibid., 159.
25 See, for instance, Ogawa Shigejirō and Tomeoka Kōsuke, "Prisons and Prisoners," in *Fifty Years of New Japan*, vol. 1, compiled by Ōkuma Shigenobu (London: Smith, Elder, 1909), 296; Johnson, *Japanese Corrections*, 191; *KHGS*, vol. 1, 50.

26 *KHGS*, vol. 1, 4, 140; Kamoshida Yasuhiro, "Kōsei hogo to shisōhan hogo kansatsu," in *Riariti to ōtō no shakaigaku: Hanzai itsudatsu to kea*, ed. Komiya Nobuo, Kamoshida Yasuhiro, and Hosoi Yōko (Tokyo: Kazama shobō, 2013): 169–203, 169–70.
27 *KHGS*, vol. 1, 156–7, 160–3.
28 On the various uses of the term *"hogo"* and *"hogo kansatsu,"* see Ogawa Tarō, *Hogo kansatsu seido ni tsuite* (Tokyo: Hōmukenshūjo, 1954), 1–3.
29 For a timeline of these events, see *KHGS*, vol. 1, 145–6. For an overview of the passage of the 1900 Reformatory Law, see Kitaba Tsutomu, "1900nen kankahō no seitei katei ni kansuru shakai seijiteki kōsai," *Shakai fukushi kenkyū* 56, no. 3 (2015): 1–13. On the relationship between private and official reformatories, see Yoshida, *Nihon shakai jigyō no rekishi*, 132–43. For a general overview of early youth reformatories, see David Ambaras, *Bad Youth: Juvenile Delinquency and the Politics of Everyday Life in Modern Japan* (Berkeley: University of California Press, 2006), 44–58 and 104–5.
30 Uchida Hirofumi, *Kōsei hogo no tenkai to kadai* (Kyoto: Hōritsu bunkasha, 2015), 6–8.
31 Ibid., 7.
32 Takahashi, *Emergence*, 39. Shigeta Shinji has shown that at this time Buddhist prison chaplains integrated philosophies of national morality, imperial veneration, and Pure Land Buddhist teachings in their experiments to reform criminals. See Shigeta Shinji, *"Aku" to tōchi no Nihon kindai: Dōtoku, shūkyō, kangoku kyōkai* (Tokyo: Hōzōkan, 2019).
33 On post–First World War economic conditions in Japan, see Takafusa Nakamura, "Depression, Recovery and War, 1920–1945," in *Cambridge History of Japan, vol. 6: The Twentieth Century*, ed. Peter Duus (Cambridge: Cambridge University Press, 1988), 451–93.
34 Michael Lewis, *Rioters and Citizens: Mass Protest in Imperial Japan* (Berkeley: University of California Press, 1990), 30.
35 On the emergence of "social work" (*shakai jigyō*) at this time, see Yoshida, *Nihon shakai jigyō no rekishi*, 171–94; and Yoshida, *Nihon shakai jigyō shisō shoshi*, 45–69. On the emergence of "social problem" (*shakai mondai*) discourse in regards to welfare, see Ikeda, *Nihon ni okeru shakai fukushi no ayumi*, 113–19. See also Ken C. Kawashima, "The Obscene, Violent Supplement of State Power: Korean Welfare and Class Warfare in Interwar Japan," *Positions: East Asia Cultures Critique* 17, no. 3 (Winter 2009): 465–87, 469.
36 On the creation of the Social Bureau, see Yamamoto Yūzō, "Shakai-kyoku secchi keika ni tsuite," *Tokyo kasei Daigaku kenkyū kiyō* 36, no. 1 (1996): 213–22.
37 Ambaras, *Bad Youth*, 100–1.

38 For a survey of developments in social work over the interwar period, see Ikeda, *Nihon ni okeru shakai fukushi no ayumi*, 121–61.
39 Minoru Shikita and Shinichi Tsuchiya, *Crime and Criminal Policy in Japan: Analysis and Evaluation of the Showa Era, 1926–1988* (New York: Springer-Verlag, 1992), 201.
40 Ibid.
41 This law is reprinted in Uchida, *Kōsei hogo no tenkai to kadai*, 10–16. For an overview of the interministerial conflicts over, and eventual passage of, this law, see Ambaras, *Bad Youth*, 104–6.
42 Shikita and Tsuchiya, *Crime and Criminal Policy in Japan*, 201.
43 For a short summary of early indeterminate sentencing practices, see ibid., 110–12; Johnson, *Japanese Corrections*, 31–4.
44 Ambaras, *Bad Youth*, 107.
45 Shikita and Tsuchiya, *Crime and Criminal Policy in Japan*, 110.
46 Ibid., 224.
47 *KHGS*, vol. 1, 168, 151. See also Shikita and Tsuchiya, *Crime and Criminal Policy in Japan*, 207.
48 Shikita and Tsuchiya, *Crime and Criminal Policy in Japan*, 175.
49 Ibid., 177.
50 On the new Relief Law, see Takahashi, *Emergence*, 42; Ishida, *Nihon shakai jigyō no rekishi*, 182–7. Ikeda notes that such policies failed to meet the dire socioeconomic conditions during the Great Depression: Ikeda, *Nihon shakai fukushi shi*, 705–34. On the reconceptualization of social work in the interwar years, see ibid., 652–8, 667–75. On the emerging welfare system at this time, see Kasza, "War and Welfare Policy in Japan," 419–21.
51 *KHGS*, vol. 1, 167 and 169. The 1924 Pardon applied to over thirty-five thousand individuals in the metropole and over fourteen thousand in colonial Korea (ibid., 167).
52 See Watanabe Ikujirō, *Kōshitsu to shakai mondai* (Tokyo: Bunsensha, 1925); Tsuji Zennosuke, *Nihon kōshitsu to shakaijigyō* (Tokyo: Sekijūjisha, 1934); Sekiya Teisaburō, *Kōshitsu to shakaijigyō* (Tokyo: Chūō shakai jigyō kyōkai, 1934).
53 See Ward, *Thought Crime*.
54 Ibid., 62–4, 73–4. On arrests in colonial Korea, see Hong Jong-wook, *Senjiki chōsen no tenkōsha-tachi: Teikoku/Shokuminchi no tōgō to kiretsu* (Tokyo: Yūshisha, 2011).
55 Ward, *Thought Crime*, 60.
56 Okudaira Yasuhiro, *Chianijihō shōshi*, new ed. (Tokyo: Iwanami shoten, 2006), 158.
57 On this development, see Ward, *Thought Crime*, 72–3.
58 Nakazawa Shunsuke, *Chianijihō: Naze seitō seiji ha 'akuhō' o unda ka* (Tokyo: Chūōkōron shinsho, 2012), 137–40.
59 Patricia Steinhoff, *Tenkō: Ideology and Societal Integration in Prewar Japan* (New York: Garland, 1999). On prison chaplains and *tenkō*, see Adam Lyons, "From

Marxism to Religion: Thought Crimes and Forced Conversions in Imperial Japan," *Japanese Journal of Religious Studies* 46, no. 2 (2019): 193–218.

60 On the development and early conceptualization of the *tenkō* policy, see Ward, *Thought Crime*, 77–111.

61 Already by 1935, the rehabilitation of thought criminals was being presented as the model for all criminal reform. See, for example, Hoseikai, ed., *Shisō hannin no hogo o chūshin to shite* (Tokyo: Hoseikai, 1935).

62 Ogawa, *Hogo kansatsu seido ni tsuite*, 2; and: KHGS, vol. 1, 21. For a detailed analysis of this law, see Kamoshida, "Kōsei hogo to Shisōhan hogo kansatsu."

63 On this law and its system of centers, see Ward, *Thought Crime*, 138–42, 149–52.

64 Moriyama Takeichirō, *Shisōhan hogo kansatsu hō kaisetsu* (Tokyo: Shōkadō shoten, 1937), 62–5. See also Ward, *Thought Crime*, 145–52.

65 Ward, *Thought Crime*, 160–72.

66 Takahashi, *Emergence*, 43; Yoshida, *Nihon shakai jigyō no rekishi*, 195–217; Yoshida, *Nihon shakai jigyō shisō shoshi*, 109–29; Ikeda, *Nihon ni okeru shakai fukushi no ayumi*, 162–9; Ikeda, *Nihon shakai fukushi shi*, 735–40.

67 Takahashi, *Emergence*, 45, 44. Indeed, Ikeda Yoshimasa explores the reconceptualization of social policy in the 1930s in the context of Japanese Fascism. See Ikeda, *Nihon shakai fukushi shi*, 652–8.

68 Hirata Isao, "Hogo kansatsu sho no shimei" (December 14, 1936), in *Shisōhan hogo kansatsu hō*, ed. Aomori Hogo Kansatsu Sho (1937), reprinted in Ogino Fujio, ed., *Chianijihō kankei shiryōshū*, vol. 3 (Tokyo: Shinnihon Shuppansha, 1996), 65–80, 78.

69 Ibid., 78; Ward, *Thought Crime*, 161–3.

70 Zennihon shihō hogo jigyō renmei, *Shihō hogo jigyō hō no hanashi* (Tokyo: Zennihon shihō hogo jigyō renmei, 1939); KHGS, vol. 1, 192–3; Uchida, *Kōsei hogo no tenkai to kadai*, 67–9.

71 On the functional relation between "rehabilitation" (*hogo*) and "supervision" (*kansatsu*), see Katō Michiko, "Senzen kara sengo fukkōki ni okeru hogo kansatsu seido no dōnyū to hensen." *Oyō shakaigaku kenkyū*, no. 55 (2013): 219–33, 223–6.

72 Shikita and Tsuchiya, *Crime and Criminal Policy in Japan*, 202. On the postwar VPO system, see Elmer H. Johnson and Carol H. Johnson, *Linking Community and Corrections in Japan* (Carbondale: Southern Illinois University Press, 2000), 288–303.

73 Shikita and Tsuchiya, *Crime and Criminal Policy in Japan*, 206.

74 GHQ/SCAP, "Seijiteki, kōminteki oyobi shūkyōteki jiyū ni taisuru seigen jokyo no ken" (October 4, 1945), in *Chianijihō kankei shiryōshū*, vol. 4, ed. Ogino Fujio (Tokyo: Shinnihon Shuppansha, 1996), 368–71.

75 For the repeal of the Peace Preservation Law, among other institutions, see reprinted orders in Ogino, *Chianijihō kankei shiryōshū*, vol. 4, 371–2. See also Ogino Fujio, *Shisō kenji* (Tokyo: Iwanami Shoten, 2000), 186.

76 Ogino, *Shisō kenji*, 186–96.
77 Excerpted in Shikita and Tsuchiya, *Crime and Criminal Policy in Japan*, 177.
78 A summary of the revised Penal Code (enforced May 3, 1947) is provided in ibid., 8. On the new prison guidelines, see ibid., 176.
79 See ibid., 16–19, 175–6.
80 *KHGS*, vol. 1, 185–7; Uchida, *Kōsei hogo no tenkai to kadai*, 129–40; Moriya Katsuhiko, *Shōnen no hikō to kyōiku: Shōnen hōsei no rekishi to genjō* (Tokyo: Keisōshobō, 1977), 152–95.
81 See Dai ikkai Kokkai Shūgiin, Shihōiin kaigi roku no. 11, August 2, 1947; https://kokkai.ndl.go.jp/#/detail?minId=100104390X01119470802&spkNum=0&single (accessed June 28, 2020).
82 On these laws, see *KHGS*, vol. 1, 8–9 and 234–42; Shikita and Tsuchiya, *Crime and Criminal Policy in Japan*, 202–5. On the Offenders Prevention and Rehabilitation Act, see Ōtsubo Yoichi, *Kōsei hogo no seiritsu* (Tokyo: Nihon kōsei hogo kyōkai, 1996); Kōsei hogo gojūnen shi henshū iinkai ed., *Kōsei hogo gojūnen shi, Dai ni hen: Chiiki shakai to tomo ni ayumu kōsei hogo* (Tokyo: Zenkoku hogoshi renmei, 2000), 449–80 (hereafter *KHGS*, vol. 2).
83 On the VPO law and system, see Shikita and Tsuchiya, *Crime and Criminal Policy in Japan*, 205–7; Ogawa Tarō, "Hogo kansatsu no shakaiteki kiso," in Kōsei hogo seido shikō jusshūnen kinen zenkoku taikai jimukyoku, ed., *Kōsei hogo ronshū* (Tokyo: Kōsei hogo seido shikō jūshūnen kinen zankoku taikai jimukyoku, 1959), 63–71 (this collection hereafter *KHR*).
84 *KHGS*, vol. 1, 239–42; Shikita and Tsuchiya, *Crime and Criminal Policy in Japan*, 204; Yanase Taizō, "Shikkō yūyo no hogo kansatsu ni tsuite," in KHR, 243–54.
85 *KHGS*, vol. 1, 231. See also the annual statistics of individuals placed in Female Rehabilitation Centers (*fujin hodōin*) and so on (*KHGS*, vol. 1, 406).
86 See Ikeda, *Nihon ni okeru shakai fukushi no ayumi*, 178–85. For a transwar history of welfare in Japan, see Kasza, *One World of Welfare*.
87 Garland, *The Culture of Control*, 33–4.
88 *KHGS*, vol. 1, 56–65.
89 Endō, *Tennōsei jikeishugi no seiritsu*.
90 John Dower, *Embracing Defeat: Japan in the Wake of World War II* (New York: Norton, 1999), 308–14.
91 Glenn D. Hook and Gavan McCormack, *Japan's Contested Constitution: Documents and Analysis* (London: Routledge, 2001), 4.
92 This double association was reinforced by the symbolism of the date chosen to issue the new constitution: November 3, the birthday of Emperor Meiji, which was soon thereafter renamed Culture Day (Bunka no hi). William Marotti, *Money, Trains, and Guillotines: Art and Revolution in 1960s Japan* (Durham, NC: Duke University Press, 2013), 55, 56.

93 Ibid., 56.
94 For example, see Dower, *Embracing Defeat*.
95 Kenneth Ruoff, *The People's Emperor: Democracy and the Japanese Monarchy, 1945–1995* (Cambridge, MA: Harvard University Press, 2003).
96 Harry Harootunian, "Hirohito Redux: Hirohito and the Making of Modern Japan by Herbert P. Bix," *Critical Asian Studies* 33, no. 4 (2001): 609–36, 615; Kan Takayuki, "Gendai shimin shakai to shōchō tennōsei," in *Tennōsei ronshū* vol. 1 (Tokyo: Ochanomizu shobō, 2014), 174–200.
97 Harootunian, "Hirohito Redux," 628.
98 See Kenneth J. Ruoff, *Japan's Imperial House in the Postwar Era, 1945–2019* (Cambridge, MA: Harvard University Press, 2020), 8.
99 Yoshimi Shunya, "The Cultural Politics of the Mass-Mediated Emperor System in Japan," in *Without Guarantees: In Honour of Stuart Hall*, ed. Paul Gilroy, Lawrence Grossberg, and Angela McRobbie (New York: Verso, 2000), 395–415.
100 See Ishida, *Nihon shakai jigyō no rekishi*, 219; Takahashi, *Emergence*, 62–6. On the drafting, debate, and translation of this welfare section in the constitution, see Kyoko Inoue, *MacArthur's Japanese Constitution: A Linguistic and Cultural Study of Its Making* (Chicago: Chicago University Press, 1991), 92–3.
101 Marotti, *Money, Trains, and Guillotines*, 72, 73. On the Daily Life Security Law and other early postwar welfare initiatives, see Ikeda, *Nihon ni okeru shakai fukushi no ayumi*, 170–7.
102 Endō, *Tennōsei jikeishugi no seiritsu*, 159–60.
103 Marotti, *Money, Trains, and Guillotines*, 58, 59.
104 *KHGS*, vol. 1, 185.
105 Endō, *Tennōsei jikeishugi no seiritsu*, 164.
106 *KHGS*, vol. 1, 51. See also Articles 7 and 73 of the (postwar) Constitution of Japan.
107 *KHGS*, vol. 1, 186.
108 Marotti, *Money, Trains, and Guillotines*, 55.
109 KHGS, vol. 1, 187. See also ibid., 188 and 50–5.
110 Ibid., 197.
111 See ibid., 197, 214, 249–50, 258, 260, 263, 265, 268, 271, 282, 285, 286, 289, 290, 307, 309. See also the "Emperor's Remarks" (Tennō heika no okotoba) opening the fiftieth anniversary celebrations of criminal reform efforts in 1999 (ibid., front matter).
112 See the annual entries for April starting in 1947 in *KHGS*, vol. 1. For parallel imperial donations to other relief and welfare groups, see Katō, *Tennōsei jikeishugi no seiritsu*, 165–72.
113 On the BBS movement, see *KHGS*, vol. 1, 110–17; Hasegawa Hiroaki, "Kōsei hogo ni okeru hanzai yobō katsudō no shinten: 'BBS undō' no shiteki tenkai katei," *Musashino Daigaku ningen kagaku kenkyūsho nenpō*, no. 1 (2012): 51–67.

114 *KHGS*, vol. 1, 267–8.
115 See ibid., 321.
116 Ibid., 261; and then Crown Princess Masako's address in 1999 to a gathering of women rehabilitation volunteers and officers, reprinted in ibid., 393. On the Kōsei hogo fujinkai and related associations, see ibid., 104–9, 274.
117 On the transwar logic of transposition, see Andrew Gordon, "Consumption, Leisure and the Middle Class in Transwar Japan," *Social Science Japan Journal* 10, no. 1 (April 2007): 1–21.
118 Akihito attended the forty-year anniversary of the establishment of criminal reform in the year that his father died (1989). See *KHGS*, vol. 1, 343. On the Heisei Emperor's relief activities, see Ruoff, *Japan's Imperial House*, 264; "Symbol of the State: Emperor's Visits to Disaster Zones Helped Define 'Heisei way,'" *Mainichi shimbun*, December 19, 2018, https://mainichi.jp/english/articles/20181219/p2a/00m/0na/002000c (accessed September 5, 2019).
119 See Jim Breen, "Abdication, Succession and Japan's Imperial Future: An Emperor's Dilemma," *Asia-Pacific Journal: Japan Focus* 17, no. 9, 3 (2019): https://apjjf.org/2019/09/Breen.html (accessed June 18, 2020).
120 See Colin Jones, "With Changes in Emperors come Amnesties, So Who Will Benefit?" *Japan Times*, June 19, 2019; Wada Takeshi, "Japan Gov't Ponders Pardons Timed for October Ceremony for New Emperor," *Mainichi*, May 2, 2019. For an overview of the changing perception of crime in contemporary Japan, see David T. Johnson, "Crime and Punishment in Contemporary Japan," *Crime and Justice* 36, no. 1 (2007): 371–423.

Afterword: Transwar as Method

Takashi Fujitani

The editors and authors of this remarkable volume on the "transwar" in Asia trouble the simple triumphalist narrative that locates 1945 as *the* moment of historical rupture that remade Asia and the world. This singular moment of disruption has not only often been told as the end to Japan's war of aggression and its colonial empire, but it has also served as a kind of origin myth for the liberation of the peoples of the Asia-Pacific and the reincorporation of Japan and the Japanese people into the civilized world. Within these freedom stories, Asian women, usually in complete disregard of their long feminist histories, have repeatedly been made to stand in for the oppressed conditions and subsequent emancipations of their nations or all the people. This idea of occupation as liberation has served time and again, as Lisa Yoneyama has emphasized in her analysis of the Occupation's discourse on Japanese women, as "the unhappiest women in the world," to legitimate not only US wars past but nearly every US war and occupation since, including the Iraq War that began in 2003.[1] Occupation by a foreign power in this way of thinking repeatedly produces new beginnings highlighted by freedom, democracy, security, and prosperity even when preceded by massive violence and destruction perpetrated by the "liberators" themselves.

In contrast to such a portable origin myth, this volume's contributors show continuities across 1945, for instance, demonstrating that agricultural policies and technologies of population management and mobilization employed under Japanese colonialism had an afterlife in US-occupied Korea and Taiwan; that militarism and police surveillance continued and in many cases intensified throughout the Asia-Pacific in the aftermath of the Hot War; that the exploitation of colonial labor did not cease; that educational institutions in liberated colonies did not suddenly emerge in a burst of newly found freedom; that wartime anticommunist ideologies found a new if transformed lease of life in postcolonial Taiwan; and that postwar liberal democracy cannot be delinked from the legacies of interwar militarism, emperorism, and practices of human rehabilitation.

We can further extrapolate from these critical interventions that we should be wary of myopic histories that isolate one country from another or contribute to the peripheralization of aggrieved communities within formal boundaries. Thus, while optimistic historians might regard the US occupation of Japan as a great success even with recognition of its imperfections, these chapters urge us to consider the broader region as a whole and the complex and entangled genealogies of war, imperialism, capitalism, social conflicts, memory making, and forgetfulness that continued across 1945 and troubled the larger region for the long period that stretched from at least the end of the First World War to the postwar period.

Such an expansive perspective that transgresses the conventional boundaries of time and space that delimit our historical knowledge should warn against confident pronouncements of progress and success, such as that all things considered the Japanese people came to "embrace defeat" and found a new and bright democratic beginning with the US occupation.[2] In a more encompassing view we find not the end to military violence but the postwar as the scene for the escalation of wars—on the Korean Peninsula, China, and Southeast Asia—with many of these wars waged by the European powers attempting to preserve their colonial empires against anti-colonial movements. This, even as their representatives at the Tokyo War Crimes Tribunal (the Dutch, British, and French) sat in judgment on Japanese war criminality. In that display of (in)justice, the crimes of all colonialisms, whether of victors or vanquished, were out of bounds for interrogation. It goes without saying that these anti-colonial wars were entangled in that other war that has been raging since at least the early twentieth century—namely, the war between the capitalist and communist camps.

On the Korean Peninsula and in Taiwan, as Bruce Cumings and others following him have pointed out, the postcolonial regimes became heirs to the developmentalist economic policies, infrastructures, and strategies to constitute disciplined and industrious human subjects that date from the period of Japan's modern colonial rule, as well as the oppressive technologies of the police states, militarism, and dictatorial rule emerging out of that very same past. North Korea even produced its own form of emperorism or *tennōsei* as well as the *chuch'e* philosophy that echoes the imperial subjectification (*kōminka*) ideology of late colonial rule.³ In metropolitan Japan, out of the ashes of imperial defeat, we find not only an exhausted and despondent (*kyodatsu*) population as some would have it. Instead, elements in the "Japanese" population who began to regain confidence in themselves as a superior and homogeneous race unleashed a renewed wave of brutality and exploitation against discriminated populations such as Okinawans, ethnic Koreans, and poor women who had been pressured or lured into prostitution.⁴

Given so many examples of the ongoing and even intensifying violence and exploitation experienced by the peoples of the Asia-Pacific across the 1945 divide, it is possible to craft an alternative narrative of continuity through time that emphasizes the unrelenting negativity of historical development. However, before unreflexively privileging narratives of continuity over disruption, it is equally necessary to critically reflect at a metahistorical level on how and why we constitute both types of stories. At the most obvious level, narratives of continuity are not inherently critical or affirmative of the past or present. For example, at one extreme of the political spectrum the writer and ultranationalist apostate from Marxism Hayashi Fusao published his version of a transwar narrative in the mid-1960s. In his *Affirmation of the Great East Asia War* (*Daitōa sensō kōteiron*) Hayashi took an even longer historical view and celebrated Japan's Great East Asia War as the culmination of a century-long battle against US imperialism that began in the mid-nineteenth century.⁵ Conversely, one of the "change with continuity" narratives criticized by this volume's editors was modernization theory, perhaps the most dominant paradigm for the study of Japan in the postwar Anglophone academy. Many of these scholars told an even more extended story of Japanese continuity than Hayashi's. Finding origins all the way back in the Edo period (1603–1868), they claimed to have discovered the roots of Japan's successful capitalist modernization in its deep history. High levels of education and literacy, a shift from *Gemeinschaft* to *Gesellschaft*, bureaucratic rationality, urbanization, impressive levels of agricultural productivity tied to a growing commercial economy, and even a Tokugawa analogue to the Protestant ethic—these elements and more seemed to point Japan toward the telos of modern capitalist development before the people living this history could even imagine or name such a goal, let alone conceive of it as a model. As John Hall, one of the most learned historians in this school put it, the Japanese were already preparing to become like the modern West even before it came knocking on their door: "The hand that opened the door [to the West] was as important as the one that produced the knock from the outside." Yet no one could completely ignore the uncomfortable reality of the 1930s and

1940s, a period that had witnessed the escalation of militarism, expansionism, and totalitarian rule. Thus, Hall explained that the Japanese pathologies that had caused such disruptions were rooted in another continuity, the continuity of "irrational inheritances out of the past."[6] Doubly continuous, Japan was figured as a model of success in the non-Western world, a kind of global model minority, but one whose accomplishments were entangled with a pathological continuum associated with its "Orientalness." Edwin O. Reischauer, one of the primary architects of Cold War Orientalism toward Japan, likewise constructed a narrative of continuity, but in his case leapfrogging over the inconvenient 1930s and 1940s by connecting the promising days of bourgeois parliamentary democracy in the 1910s and 1920s directly to the rebirth of Japanese democracy in the postwar.[7]

Narratives of historical continuity or discontinuity, of origins or devolutions, do not exist "out there," waiting for clever historians to find them. Hayashi clearly crafted a story to figure Japan's nationalism, imperialism, and war of aggression as a struggle against Western imperialism, while the will to knowledge of the modernization theorists stemmed from their desire to reconstitute Japan from an aberrant enemy to America's best if somewhat strange friend in Asia. But the admission that "knowledge is perspective"[8] need not lead to historical relativism or nihilism if we understand that history is not about the recuperation of history as it was but about constructing an effective history for now, and that this perspectival history must be able to withstand empirically based scrutiny. In this way, if I am not mistaken, the authors and editors of this volume have been guided in their desire to cast a critical eye on conventional celebratory stories of the end of the Second World War, not out of a passion for objectivist neutrality but out of an empirically grounded commitment to a political life. This is a stance that has also guided my own work. In my view, the transwar is most effective when we understand that it is not a thing to be discovered but a method for exposing repressed histories of violence as well as for revisiting the myriad of alternative possibilities that existed at the 1945 conjuncture.

As a segue way from these abstract thoughts to the question of empires at war, I turn first to Michel Foucault's essay "Nietzsche, Genealogy, History." Interestingly, in this well-known meditation on Nietzsche's critique of history, Foucault briefly took up the issue of total war and its ending as an example of how his genealogical method would proceed to expose the myth that equates the termination of war with peace and reconciliation. He wrote:

It would be false to think that total war exhausts itself in its own contradictions and ends by renouncing violence and submitting to civil laws. On the contrary, the law is a calculated and relentless pleasure, delight in the promised blood, which permits the perpetual instigation of new dominations and staging of meticulously repeated scenes of violence. The desire for peace, the serenity of compromise, and the tacit acceptance of the law, far from representing a major moral conversion or a utilitarian calculation that gave rise to the law are but its result and, in point of it, its perversion. ... Humanity does not gradually progress from combat to combat until it arrives at a universal reciprocity, where the rule of law finally replaces warfare; humanity installs each of its violences in a system of rules and thus proceeds from domination to domination.[9]

Elsewhere, providing a similar insight, Foucault reversed Carl von Clausewitz's now commonsensical definition of war—that it is the extension of politics by other means—by insisting that politics is nothing other than war by other means. In short, the termination of hostilities by treaties does not end violence but inaugurates another instantiation of it and a new set of dominations. Or as Foucault put it, "We are always writing the history of the same war, even when we are writing the history of peace and its institutions." Like Walter Benjamin, who elaborated on the violence of law making, Foucault recognized the violence that continues in the name of law and order.[10]

Thus, at that conjuncture of possibilities that came together in 1945, the most powerful warring empires in the Asia-Pacific—that is, Japan and the United States—made peace while crushing the dreams of so many throughout the region and unleashing another regional system of domination based on new rules and turning up the heat on what is misleadingly called the Cold War. As such, we may view 1945 not as a point of origin for peace and freedom, or the war itself as a momentary disruption along an otherwise smooth path toward the telos of capitalist liberal democracy. Instead, 1945 was a transit point or a conjuncture during which the workings of power among the empires, both winners and losers, bumped up against the many hopes of the liberated while enabling or disabling the multiplicity of possible routes into the future. These were desires for postcoloniality without violence and with civil rights, self-determination, and democracy; not of military dictatorships and neocolonialism. And in so many cases, throughout the Asia-Pacific, aspirations for self-determination came to be severely compromised by a system that turned formal colonies of Japan, the United States, and the European powers into client states, proxies, sub-imperial nations, or disprivileged appendages of metropolitan nations.

In some instances, the United States transformed citizens of newly liberated nations into agents of the reconstituted American Empire—a blob-like entity that absorbed sovereignties even while it disavowed territorial aggrandizement. Simeon Man has shown, for example, how almost one hundred thousand military personnel from South Korea, Taiwan, the Philippines, and South Vietnam received military training in the United States during the supposedly decolonizing years, and that at the height of the war in Vietnam some six thousand Filipino soldiers and fifty thousand South Koreans were deployed to Vietnam every year to assist in the US war effort.[11] In the course of my own research, I had an opportunity to meet one of those US-trained South Korean soldiers. Chŏn Sang-yŏp's tumultuous life embodies (in both a literal and a figurative sense) what should be thought of not as the defeat of the Japanese Empire but rather as its transwar absorption into the postwar US Empire, for the United States was not the first empire to provide him with military training. Near the end of the colonial period, with Japan engaged in total war, Chŏn had become a soldier in the Japanese Imperial Army. In the harrowing story that he told me and that I was able to confirm through a copy of his Japanese court martial record, after becoming a Japanese soldier he took part in a planned mutiny of Korean soldiers stationed in Pyŏngyang. If successful, it would have been the largest insurrection involving Japanese soldiers since the well-known February 26 (1936) coup d'état attempt of young officers in Tokyo. Unfortunately for him, the military police discovered this plot, and he was arrested along with more than seventy comrades. Although he was found guilty for his participation in the planned insurrection, he miraculously escaped from jail. Clearly, he sought freedom not just from military confinement but from the grip of the Japanese Empire. But just as he was about to find that space of liberation beyond the northern border of the Korean colony, he was recaptured and once again imprisoned. Luckily for him, or so he initially thought, he did not spend a long time in confinement because the war soon ended. But his release marked only another moment in his experiences as a soldier of two empires since he then traveled to the United States for military training, only to see combat in the Korean War. During that war he suffered a severe gunshot wound to the chest. In other words, liberation from the militarism of the Japanese Empire meant not the end of violence, but rather participation in yet another war that was routed through the United States.[12]

Despite the common naming of the Second World War in the Asia-Pacific as the Asia-Pacific War, the peoples of the Pacific Islands are all too often forgotten or at best marginalized in these histories. But in recent years scholars such as Setsu Shigematsu, Keith Camacho, and others have stressed how the fates of Pacific Islanders have been inextricably entangled in the militarized and capitalist networks that have bound together places as distant from each other as Okinawa, Guam, and Hawaii; Seoul and Saipan; New Mexico and Tinian; Tokyo and Washington; Vietnam and the Philippines.[13] The islands and the seas around them became the scenes of some of the fiercest battles of the Second World War; and as the Japanese and US empires traded places as insular occupiers, their competing demands for service and loyalty ripped apart the lives of the indigenous peoples. Near the end of the war the Tinian airfields from which US bombers took off for their bombing runs to the Japanese archipelago comprised what some argue was the busiest operational air base in the world, finally providing the launching pad for the bombers that delivered the atomic bombs dropped on Hiroshima and Nagasaki.[14] While many continue to find gratification in believing that dropping the atomic bombs on Japan contributed to lasting world peace, for the Marshallese whose atolls became subjected to massive nuclear testing by the United States beginning shortly after the war, 1945 represents not the beginning of peace and security but a transit point for repetitive acts of nuclear violence on their lives and environment. In Hawaii, indigenous desires for emancipation from US colonial rule—as seemingly promised by the United Nations Charter (1946) in its designation of Hawaii as a "non-self-governing territory" that should be nurtured toward self-government—were dashed by statehood. Like the reversion of Okinawa to Japan in 1972, the granting of Hawaiian statehood exemplifies how the apparently progressive act of inclusion resulted in the neocolonial annexation of indigenous peoples and lands in the name of national inclusivity.[15]

Of course, this is not to deny that life has improved for many. But the transwar as method allows us to see 1945 as a junction for exchanges among the empires that had been at war with each other, who recomposed themselves into a new formation that marginalized those who had been subordinated throughout the course of the twentieth century. For instance, while it is evident that the Okinawan people have been forced to bear the overwhelming weight of the postwar US military presence in the country with some 75 percent of the US military facilities in Japan now based in their prefecture, critical scholars have also observed that this wildly disproportionate burden is tightly linked to the apparent success of the anti-base movement on the main Japanese islands. In other words, military personnel and installations have disappeared from many "backyards" on the main islands, only to reappear as a daily and often deadly presence in Okinawa, which comprises only 1 percent of the country's landmass.[16] The remilitarization of Okinawa and the ongoing endangerment to the local people and natural environment was not simply a one-time, if obscene, supplement to mainland Japan's peace and prosperity along the way to happiness for all. Rather, it continued a seemingly permanent structure of sacrifice that had already been part of Japanese imperialism since the late nineteenth century and that became tragically salient near the close of the Second World War when Okinawa lost one-quarter or more of its population to the US marines' only land invasion of Japan. Other examples of such exchanges include suffrage for Japanese women in conjunction with the disenfranchisement of adult male Koreans and Taiwanese; the end of the "comfort women" system and the establishment of "camp towns" next to US bases; the Japanese emperor and economic czar of Manchukuo, Kishi Nobusuke, given a pass on the Tokyo War Crimes Tribunal to become "symbolic emperor" and prime minister, respectively, but Korean and Taiwanese POW guards executed as war criminals; the official liberation of Japanese and US colonies in exchange for America's expansion of its empire of bases, and so on.[17]

Recognizing the persistent forces that derailed alternative possibilities around 1945, in our historical analyses we might more effectively employ a past conditional temporal lens, "what might have been," in addition to what we have become.[18] Such an approach would reconsider, for instance, the Tokyo War Crimes Tribunal, as if it had taken up the "comfort women" issue as a war crime. Indeed, in the Women's International War Crimes Tribunal on Japan's Military Sexual Slavery (December 2000), this is precisely what the learned justices on that tribunal attempted as they put Hirohito on trial and found him guilty as charged.[19] Likewise, as historians, we might try to recuperate attempts to forge unexpected alliances against racism, sexism, and imperialism, as some are doing by excavating Asian (including Japanese)/Black solidarities across time.[20] To take such an approach would be to recognize that afterward, after everything seems to have been said and done, the transwar as *method* opens up the possibility that neither the past nor the future is set in stone.

Notes

1 Lisa Yoneyama, "Liberation under Siege: Japanese Women," in *Cold War Ruins*, ed. Lisa Yoneyama (Durham, NC: Duke University Press, 2016), 81–107.
2 See John W. Dower's *Embracing Defeat: Japan in the Wake of World War II* (New York: W. W. Norton, 1999); and for a more critical view of the postwar whose

title is a subtle jab at Dower, see Gavan McCormack, *Client State: Japan in American Embrace* (London: Verso, 2007).

3 While Bruce Cumings had taken up these themes in his earlier work, for a concise essay connecting the colonial with the postcolonial in Korea, Taiwan, and Vietnam, see Bruce Cumings, "Colonial Formations and Deformations: Korea, Taiwan, and Vietnam," in *Parallax Visions: Making Sense of American-East Asian Relations at the End of the Century* (Durham, NC: Duke University Press, 1999), 69–94.

4 Oguma Eiji has argued that the idea of the Japanese as a homogeneous race was one among several racial discourses in the prewar and wartime period and that it became more dominant after the war: *A Genealogy of "Japanese" Self-Images*, trans. David Askew (Melbourne: Trans Pacific, 2002). Choi Deokhyo, "The Empire Strikes Back from Within: Colonial Liberation and the Korean Minority Question at the Birth of Postwar Japan, 1945–1947," *American Historical Review* (forthcoming); Sarah Kovner, *Occupying Power: Sex Work and Servicemen in Postwar Japan* (Stanford, CA: Stanford University Press, 2012); Robert Kramm, *Sanitized Sex: Regulating Prostitution, Venereal Disease, and Intimacy in Occupied Japan, 1945–1952* (Oakland: University of California Press, 2017).

5 Hayashi Fusao, *Daitōa sensō kōteiron*, vols. 1 & 2 (1964–65; reprint ed. Tokyo: Miki shobō, 1984).

6 For the quotes, see John Whitney Hall, "Changing Japanese Attitudes toward Modernization," in *Changing Japanese Attitudes toward Modernization*, ed. Marius B. Jansen (Princeton, NJ: Princeton University Press, 1965), 36; and "A Monarch for Modern Japan," in *Political Development in Modern Japan*, ed. Robert E. Ward (Princeton, NJ: Princeton University Press, 1968), 64.

7 E. O. Reischauer, "What Went Wrong," in *Dilemmas of Growth in Prewar Japan*, ed. James W. Morley (Princeton, NJ: Princeton University Press, 1971), 489–510.

8 Michel Foucault, "Nietzsche, Genealogy, History," in *Language, Counter-Memory, Practice*, ed. with an intro. Donald F. Bouchard, trans. Donald F. Bouchard and Sherry Simon (Ithaca, NY: Cornell University Press, 1980), 156.

9 Ibid., 150–1.

10 Michel Foucault, *Society Must Be Defended: Lectures at the College de France, 1975–76*, ed. Mauro Bertaini and Alessandro Fontana, trans. David Macy (New York: Picador, 2003), 16; Walter Benjamin, "Critique of Violence," in *Walter Benjamin: Selected Writings Volume 1, 1913–1926*, ed. Marcus Bullock and Michael W. Jennings (Cambridge, MA: Harvard University Press, 1996), 236–52.

11 Simeon Man, *Soldiering through Empire: Race and the Making of the Decolonizing Pacific* (Oakland: University of California Press, 2018), 4.

12 It is also known that a large number of Koreans served as officers in both the Japanese Imperial Army and the South Korean military, including Kim Sŏk-wŏn, who at one time was deployed with the infamous "Tiger of Malaya" Major General

Yamashita Tomoyuki and then became a divisional commander in the South Korean forces. For this and Chŏn, see Takashi Fujitani, *Race for Empire: Koreans as Japanese and Japanese as Americans during WWII* (Berkeley: University of California Press, 2011), 285–6, 295, 378–9.

13 Setsu Shigematsu and Keith L. Camacho, eds., *Militarized Currents: Toward a Decolonized Future in Asia and the Pacific* (Minneapolis: University of Minnesota Press, 2010).

14 Don A. Farrell, *Tinian: A Brief History* (Honolulu: Pacific Historic Parks, 2012), 68, 72–81.

15 Dean Itsuji Saranillio, *Unsustainable Empire: Alternative Histories of Hawai'i Statehood* (Durham, NC: Duke University Press, 2018).

16 Annmaria M. Shimabuku, *Alegal: Biopolitics and the Unintelligibility of Okinawan Life* (New York: Fordham University Press, 2019).

17 Many of these facts are known but not juxtaposed as exchanges. It is not commonly known that adult male Koreans who could establish residency in the metropole had the right to vote and hold office. See Matsuda Toshihiko, *Senzenki no Zainichi Chōsenjin to sanseiken* (Tokyo: Akashi shoten, 1995). On the empire of bases, see Chalmers Johnson, *The Sorrows of Empire: Militarism, Secrecy, and the End of the Republic* (New York: Metropolitan Books, 2004).

18 This is Lisa Lowe's rephrasing (*Intimacies of Four Continents* [Durham, NC: Duke University Press, 2015], 40) of a method articulated by Stephanie Smallwood (*Saltwater Slavery: A Middle Passage from Africa to the American Diaspora* [Cambridge, MA: Harvard University Press, 2009]).

19 On the alternative trial and NHK's (Japan's public broadcaster) problematic coverage of the trial, see Lisa Yoneyama, "Sovereignty, Apology, Forgiveness: Revisionisms," in Yoneyama, *Cold War Ruins*, 121–9.

20 Among efforts to recuperate possibilities in such efforts despite their imperfections, see George Lipsitz, "'Frantic to Join … the Japanese Army': Black Soldiers and Civilians Confront the Asia-Pacific War," in *Perilous Memories: The Asia-Pacific War(s)*, ed. T. Fujitani, Geoffrey W. White, and Lisa Yoneyama (Durham, NC: Duke University Press, 2001), 347–77; Nahum Dimitri Chandler, "Introduction: On the Virtues of Seeing—At Least, But Never Only—Double," *CR: The New Centennial Review* 12, no. 1 (Spring 2012): 1–39; Yuichiro Onishi and Fumiko Sakashita, eds., *Transpacific Correspondences: Dispatches from Japan's Black Studies* (Cham: Springer International, 2019).

Bibliography

Abel, Jonathan. *Redacted: The Archives of Censorship in Transwar Japan*. Berkeley, CA: University of California Press, 2012.

Ai'ai Changbai. *WeiMan junxiao xuesheng huiyilu*. Changchun: Jilin sheng qingnian yundong shi gong zuo weiyuanhui, 2000.

Ambaras, David. *Bad Youth: Juvenile Delinquency and the Politics of Everyday Life in Modern Japan*. Berkeley, CA: University of California Press, 2006.

Aspinall, Edward. *Opposing Suharto: Compromise, Resistance, and Regime Change in Indonesia*. Stanford, CA: Stanford University Press, 2005.

Azuma Eiichiro. *In Search of Our Frontier: Japanese America and Settler Colonialism in the Construction of Japan's Borderless Empire*. Berkeley: University of California Press, 2019.

Barlow, Tani, ed. *Formations of Colonial Modernity in East Asia*. Durham, NC: Duke University Press, 1997.

Barnard, F. "National Culture and Political Legitimacy: Herder and Rousseau." *Journal of the History of Ideas* 44, no. 2 (1983): 231–53.

Benesch, Oleg. *Inventing the Way of the Samurai. Nationalism, Internationalism, and Bushido in Modern Japan*. Oxford: Oxford University Press, 2014.

Benesch, Oleg. "The Samurai Next Door: Chinese Examinations of the Japanese Martial Spirit." *Extrême-Orient Extrême-Occident* 38 (2014): 129–68.

Benjamin, Walter. "Critique of Violence." In *Walter Benjamin: Selected Writings Volume 1, 1913–1926*, edited by Marcus Bullock and Michael W. Jennings. Cambridge, MA: Belknap Press of Harvard University Press, 1996, 236–52.

Bergère, Marie-Claire. *Sun Yat-sen*. Stanford, CA: Stanford University Press, 1998.

Bourchier, David. *Illiberal Democracy in Indonesia: The Ideology of the Family State*. London: Routledge, 2015.

Bourchier, David. "The Romance of Adat in the Indonesian Political Imagination and the Current Revival." In *The Revival of Tradition in Indonesian Politics: The Deployment of Adat from Colonialism to Indigenism*, edited by Jamie Davidson and David Henley. London: Routledge, 2007, 113–29.

Bourchier, David, and Vedi Hadiz, eds. *Indonesian Politics and Society: A Reader*. London: RoutledgeCurzon, 2003.

Breen, Jim. "Abdication, Succession and Japan's Imperial Future: An Emperor's Dilemma." *Asia-Pacific Journal: Japan Focus* 17 (2019): 9.

Burns, Peter. *The Leiden Legacy: Concepts of Law in Indonesia*. Leiden: KITLV, 2004.

Chandler, Nahum Dimitri. "Introduction: On the Virtues of Seeing—At Least, but Never Only—Double." *CR: The New Centennial Review* 12, no. 1 (Spring 2012): 1–39.

Chatani, Sayaka. *Nation-Empire: Ideology and Rural Youth Mobilization in Japan and Its Colonies*. Ithaca, NY: Cornell University Press, 2018.

Chen Cheng. *Land Reform in Taiwan*. Taipei: China Publishing, 1961.

Chen Yunqian. *Chongbai yu jiyi: Sun Zhongshan fuhao de jian'gou yu chuanbo*. Nanjing: Nanjing daxue chuabshe, 2009.

Chen Yun-Ru. "Family Law as a Repository of *Volksgeist*: The Germany-Japan Genealogy." *Comparative Law Review* 4, no. 2 (2013): 1–34.

Cheng Jingfu. *Sanmin zhuyi zhi lilun ji shiti jieda*. Taipei: Banyue wenyi she, 1957.

Chiang Kai-shek. *China's Destiny*. Trans. Wang Chung-hui. New York: Macmillan, 1947.

Chiang Kai-shek. *China's Destiny and Chinese Economic Theory*. New York: Roy, 1947.

Chiang Kai-shek. *Zongtong Jianggong sixiang yanlun zongji*. http://www.ccfd.org.tw/ccef001/index.php?option=com_content&view=categories&id=103&Itemid=256. Accessed April 15, 2020.

Ching Leo. *Becoming "Japanese": Colonial Taiwan and the Politics of Identity Formation*. Berkeley, CA: University of California Press, 2001.

Cho Eunjin. "The Government Specialized School System Establishment and Management in Korea during 1910s–1920s" [in Korean]. MA diss., Seoul National University, 2015.

Choi Deokhyo. "The Empire Strikes Back from Within: Colonial Liberation and the Korean Minority Question at the Birth of Postwar Japan, 1945–1947," *American Historical Review* (forthcoming).

Chu Chong-Hwan. "Ilche chosŏn t'ojijosasaŏbe kwanhan 'shingminjigŭndaehwaron' pip'an." *Critical Review of History* 47 (1999): 198–225.

Chung, Jin-A. "The Trends of the Circle of Economics in Korea and Economics Education in the College of Commerce and Economics of Yonsei University during the 20 Years after the Liberation (1945–1965)." *Korean Journal of Economics* 22, no. 3 (2015): 451–95.

Conrad, Sebastian. "'The Colonial Ties Are Liquidated': Modernization Theory, Post-War Japan and the Global Cold War." *Past & Present* 216, no. 1 (August 2012): 181–214.

Cui Shuqin. *Sanmin zhuyi xinlun*. Taipei: Taiwan shangwu yinshuguan, 1987.

Cullather, Nick. "'Fuel for the Good Dragon': The United States and Industrial Policy in Taiwan, 1950–1965." *Diplomatic History* 20 (1996): 1–25.

Cumings, Bruce. "Boundary Displacement: The State, the Foundations, and Area Studies during and after the Cold War." In *Learning Places: The Afterlives of Area Studies*, edited by Masao Miyoshi and H. D. Harootunian. Durham, NC: Duke University Press, 2002, 206–303.

Cumings, Bruce. "Japan's Position in the World System." In *Postwar Japan as History*, edited by Andrew Gordon. Berkeley, CA: University of California Press, 1993, 34–63.

Cumings, Bruce. *The Origins of the Korean War: Liberation and the Emergence of Separate Regimes, 1945–1947*. Princeton, NJ: Princeton University Press, 1981.

Cumings, Bruce. *Parallax Visions: Making Sense of American-East Asian Relations at the End of the Century*. Durham, NC: Duke University Press, 1999.

Dai Jitao. *Sun Wen zhuyi zhi zhexue de jichu*. Taipei: Zhongyang gaizao weiyuanhui wenwu gongying chu, 1951.

Dale, Peter. *The Myth of Japanese Uniqueness*. London: Routledge, 1990.

Departemen Penerangan. *Peningkatan Penerangan yang Berwibawa, Himpunan Pidato Menteri Penerangan RI 1978–82*. Jakarta: Departemen Penerangan, 1983.

Dirlik, Arif. *Culture and History in Postrevolutionary China: The Perspective of Global Modernity*. Hong Kong: Chinese University Press, 2011.

Dirlik, Arif. "T'ao Hsi-sheng: The Social Limits of Change." In *The Limits of Change: Essays on Conservative Alternatives in Republican China*, edited by Charlotte Furth. Cambridge, MA: Harvard University Press, 1976, 305–31.

Djoyoadisuryo, Subardjo. *Kesadaran Nasional: Otobiografi*. Jakarta: Gunung Agung, 1978.

Dongbei minbing sanshiwu nian (1949–1984). Shenyang: Shenyang junqu silingbu dongyuanbu, 1985.

Dornetti, Filippo. "Chiiki shakai ni okeru Manshūkoku Kyōwakai no tenkai to nōmin no dōkō: Hōten shō Bujun ken wo chūshin ni." *Mita gakkai zasshi* 110 (2017): 83–107.

Dower, John. *Embracing Defeat: Japan in the Wake of World War II*. New York: Norton, 1999.

Dower, John W. "The Useful War." *Daedalus* 119, no. 3 (Summer 1990): 49–70.

Eckert, Carter. *Park Chung-hee and Modern Korea: The Roots of Militarism, 1866–1945*. Cambridge, MA: Harvard University Press, 2016.

Eckert, Carter J. *Offspring of Empire: The Koch'ang Kims and the Colonial Origins of Korean Capitalism, 1876–1945*. Seattle: University of Washington Press, 1991.

Eckert, Carter J., Ki-Baik Lee, Young Ick Lew, Michael Robinson, and Edward W. Wagner. *Korea Old and New: A History*. Cambridge, MA: Harvard Korea Institute, 1990.

Elias, Norbert. *The Civilizing Process*. Oxford: Blackwell, 2000.

Endō Kōichi. *Tennōsei jikeishugi no seiritsu*. Tokyo: Gakubunsha, 2010.

Eubanks, Charlotte. *The Art of Persistence: Akamatsu Toshiko and the Visual Cultures of Transwar Japan*. Honolulu: University of Hawai'i Press, 2019.

Farrell, Don A. *Tinian: A Brief History*. Honolulu: Pacific Historic Parks, 2012.

Fasseur, Cees. "Colonial Dilemma." In *The Revival of Tradition in Indonesian Politics: The Deployment of Adat from Colonialism to Indigenism*, edited by Jamie Davidson and David Henley. London: Routledge, 2007, 50–67.

Feith, Herbert. *The Decline of Constitutional Democracy in Indonesia*. Ithaca, NY: Cornell University Press, 1962.

Feith, Herbert, and Lance Castles, eds. *Indonesian Political Thinking, 1945–1965*. Ithaca, NY: Cornell University Press, 1970.

Foote, Daniel H. "The Benevolent Paternalism of Japanese Criminal Justice." *California Law Review* 80, no. 2 (March 1992): 317–90.

Foucault, Michel. "Nietzsche, Genealogy, History." In *Language, Counter-Memory, Practice*, edited with an introduction by Donald F. Bouchard, translated by Donald F. Bouchard and Sherry Simon. Ithaca, NY: Cornell University Press, 1980, 139–64.

Foucault, Michel. *Society Must Be Defended: Lectures at the College de France, 1975–76*. Edited by Mauro Bertaini and Alessandro Fontana. Translated by David Macy. New York: Picador, 2003.

Fu Dazhong. *Wei Manzhouguo jun jianshi*. Changchun: Jilin wenshi chubanshe, 1999.

Fujitani Takashi. *Race for Empire: Koreans as Japanese and Japanese as Americans during World War II*. Berkeley: University of California Press, 2011.

Garland, David. *The Culture of Control: Crime and Social Order in Contemporary Society*. Chicago: University of Chicago Press, 2001.

Gayn, Mark. *Japan Diary*. New York: W. Sloane, 1948.

Gluck, Carol. *Japan's Modern Myths: Ideology in the Late Meiji Period*. Studies of the East Asian Institute. Princeton, NJ: Princeton University Press, 1985.

Gluck, Carol. "The Past in the Present." In Gordon, *Postwar Japan as History*, 64–95.

Goodman, Roger. "The 'Japanese-Style Welfare State' and the Delivery of Personal Social Services." In *The East Asian Welfare Model: Welfare Orientalism and the State*, edited by Roger Goodman, Huck-ju Kwon, and Gordon White. London: Routledge, 1998, 139–58.

Gordon, Andrew. "Conclusion." In Gordon, *Postwar Japan as History*, 449–64.

Gordon, Andrew. "Consumption, Leisure and the Middle Class in Transwar Japan." *Social Science Japan Journal*, vol. 10, no. 1 (April 2007): 1–21.

Gordon, Andrew, ed. *Postwar Japan as History*. Berkeley: University of California Press, 1993.

Gordon, Robert. "The White Man's Burden: Ersatz Customary Law and Internal Pacification in South Africa." *Journal of Historical Sociology* 2, no. 1 (1989): 41–65.

Goto Ken'ichi. *"Returning to Asia": Japan-Indonesia Relations, 1930s–1942*. Tokyo: Ryukei shosha, 1997.

Gunseikanboe. *Orang Indonesia jang terkemoeka di Djawa*. Jakarta: Gunseikanboe, 1944.

Ha Yu-Sik, and Jong-Bong Lee. "A Research on the Fluctuation of Land Ownership before Agricultural Land Reform in Wongchon-myon, Ulsan-gun." *Taegusahak* 123 (2016): 87–131.

Hall, Andrew. "The Word Is Mightier than the Throne: Bucking Colonial Education Trends in Manchukuo." *Journal of Asian Studies* 68, no. 3 (August 2009): 895–925.

Hall, John Whitney. "Changing Japanese Attitudes toward Modernization." In *Changing Japanese Attitudes toward Modernization*, edited by Marius B. Jansen. Princeton, NJ: Princeton University Press, 1965, 7–42.

Hall, John Whitney. "A Monarch for Modern Japan." In *Political Development in Modern Japan*, edited by Robert E. Ward. Princeton, NJ: Princeton University Press, 1968, 11–67.

Harootunian, Harry. 2001. "Hirohito Redux: Hirohito and the Making of Modern Japan by Herbert P. Bix." *Critical Asian Studies* 33, no. 4 (2001): 609–36.

Hasegawa Hiroaki. "Kōsei hogo ni okeru hanzai yobō katsudō no shinten: 'BBS undō' no shiteki tenkai katei." *Musashino Daigaku ningen kagaku kenkyūsho nenpō*, no. 1 (2012): 51–67.

Hayashi Fusao. *Daitōa sensō kōteiron*, vols. 1 and 2. 1964–1965. Reprint, Tokyo: Miki Shobō, 1984.

Hirata Isao. "Hogo kansatsu sho no shimei" (December 14, 1936). In *Shisōhan hogo kansatsu hō*, edited by Aomori Hogo Kansatsu Sho (1937). Reprinted in Ogino Fujio, ed., *Chianijihō kankei shiryōshū*, vol. 3. Tokyo: Shinnihon Shuppansha, 1996, 65–80.

History Net. s.v. "1946nyeon bukan toji gaehyeoge daehan beomnyeong." http://contents.history.go.kr/front/hm/view.do?treeId=020208&tabId=01&levelId=hm_157_0010. Accessed September 1, 2020.

History Net. s.v. "Yonhi Professional School." http://contents.history.go.kr/front/tg/view.do?treeId=0202&levelId=tg_004_2270&ganada=&pageUnit=10. Accessed September 1, 2020.

Hobsbawm, Eric. *Age of Extremes: A History of the World, 1914–1991*. New York: Vintage, 1996.

Hong Jong-wook. *Senjiki chōsen no tenkōsha-tachi: Teikoku/Shokuminchi no tōgō to kiretsu*. Tokyo: Yūshisha, 2011.

Hong Sung-Chan. "1940nyŏndae chŏnban ilcheŭi han'gungnongŏp chaep'yŏnch'aek." *Kuksagwan nonch'ong* 38 (1992): 205–41.

Hong Sun-Pyo. "Ilcheha migukyuhakyŏn'gu." *Kuksagwan nonch'ong* 96 (2001): 151–81.

Hook, Glenn D., and Gavan McCormack. *Japan's Contested Constitution: Documents and Analysis*. London: Routledge, 2001.

Hoseikai, ed. *Shisō hannin no hogo o chūshin to shite*. Tokyo: Hoseikai, 1935.

Hoskins, Janet Alison, and Viet Thanh Nguyen, eds. *Transpacific Studies: Framing an Emerging Field*. Honolulu: University of Hawai'i Press, 2014.

Hsu Hsueh-chi. *Gaoxiong shi Er'erba xiangguan renwu fangwen jilu*. Taipei: Academia Sinica, 1995.

Hwang Jyn-lin. *Zhanzheng, shenti, xiandaixing: Jindai Taiwan de junshi zhili yu shenti, 1895–2005*. Taipei: Lianjing, 2009.

Ikeda Yoshimasa. *Nihon ni okeru shakai fukushi no ayumi*. Kyoto: Hōken ritsu bunkasha, 1994.

Ikeda Yoshimasa. *Nihon no shakai fukushi shi*. Kyoto: Hōritsu bunka sha, 1986.

Inoue Kyoko. *MacArthur's Japanese Constitution: A Linguistic and Cultural Study of Its Making*. Chicago: Chicago University Press, 1991.

Jang Sang-Hwan. "Land Reform and Capitalist Development in Korea." In *Marxist Perspectives on South Korea in the Global Economy*, edited by Martin Hart-Landsberg, Richard Westra, and Seongjin Jeong. Aldershot: Ashgate, 2007, 157–82.

Jang Sang-Jin. "Land Reform." In *Encyclopedia of Korean Culture*. Seongnam, South Korea: Academy of Korean Studies, 1995. http://encykorea.aks.ac.kr/Contents/Index?contents_id=E0059210.

Jang Shin. "Study of Bureaucracy of the Japanese Colonial Empire." *Kokusai shinpojūmu* 30 (2008): 367–84.

Jang Si-Won. "Study on the Mode of Existence of the Large Landowners during the Colonial Period in Korea" [in Korean]. PhD diss., Seoul National University, Seoul, 1989.

Japanese Government-General of Korea. *Statistical Yearbook 1939*. Seoul: Japanese Government-General of Korea, 1939.

Japanese Government-General of Korea. *Statistical Yearbook 1943*. Seoul: Japanese Government-General of Korea, 1943.

The Jeju 4.3 Incident Investigation Report. Jeju-si: Jeju 4.3 Peace Foundation, 2014.

Jenkins, David. *Suharto and His Generals: Indonesian Military Politics, 1975–1983*. Ithaca, NY: Cornell University Press, 1984.

Jeong Miae. "A Study on the Effect of the Change of Landed Classes by Land Reform after Korean Liberation." MA diss., Ewha Womans University, Seoul, 1991.

Jiefang zhanzheng shiqi de Tonghua. Tonghua: Tonghua shiwei dangshi yanjiushi, 2000.

Johnson, Chalmers. *MITI and the Japanese Miracle: The Growth of Industrial Policy, 1925–1975*. Stanford, CA: Stanford University Press, 1983.

Johnson, Chalmers. *The Sorrows of Empire: Militarism, Secrecy, and the End of the Republic*. New York: Metropolitan Books, 2004.

Johnson, David T. "Crime and Punishment in Contemporary Japan." *Crime and Justice* 36, no. 1 (2007): 371–423.

Johnson, Elmer H. *Japanese Corrections: Managing Convicted Offenders in an Orderly Society*. Carbondale: Southern Illinois University Press, 1996.

Johnson, Elmer H., and Carol H. Johnson. *Linking Community and Corrections in Japan*. Carbondale: Southern Illinois University Press, 2000.

Kadia, Miriam Kingsberg. *Into the Field: Human Scientists of Transwar Japan*. Stanford, CA: Stanford University Press, 2020.

Kan Takayuki. "Gendai shimin shakai to shōchō tennōsei." In *Tennōsei ronshū*, vol. 1. Tokyo: Ochanomizu shobō, 2014, 174–200.

Kang Man-Gil. *Han'guksa*. Seoul: Han'gilsa, 1994.
Kang Myung-Sook. *Sarip'akkyoŭi kiwŏn*. Seoul: Communication Books, 2015.
Kang Myung-Sook. "Setting of Private College or University and Expansion of Higher Education Opportunity under the USAMGIK." *Asian Journal of Education* 4, no. 1 (2003): 155–79.
Kang Myung-Sook. "A Study on the Private Primary School in the 1910s." *Korean Journal of History of Education* 33, no. 2 (2011): 1–26.
Karatani Kojin. *History and Repetition*. Translated by Seiji Lippit. New York: Columbia University Press, 2012.
Karl, Rebecca E. "'Serve the People': An Exemplary Chinese Socialist Text of 1944." In *Reading the Postwar Future: Textual Turning Points from 1944*, edited by Kirrily Freeman and John Munro. London: Bloomsbury, 2019, 215–30.
Kartohadikoesoemo, Soetardjo. *Desa*. 1953. Bandung: Sumur Bandung, 1965.
Kartohadiprodjo, Soediman. *Beberapa pikiran sekitar Pantja Sila*. Bandung: Alumni, 1970.
Kasza, Gregory. *One World of Welfare: Japan in Comparative Perspective*. Ithaca, NY: Cornell University Press, 2006.
Kasza, Gregory. "War and Welfare Policy in Japan." *Journal of Asian Studies* 61, no. 2 (May 2002): 417–35.
Katō Michiko. "Senzen kara sengo fukkōki ni okeru hogo kansatsu seido no dōnyū to hensen." *Oyō shakaigaku kenkyū*, no. 55 (2013): 219–33.
Kawashima, Ken C. "The Obscene, Violent Supplement of State Power: Korean Welfare and Class Warfare in Interwar Japan." *Positions: East Asia Cultures Critique* 17, no. 3 (Winter 2009): 465–87, 469.
Kim Bong-jin. "Paramilitary Politics under the USAMGIK and the Establishment of the Republic of Korea." *Korea Journal* 43 (2003): 289–322.
Kim Do-Hyung. "Nationalism of Severance Medical College in Modern Korea." *Yonsei Journal of Medical History* 22 (2019): 7–33.
Kim Dong-Hwan. "A Study on the Entrance-Examination-Oriented Education in Japanese Colonized Period." *Korean Journal of Sociology of Education* 12, no. 3 (2002): 25–53.
Kim Inhan. "Land Reform in South Korea under the U.S. Military Occupation, 1945–1948." *Journal of Cold War Studies* 18, no. 2 (2016): 97–129.
Kim Jeong-In. "Han'guk sahak hyŏngsŏngŭi yŏksawa kujojŏk t'ŭksŏng." In *Sahangmunjeŭi haedabŭl mosaek'anda*, edited by Sahangmunje haegyŏrŭl wihan yŏn'guhoe. Seoul: Shilch'ŏnmunhak, 2012, 29–45.
Kim Seongho, Gyeongsik Jeon, Sanghwan Jang, and Seokdu Park. *Nongjigaehyŏksa yŏn'gu*. Seoul: Korea Rural Economic Institute, 1989.
Kim Sŏn-mi, "1930 nyŏndae migok chŏngch'aek kwa singminji chijuje ŭi chŏn'gae," *Pusan Sahak* 18 (1994).
Kim Suk Joon. *Migunjŏng shidaeŭi kukkawa haengjŏng: Pundan kukkaŭi hyŏngsŏnggwa haengjŏng ch'ejeŭi chŏngbi*. Seoul: Ewha Womans University Press, 1996.

Kim, Suzy. *Everyday Life in the North Korean Revolution, 1945–1950*. Ithaca, NY: Cornell University Press, 2013.
Kim Yong Sop. "Modern Agrarian Reforms Claimed by the Reformist in 1884–94." *Tongbanghakchi* 15 (1974): 125–95.
Kim Young-Chul, Jeong-Gyu Lee, and Gyu-Tae Kim. *An Analytical Study on Demand for Higher Education*. Seoul: Korea Educational Development Institute, 2000.
Kitaba Tsutomu. "1900nen kankahō no seitei katei ni kansuru shakai seijiteki kōsai." *Shakai fukushi kenkyū* 56, no. 3 (2015): 1–13.
Kleeman, Faye Yuan. *Under an Imperial Sun: Japanese Colonial Literature of Taiwan and the South*. Honolulu: University of Hawai'i Press, 2005.
Komagome, Takeshi. *Shokuminchi teikoku Nihon no bunka tōgō*. Tokyo: Iwanami shoten, 1996.
Komagome Takeshi, and J. A. Mangan. "Militarism, Sacrifice and Emperor Worship: The Expendable Male Body in Fascist Japanese Martial Culture." *International Journal of the History of Sport* 16 (1999): 181–204.
Kondō Masami. *Sōryokusen to Taiwan: Nihon shokuminchi hōkai no kenkyū*. Tokyo: Tōsui shobo, 1996.
Korea Democracy Foundation. *Han'gungminjuhwaundongsa 1*. Paju, South Korea: Tolbegae, 2008.
Korea Higher Education Research Institute. "Number of Universities in South Korea." *KHEI Statistics*, March 10, 2013. https://khei-khei.tistory.com/579.
Korea Higher Education Research Institute. "Number of University Students in South Korea." *KHEI Statistics*, April 11, 2013. https://khei-khei.tistory.com/585.
Korea Higher Education Research Institute. "Number of University Students in South Korea." *KHEI Statistics*, September 17, 2018. https://khei-khei.tistory.com/2279.
Korean History Society Modern History Research Unit. *Han'guk'yŏndaesa 1*. Seoul: P'ulbit, 1991.
Kōsei hogo gojūnen shi henshū iinkai, ed., *Kōsei hogo gojūnen shi: Chiiki shakai to tomo ni ayamu kōsei hogo*, vols 1 and 2. Tokyo: Zenkoku hogoshi renmei, 2000.
Kōsei hogo seido shikō jūshūnen kinen zankoku taikai jimukyoku, ed. *Kōsei hogo ronshū*. Tokyo: Kōsei hogo seido shikō jūshūnen kinen zankoku taikai jimukyoku, 1959.
Kovner, Sarah. *Occupying Power: Sex Work and Servicemen in Postwar Japan*. Stanford, CA: Stanford University Press, 2012.
Kozawa Shinkō. *Hishi Manshūkoku gun: Nikkei gunkan no yakuwari*. Tokyo: Kashiwa shobō, 1976.
Kramm, Robert. *Sanitized Sex: Regulating Prostitution, Venereal Disease, and Intimacy in Occupied Japan, 1945–1952*. Berkeley: University of California Press, 2017.
Kurasawa Aiko. "Marilah Kita Bersatu! Japanese Propaganda in Java, 1942–45." In *Asian Panorama: Essays in Asian History, Past and Present*, edited by K. M. de Silva, Sirima Kiribamune, and C. R. de Silva. New Delhi: Executive Committee, 11th Conference of the International Association of Historians, 1990, 486–97.

Kushner, Barak. "Ghosts of the Japanese Imperial Army: The 'White Group' (*Baituan*) and Early Post-war Sino-Japanese Relations." *Past & Present* 218 (2013): 117–50.

Kushner, Barak, and Sherzod Muminov, eds. *The Dismantling of Japan's Empire in East Asia: Deimperialization, Postwar Legitimation and Imperial Afterlife.* London: Routledge, 2018.

Kusuma, A. B., ed. *Lahirnya Undang-Undang Dasar 1945: Memuat Salinan Dokumen Otentik Badan Oentoek Menyelidiki Oesaha-2 Persiapan Kemerdekaan.* Jakarta: Badan Penerbit Fakultas Hukum Universitas Indonesia, 2004.

Lee, Chang Eun. "Socio-political Terms and Micro-Factors as to 'April 18th Non-violent Direct Actions' Waged by Students at Korea University—Focused on Broad Struggle Frameworks and Active Networks." *Sa-Chʻong* 71 (2010): 1–36.

Lee, Gwang Ho. "Haebangjikʻu kodŭnggyoyukkigwan sŏllip chʻujinseryŏgŭi sahoejŏk paegyŏng." *Yonsei Review of Education* 5, no. 1 (1992): 63–85.

Lee, Hui-Jei. "Capital Accumulation of Korean Landlord in Colonial Period." MA diss., Yonsei University, Seoul, 2000.

Lee, Ki-Hoon. "Avison and Higher Education under Japanese Occupation." *Yonsei Journal of Medical History* 13, no. 1 (2010): 15–25.

Lee, Sang-Chul. "The Analysis of Amendment Process and Major Contents of Private School Law." *Journal of Educational Administration* 24, no. 1 (2006): 197–224.

Lee, Se-Young. "The Structural Change of Landownership in Naeseo-myeon Changweon-gun Gyeongsangnam-do from 1910 to 1945." *Journal of Korean History* 21 (2007): 5–73.

Lev, Daniel. "Colonial Law and the Genesis of the Indonesian State." *Indonesia* 40 (1985): 57–74.

Levine, Steven. *Anvil of Victory: The Communist Revolution in Manchuria, 1945–1948.* New York: Columbia University Press, 1987.

Lewis, Michael. *Rioters and Citizens: Mass Protest in Imperial Japan.* Berkeley: University of California Press, 1990.

Lin, Cheng-hui. *Taiwan kejia de xingsu licheng: Qing dai zhi zhanhou de zhuisuo.* Taipei: Guoli Taiwan daxue chuban zhongxin, 2015.

Lin, Jiwen. *Riben juTai moqi (1930–1945): zhanzheng dongyuan tixi zhi yanjiu.* Taipei: Daoxiang, 1996.

Lin, Pei-Yin, and Su Yun Kim. "Introduction." In *East Asian Transwar Popular Culture: Literature and Film from Taiwan and Korea*, edited by Pei-Yin Lin and Su Yun Kim. Singapore: Palgrave Macmillan, 2019, 1–20.

Lipsitz, George. "'Frantic to Join ... the Japanese Army': Black Soldiers and Civilians Confront the Asia-Pacific War." In *Perilous Memories: The Asia-Pacific War(s)*, edited by T. Fujitani, Geoffrey W. White, and Lisa Yoneyama. Durham, NC: Duke University Press, 2001, 347–77.

Liu, Hsi-ming. *Weijun: Qiangquan jingzhu xia de zuzi (1937–1949).* Taipei: Daoxiang, 2011.'

Liu, Jennifer. "Indoctrinating the Youth: Guomindang Policy on Secondary Education in Wartime China and Postwar Taiwan, 1937–1960." PhD diss., University of California, Irvine, 2010.

Liu Xiuru. *Sanmin zhuyi jiaocheng*. Chongqing: Zhengzhong shuju, 1943.

Louzon, Victor. "Colonial Legacy and War Aftermaths in Taiwan, 1945–1947." In *In the Ruins of the Japanese Empire: Imperial Violence, State Destruction, and the Reordering of Modern East Asia*, edited by Barak Kushner and Andrew Levidis. Hong Kong: Hong Kong University Press, 2020, 76–97.

Louzon, Victor. "From Japanese Soldierrs to Chinese Rebels: War Experience and Remobilization during the 1947 Taiwanese Rebellion." *Journal of Asian Studies* 77 (2018): 161–79.

Lowe, Lisa. *Intimacies of Four Continents*. Durham, NC: Duke University Press, 2015.

Lü Fangshang. *Jiang Zhongzheng xiansheng nianpu changbian*. Taipei: Guoshiguan, Guoli Zhongzheng jiniantang guanlichu and Caituan faren Zhongzheng wenjiao jijin hui, 2015.

Lyons, Adam. "From Marxism to Religion: Thought Crimes and Forced Conversions in Imperial Japan." *Japanese Journal of Religious Studies* 46, no. 2 (2019): 193–218.

Ma, Tehyun. "Making Taiwan Chinese, 1945–60." In *Routledge Handbook of Revolutionary China*, edited by Alan Baumler. London: Routledge, 2019, 202–16.

Man, Simeon. *Soldiering through Empire: Race and the Making of the Decolonizing Pacific*. Berkeley: University of California Press, 2018.

Mandel, Ernest. *The Meaning of the Second World War*. Verso: London, 1986.

"Manshū-Manshūkoku" kyōiku shiryō shūsei. Tokyo: Emuti shuppan, 1993.

Mark, Ethan. "'Asia's' Transwar Lineage: Nationalism, Marxism, and 'Greater Asia' in an Indonesian Inflection." *Journal of Asian Studies* 65, no. 3 (August 2006): 461–93.

Marotti, William. *Money, Trains, and Guillotines: Art and Revolution in 1960s Japan*. Durham, NC: Duke University Press, 2013.

Matsuda Toshihiko. *Senzenki no Zainichi Chōsenjin to sanseiken*. Tokyo: Akashi Shoten, 1995.

McCormack, Gavan. *Client State: Japan in American Embrace*. London: Verso, 2007.

Mizuno, Hiromi, Aaron S. Moore, and John DiMoia, eds. *Engineering Asia: Technology, Colonial Development, and the Cold War Order*. London: Bloomsbury, 2020.

Moon, So-Jeong. "Formation of Japanese Landlordism under the Korean Empire" [in Korean]. *Han'guksahoesahak'oenonmunjip* 2 (1986): 57–79.

Moore, Aaron S. *Constructing East Asia: Technology, Ideology, and Empire in Japan's Wartime Era, 1931–1945*. Stanford, CA: Stanford University Press, 2013.

Morfit, Michael. "Pancasila: The Indonesian State Ideology According to the New Order Government." *Asian Survey* 21, no. 8 (1981): 838–51.

Moriya Katsuhiko. *Shōnen no hikō to kyōiku: Shōnen hōsei no rekishi to genjō*. Tokyo: Keisōshobō, 1977.

Moriyama Takeichirō. *Shisōhan hogo kansatsu hō kaisetsu*. Tokyo: Shōkadō shoten, 1937.

Morrow, Robert B., and Kenneth H. Sherper. *Land Reform in South Korea*. Washington, DC: Agency for International Development, 1970.

Najita, Tetsuo, and H. Harootunian. "Japanese Revolt against the West: Political and Cultural Criticism in the Twentieth Century." In *The Cambridge History of Japan*, vol. 6, edited by Peter Duus. Cambridge: Cambridge University Press, 1989, 711–74.

Nakamura, Takafusa. "Depression, Recovery and War, 1920–1945." In *Cambridge History of Japan, vol. 6: The Twentieth Century*, edited by Peter Duus. Cambridge: Cambridge University Press, 1988, 451–93.

Nakazawa Shunsuke. *Chianijihō: Naze seitō seiji ha 'akuhō' o unda ka*. Tokyo: Chūōkōron shinsho, 2012.

Nasution, Adnan Buyung. *The Aspiration for Constitutional Government in Indonesia: A Socio-legal Study of the Indonesian Konstituante 1956–1959*. Jakarta: Pustaka Sinar Harapan, 1992.

National Institute of Korean History. *New Edition of Koran History 47*. Gwacheon, South Korea: National Institute of Korean History, 2001.

Ogawa Tarō. "Hogo kansatsu no shakaiteki kiso." In *Kōsei hogo seido shikō jūshūnen kinen zankoku taikai jimukyoku*, ed., 63–71, 1959.

Ogawa Tarō. *Hogo kansatsu seido ni tsuite*. Tokyo: Hōmukenshūjo, 1954.

Ogino Fujio, ed. *Chianijihō kankei shiryōshū*, 4 vols. Tokyo: Shinnihon shuppansha, 1996.

Ogino Fujio. *Shisō kenji*. Tokyo: Iwanami shoten, 2000.

Oguma Eiji. *A Genealogy of "Japanese" Self-Images*. Translated by David Askew. Melbourne: TransPacific, 2002.

Oh, Do Young. "The University and East Asian Cities: The Variegated Origins of Urban Universities in Colonial Seoul and Singapore." *Journal of Urban History*, July 20, 2020 (published electronically). doi:10.1177/0096144220941199.

Oh, Ookwhan. *Han'guksahoeŭi kyoyukyŏl: Kiwŏn'gwa shimhwa*. Seoul: Kyoyukkwahaksa, 2000.

Oh, Seong Cheol. *Shingminji ch'odŭnggyoyuguŭi hyŏngsŏng*. Seoul: Kyoyukkwahaksa, 2000.

Oh, Seong Cheol. "Shingminjigiŭi kyoyukchŏk yusan." *History of Education* 8 (1998): 221–44.

Oh, Sung-Bae. "Exploration of Private University Expansion Process: Based on Land Reform after the Liberation." *Journal of Korean Education* 31, no. 3 (2004): 53–73.

Okudaira Yasuhiro. "Nihonkoku kempō to 'uchi naru tennōsei.'" *Sekai*, no. 523 (January 1989): 111–30.

Okudaira Yasuhiro. *Chianijihō shōshi*, new ed. Tokyo: Iwanami shoten, 2006.

Onishi, Yuichiro, and Fumiko Sakashita, eds. *Transpacific Correspondences: Dispatches from Japan's Black Studies*. Cham: Springer International; Imprint: Palgrave Macmillan, 2019.

Ōtsubo Yoichi. *Kōsei hogo no seiritsu*. Tokyo: Nihon kōsei hogo kyōkai, 1996.

Palmer, Brandon. *Fighting for the Enemy: Koreans in Japan's War, 1937–1945*. Seattle: University of Washington Press, 2013.

Park, Chan-Seung. *The Writing of Korean History in the 21st Century*. Seoul: Hanyang University Press, 2019.

Park, Jhungsoo, Heejung Hong, and Hyunjung Lee. *Taehaktŭngnokkŭm munjewa taehakchaejŏngjiwŏnjŏngch'aek kaesŏnbangan*. Seoul: National Assembly Budget Office, 2009.

Park, Keong-Suk. "Population Dynamics of Korea during the Colonialization Period (1910–1945)." *Korea Journal of Population Studies* 32, no. 2 (2009): 29–58.

Park, Myungho. *Land Reform in Korea*. Sejong, South Korea: Korea Ministry of Strategy and Finance, 2013.

Pavone, Claudio. *Alle origini della Repubblica. Scritti su fascismo, antifascismo e continuità dello Stato*. Turin: Bollati Boringhieri, 1995.

Qu Wanwen. *Taiwan zhanhou jingji fazhan de yuanqi: houjin fazhan de weihe yu ruhe*. Taipei: Lianjing, 2017.

Reeve, David. *Golkar of Indonesia: An Alternative to the Party System*. Singapore: Oxford University Press, 1985.

Rehabilitation Bureau. *Non-institutional Treatment of Offenders in Japan*. Tokyo: Ministry of Justice Rehabilitation Bureau, 1974.

Reischauer, Edwin O. "What Went Wrong?" In *Dilemmas of Growth in Prewar Japan*, edited by James W. Morley. Princeton, NJ: Princeton University Press, 1971, 489–510.

Rensei no michi: kokumin rensei no shidō ni tsuite. Taipei: Taiwan sōtokufu kokumin seishin kenkyūjo, 1942.

Renshō no kōgun. Taipei: Taiwan sōtokufu bunkyōkyoku shakaika, 1937.

Rose, Mavis. *Indonesia Free: A Political Biography of Mohammad Hatta*. Cornell Modern Indonesia Project Monograph Series 67. Ithaca, NY: Cornell University Press, 1987.

Ruoff, Kenneth. *Japan's Imperial House in the Postwar Era, 1945–2019*. Cambridge, MA: Harvard University Press, 2020.

Saiseikai, ed. *Onshi zaidan saiseikai shi*. Tokyo: Saiseikai, 1937.

Sansom, Brenda. "'Minsheng' and National Liberation: Socialist Theory in the Guomindang, 1919–1931." PhD diss., University of Wisconsin–Madison, 1988.

Saranillio, Dean Itsuji. *Unsustainable Empire: Alternative Histories of Hawai'i Statehood*. Durham, NC: Duke University Press, 2018.

Sawyer, Robert. *Military Advisors in Korea: KMAG in Peace and War*. Washington, DC: Center of Military History, 1962.

Schmid, Andre. "Colonialism and the 'Korea Problem' in the Historiography of Modern Japan: A Review Article." *Journal of Asian Studies* 59, no. 4 (2000): 951–76.
Sekiya Teisaburō. *Kōshitsu to shakaijigyō*. Tokyo: Chūō shakai jigyō kyōkai, 1934.
Seo, Chan Su. "Han'gugŭi injŏkchabonch'ukchŏkkwajŏnggwa kŭ yoin." *Journal of Korean National Economy* 5 (1987): 69–90.
Seth, Michael J. *Education Fever: Society, Politics, and the Pursuit of Schooling in South Korea*. Honolulu: University of Hawai'i Press, 2002.
Shigematsu Setsu and Keith L. Camacho, eds. *Militarized Currents: Toward a Decolonized Future in Asia and the Pacific*. Minneapolis: University of Minnesota Press, 2010.
Shigeta Shinji. *"Aku" to tōchi no Nihon kindai: Dōtoku, shūkyō, kangoku kyōkai*. Tokyo: Hōzōkan, 2019.
Shikita Minoru and Shinichi Tsuchiya. *Crime and Criminal Policy in Japan: Analysis and Evaluation of the Showa Era, 1926–1988*. New York: Springer-Verlag, 1992.
Shimabuku, Annmaria M. *Alegal: Biopolitics and the Unintelligibility of Okinawan Life*. New York: Fordham University Press, 2019.
Shimizu Ryōtarō. "Manshūkoku tōchi kikō ni okeru senden/senfu kōsaku." *Senshi kenkyū nenpō* 17 (2014): 49–75.
Shin, Gi-Wook. *Peasant Protest and Social Change in Colonial Korea*. Seattle: University of Washington Press, 2014.
Shirane, Seiji. "Mediated Empire: Colonial Taiwan in Japan's Imperial Expansion into South China and Southeast Asia, 1895–1945." PhD diss., Princeton University, 2014.
Sjahrir, Sutan. *Indonesische Overpeinzingen*. Written under the pseudonym Sjahrazad. Amsterdam: De Bezige Bij, 1948.
Smallwood, Stephanie. *Saltwater Slavery: A Middle Passage from Africa to the American Diaspora*. Cambridge, MA: Harvard University Press, 2009.
Soebagijo, I. N., ed. *Mr. Sudjono, Mendarat dengan Pasukan Jepang di Banten 1942*. Jakarta: Gunung Agung, 1983.
Soegomo, Yoga. *Perbandingan antara Demokrasi Eropa dan Demokrasi Pancasila di Indonesia sebagai Subyek Penelitian Demokrasi*. Jakarta: Pustaka Kartini/PT Sarana Bakti Semesta, 1986.
Soeharto. *Soeharto: Pikiran, Ucapan dan Tindakan Saya*. Autobiography, as told to G. Dwipayana and K. H. Ramandan. Jakarta: PT Citra Lantoro Gung Persada, 1988.
Song, Seun-Won. "Back to Basics in Indonesia? Reassessing the Pancasila and Pancasila State and Society, 1945–2007." Unpublished PhD diss., College of Arts and Sciences, Ohio University, Athens, 2008.
Sōtei dokuhon. Taipei: Taiwan sōtokufu, 1944.
Steinhoff, Patricia. *Tenkō: Ideology and Societal Integration in Prewar Japan*. New York: Garland, 1999.
Stoler, Ann Laura. "Imperial Debris: Reflections on Ruins and Ruination." *Cultural Anthropolgy* 23, no. 2 (2008): 191–219.

Strauss, Julia C. "Campaigns of Redistribution: Land Reform and State Building in China and Taiwan, 1950–1953." In *States in the Developing World*, edited by Miguel A. Centeno, Atul Kohli, and Deborah J. Yashar. Cambridge: Cambridge University Press, 2017, 339–62.

Strawn, Perri Johanna. "Teaching Nationalism in the Crucible: Changing Identities in Taiwan High Schools after Martial Law." PhD diss., Yale University, 1999.

Sun, Bang, ed. *WeiMan fuwang*. Changchun: Jilin renmin chubanshe, 1993.

Sun Yat-sen. *San Min Chu I: The Three Principles of the People*. Chungking: Ministry of Information of the Republic of China, 1943.

Sutjipto. *Tumbuhnya Tunas Baru diatas Humus dari Daun Tua-Kering jang Berguguran: Sebuah Capita Selecta*. Jakarta: Penerbit Fakta, 1967.

Szonyi, Michael. *Cold War Island: Quemoy on the Frontline*. New York: Cambridge University Press, 2008.

Taiwan no shakai kyōiku. Taipei: Taiwan sōtokufu, 1942.

Takahashi Mutsuko. *The Emergence of Welfare Society in Japan*. Aldershot: Avebury, 1997.

Tang, Xiyong. "Tuoli kunjing: zhanhou chuqi Hainandao zhi Taiwanren de fanTai." *Taiwan shi yanjiu* 12 (2005): 167–208.

Tao Jinsheng. *Tao Xisheng riji: Zhongguo minguo lizu Tai, Peng, Jin, Ma de lishi jianzheng*. Taipei: Lianjing, 2014.

Tao Tailai and Tao Jinsheng. *Tao Xisheng nianbiao*. Taipei: Lianjing, 2017.

Tao Xisheng. *Chaoliu yu diandi*. Taipei: Zhuanji wenxue chubanshe, 1964.

Tertitskiy, Fyodor. "Study of Soviet Influence on the Formation of the North Korean Army." *Acta Koreana* 20, no. 1 (2017): 195–219.

Tikhonov, Vladimir. "Militarism and Anti-militarism in South Korea: 'Militarized Masculinity' and the Conscientious Objector Movement." *Japan Focus* 7, no. 12 (2009): https://apjjf.org/-Vladimir-Tikhonov/3087/article.html.

Ts'ai, Hui-yu, ed. *Zou guo liang ge shidai de ren: Taiwan Riben bing*. Taipei: Academia Sinica, 2008.

Tsui, Brian. *China's Conservative Revolution: The Quest for a New Order*. Cambridge: Cambridge University Press, 2018.

Tsuji Zennosuke. *Nihon kōshitsu to shakaijigyō*. Tokyo: Sekijūjisha, 1934.

Tu, Kuo-ch'ing, and Terence Russell, eds. *Taiwan Literature: English Translation Series* 37 (2016).

Uchida Hirofumi. *Kōsei hogo no tenkai to kadai*. Kyoto: Hōritsu bunkasha, 2015.

US Department of State, Division of Research for Far East. *The Redistribution of Korean-Owned Farm Lands in South Korea*, OIR Report No. 4863 (preliminary version), 1948. http://archive.history.go.kr/image/viewer.do?system_id=000001041487.

Usui Shigeru. *Nan Manshū no nōson*. Tokyo: Chijin shokan, 1940.

Wakabayashi Masahiro. *Taiwan no seiji: Chûka Minkoku Taiwan-ka no sengoshi*. Tokyo: Tôkyô daigaku shuppankai, 2008.

Wang, Chaoguang. *He yu zhan de jueze: Zhanhou Guomindang de Dongbei juece.* Beijing: Renmin daxue chubanshe, 2016.
Wang Hui. *The Politics of Imagining Asia.* Cambridge, MA: Harvard University Press, 2011.
Ward, Ken. "Soeharto's Javanese Pancasila." In *Soeharto's New Order and Its Legacy: Essays in Honour of Harold Crouch*, edited by Edward Aspinall and Greg Fealy. Asian Studies Monograph 2. Canberra: ANU E-Press, 2010, 27–38.
Ward, Max. *Thought Crime: Ideology and State Power in Interwar Japan.* Durham, NC: Duke University Press, 2019.
Westad, Odd Arne. *The Global Cold War: Third World Interventions and the Making of Our Times.* Cambridge: Cambridge University Press, 2005.
Watanabe Ikujirō. *Kōshitsu to shakai mondai.* Tokyo: Bunsensha, 1925.
Wo suo zhidao de Wei Man zhengquan. Beijing: Zhongguo wenshi chubanshe, 2017.
Xin shi zhengjun yundong. Beijing: Jiefangjun chubanshe, 1995.
Xu Zhaorong. *Taiji laobing de xie lei hen.* Taipei: Qianwei, 1995.
Yamamoto Yūzō. "Shakai-kyoku secchi keika ni tsuite." *Tokyo kasei Daigaku kenkyū kiyō* 36, no. 1 (1996): 213–22.
Yanase Taizō. "Shikkō yūyo no hogo kansatsu ni tsuite." In *Kōsei hogo seido shikō jūshūnen kinen zankoku taikai jimukyoku*, ed., 1959, 243–54.
Yang Jonghoe. "Colonial Legacy and Modern Economic Growth in Korea: A Critical Examination of Their Relationships." *Development and Society* 33, no. 1 (June 2004): 1–24.
Yasumaru Yoshio. *Kindai tennō-zō no keisei.* Tokyo: Iwanami, 2017.
Ying, Feng-Huang. "Reassessing Taiwan's Literary Field of the 1950s." PhD diss., University of Texas at Austin, 2000.
Ying, Feng-Huang. *Wuling niandai wenxue chuban xianying.* Taipei County: Taibei xian wenhua ju, 2006.
Yoneyama, Lisa. *Cold War Ruins: Transpacific Critique of American Justice and Japanese War Crimes.* Durham, NC: Duke University Press, 2016.
Yoshida Kyūichi. *Nihon shakai jigyō no rekishi.* Tokyo: Keisō shobō, 1989.
Yoshimi Shunya. "The Cultural Politics of the Mass-Mediated Emperor System in Japan." In *Without Guarantees: In Honour of Stuart Hall*, edited by Paul Gilroy, Lawrence Grossberg, and Angela McRobbie. New York: Verso, 2000, 395–415.
Yoshino Kosaku. *Cultural Nationalism in Contemporary Japan: A Sociological Enquiry.* London: Routledge, 1992.
Young, Louise. "When Fascism Met Empire in Japanese-Occupied Manchuria." *Journal of Global History* 12, no. 2 (2017): 274–96.
Yun, Hae-Dong. *Shingminjiŭi hoesaekchidae.* Seoul: Yŏksabip'yŏnsa, 2003.
Zanasi, Margherita. *Saving the Nation: Economic Modernity in Republican China.* Chicago: University of Chicago Press, 2006.

Zennihon shihō hogo jigyō renmei. *Shihō hogo jigyō hō no hanashi.* Tokyo: Zennihon shihō hogo jigyō renmei, 1939.

Zheyin shenshen: yi ge Wei Man junguan de riji. Changchun: Jilin sheng zhengxie wenshiziliao weiyuanhui, 2011.

Newspapers

Chosŏn Ilbo. June 24, 1920; August 6, 1948; September 16, 1949; May 15, 1953; June 8, 1953.

Han'gyore 21. July 25, 2016.

Japan Times. June 19, 2019.

Kyŏng Hyang Sinmun. May 8, 1953; June 19, 2019.

The Mainichi. May 2, 2019.

Mainichi shimbun. December 19, 2018.

Manila Chronicle. February 3, 1948.

New York Times. July 22, 1945; September 21, 1952.

Newstapa. July 25, 2019. https://newstapa.org/article/xTHN6.

Ohmynews. August 5, 2009. http://www.ohmynews.com/NWS_Web/View/at_pg.aspx?CNTN_CD=A0001190266.

Tonga Ilbo. March 12, 1928; January 21, 1949; May 19, 1955; December 21, 1956; March 26, 1957; January 21, 1969; May 9, 1974.

Contributors

David Bourchier is an associate professor at the University of Western Australia where he teaches Indonesian and Asian studies. A graduate of Monash University, he has published widely on contemporary Indonesian politics, law, and ideology and is currently working on the history of liberalism in Indonesia.

Takashi Fujitani holds the Dr. David Chu Chair in Asia Pacific Studies at the University of Toronto, where he is also Professor of History. His major works include *Splendid Monarchy* (1996); *Race for Empire: Koreans as Japanese and Japanese as Americans during WWII* (2011); and *Perilous Memories: The Asia Pacific War(s)* (coedited, 2001). He is editor of the book series Asia Pacific Modern and has held numerous fellowships, including from the John S. Guggenheim Foundation. He is currently working on several books, including *Whose "Good War"? A Postnationalist History of WWII in the Asia-Pacific* and *Cold War Clint: Asians, "Indians" and Others in an American Political (Un)conscious*.

Reto Hofmann is a senior lecturer in Asian Studies at the University of Western Australia. He specializes in modern Japanese and international history. His first monograph was titled *The Fascist Effect: Japan and Italy, 1915–1952* (2015). His research on fascism, empire, and war has been published in the *Journal of Contemporary History*, *Journal of Global History*, *Japan Forum*, and *Journal of Asian Studies*. Hofmann is currently writing a transwar history of right-wing politics entitled *Afterlives of Empire: The Right and the Making of Postwar Japan*.

Victor Louzon is an assistant professor in East Asian history at Sorbonne University, Paris. His current work focuses on militarization and violence in twentieth-century Greater China, with a particular interest in areas of contact between Chinese nationalism and the Japanese empire. He has published on postwar Taiwan and East Asia, as well as on the political uses of the past in the region. He is now working on a book manuscript on colonial legacies, wartime memories, and political violence during the February 28 incident in 1947 in Taiwan.

Yumi Moon is an associate professor in the Department of History at Stanford University. She is the author of *Populist Collaborators: The Ilchinhoe and the Japanese Colonization of Korea, 1896–1910* (Cornell University Press, 2013; Japanese translation published by Akashi Shoten, 2018). She is currently writing a book on Korea's transition from the wartime colonial period to the

US Occupation, tentatively entitled *Toward a Free State: Imperial Shift and the Making of Postwar South Korea, 1937–1950*.

Do Young Oh is a research assistant professor at the School of Graduate Studies, Lingnan University, Hong Kong. He was previously a research officer, based jointly at the Saw Swee Hock Southeast Asia Centre and the Middle East Centre at the London School of Economics and Political Science, where he finished his PhD in regional and urban planning. His research interests focus on comparative urbanism and postcolonialism in East Asia. His doctoral thesis investigated the evolving university–city relationship through a comparative analysis of East Asian urbanization processes and was short-listed for the biennial ICAS Book Prize in 2019 (Dissertation in the Social Sciences). Oh has published in major international journals, including the *Journal of Urban History* and *Cities*.

Brian Tsui is an associate professor at the Department of Chinese Culture, the Hong Kong Polytechnic University. He studies modern Chinese revolutionary politics on the left and the right and their influences on domestic and international politics. Along with journal articles, his works include the monograph *China's Conservative Revolution: The Search for a New Order, 1927–1949* (2018). He is also coeditor, with Tansen Sen, of the forthcoming volume *Beyond Pan-Asianism: Connecting China and India, 1840s–1960s*. Tsui is working on how influential cultural and religious figures outside the Chinese mainland understood and sympathized with the People's Republic in the 1950s and 1960s.

Max Ward is an associate professor of Japanese History at Middlebury College, Vermont, author of *Thought Crime: Ideology and State Power in Interwar Japan* (2019), and coeditor of *Confronting Capital and Empire: Rethinking Kyoto School Philosophy* (2017). He has written on various topics related to Japan and social theory, including Japanese fascism, postwar Japanese cinema, postcolonial theory, and policing in Imperial Japan, and is currently working on a new book tentatively titled *Police Power in Modern Japan*.

Colleen Woods is an associate professor of History at the University of Maryland. Her research focuses on US imperial history, war and transnational politics, decolonization, and global imperial history. Her first book, *Freedom Incorporated: American Imperialism and Decolonization in the Age of Philippine Independence*, was published in May 2020. She has also published pieces in the *Journal of Contemporary History*, *LABOR: Studies of Working-Class History*, and the *Companion to U.S. Foreign Relations, Colonial Era to the Present*. Woods is currently working on a second project that will bring together histories of US foreign affairs, labor, and capitalism through a study of US military and military contractors' recruitment of and reliance on low-wage Filipino labor in the postwar Pacific.

Index

allied forces, 20
American Federation of Labor (AFL), 81
American sponsors, Guomindang (GMD), 127
anti-colonialism, 62, 125
anti-communism, 108, 125, 128
anti-imperialism, 68
anti-Japanese resistance, 60
April Revolution, 116
asset-accumulating behaviors, 101

Bill, Bacon, 79
black markets, 28
Blitzkrieg, 25, 27
British Empire, 52
British Labour Party, 138
Bureau of Agricultural Affairs, Northern Kyongsang Province, 27
Burnham, Daniel, 83
bushido spirit, 57

caciquism, 81
catechism, 135
Cavite Naval Yard, 81
Children Army, 55
Children Corps, 55
China's anti-Japanese resistance, 134
China's Destiny, 134–138
China Youth Anti-Communist Corps, 128
Chinese Civil War, 107, 125, 126
Chinese Communist Party (CCP), 62–64, 129
Chinese Literary Association, 129
Chinese youth organizations, 55
Chinese Youth Writing Association, 129
Chosen Christian College, 108
CINCFE, 85, 91
civil war, 63–64
Cold War, 49, 62, 68, 70, 77, 82, 107
    American Empire, 78
    expansion, 85–88

geopolitics, 127
    Indonesia, 147
    violence, 88
collaboration, 70
colonialism, 17, 19, 38
    capitalism, 104
    colonial government, 22, 26, 27, 28
    educators, 110
    government, 105
    higher education, 105–107
    labor, 78–81
    militarism (*See* militarism, colonial)
    soldiers, 61
Commonwealth, 80
communism, 126, 127, 133, 138
Communist Party of Korea, 108
CONCOR, 84
confucianism, 139
conservative revolution, China, 125, 128
    communism, 131
    Marxism, 131
    regional hegemon, 127
    reorientation, 137–141
    Second Sino-Japanese War, 128
    Soviet Russia, 131
constitutionalism, 148, 160
conversion, 58, 178
corporatism, 133
criminal justice systems, 170
criminal reform, Japan, 177–178
    imperial benevolence, 177–178
    laws, 182
    Memorial Day, 182
    recalibration, 180–182
    symbolic emperor, 184–186
criminal rehabilitation, 174–177
    wartime consolidation, 178–180
cross-strait standoff, 68
Cui Shuqin, 130, 131
cultural policy, 57, 106
Cumings, Bruce, 108

Dai Jitao, 133
Declaration of Humanity, 183
decolonization, 17
demobilization, 61
democracy, 18, 83, 126, 148, 157–158, 162, 169, 181
Department of Defense (DOD), United States, 90
depression, economic, 35, 82
developmentalism, 160

Educational Foundation Association, 112, 113
Education Committee, 110
Europe, 147, 151–152, 155
explicit colonial rule, 80
exploitation, 49, 103, 131
extraterritoriality, 57

families consumption, 35
Far East Air Forces, 86
Farmland Reform Act, 1949, Korea, 112
February Eighth Movement, Korea, 107
February 28 Incident, Taiwan, 66
Fengtian Province, 55
Filipino labor, 77, 82
Finance and Agricultural Buildings, 83
First Sino-Japanese War, 50
food
    crisis, 17, 34
    Food Administration Bureau, 36
    Food Control Law, 21, 26
    management, 25
    supply, 21
Forbes planned social reform, 139
Free China, 125, 128, 130
free world, 127
Fujian Province, 127

gemeinschaft capitalism, 183
General Headquarters (GHQ), 29, 180
Government-General of Korea (GGK), 53
Government-General of Taiwan (GGT), 51
grains, 25
Greater Indonesia Unity Party (PIR), 157
Guadalcanal Campaign, 20
Guided Democracy, 148
Guomindang (GMD), 125, 127

Chinese Communist Party (CCP), 129
Cold War, 130
land reform, 132
minsheng, 130
rule, 125
social-building strategies, 127
supplement, 136
Taiwan, 126, 128
Three People's Principles, 126
youth movement, 137

higher education, 60, 101, 102, 105–107, 116
human rights, 181
hypermilitarism, 49, 53, 59

immigration policies, 86
Imperial Army, Japan, 53, 54, 56
imperial benevolence, 172–174, 177–178
    criminal justice reforms, 176
    criminal reform, 177–178
    state relief, 172–174
    symbolic emperor system, 182–184
    welfare, 177–178
imperialization, 59
    Japan, 107
    militaristic program, 60
    network, 21
    subject, 60
Indonesia
    Cold War, 147
    indigenous democracy, 157
    integralist, 148
    philosophies, 148
    Supomo, 154–156
industrialization, 138
International Confederation of Free Trade Unions, 91

Japan
    China, 170
    cultural nationalism, 147
    Empire, 17, 19, 38
    government, 21
    Government-General of Korea (GGK), 53
    imperialism, 50
    Korea, 30–31, 51, 53
    Manchuria, 20

militarism, 49
political culture, 49
rice farmers, 21
Savigny concept, 151–154
spirit, 58, 67
Taiwan, 51, 54
wartime administration, 17
welfare state, 170
Joseon Dynasty, 103, 107
June Democratic Uprising, 116
Juvenile Law, 180

Kangwon provincial government, 25
Kasza, Gregory, 170
Kazushige, Ugaki, 20
Keijo Imperial University, 105
Kingly Way, 56
kominka. *See* Imperialization
Konkuk University, 114
Korea, 17
    food management in, 25
    independence of, 19
    Japan, 20, 30–31
    Japanese imperial market, 19
    Manchuria, 20
    population, 106
    revolution, 18
    rice-control policies, 21
    Rice Market Company, 23, 24, 25
    rice production program, 19, 20
    Taiwan, 55
    University, 103, 111
    US occupation, 19
    War, 109, 111
Korea Democratic Party, 108, 110
Korea Foodstuff Control Corporation, 29
Korean Committee on Education, 110
Korean Commodity Company, 30
Korean Democratic Party, 32
Korean Food Company, 25, 26
Kwangmu Land Reform, 103
Kyonggi provincial government, 22
Kyongsang region, 109
Kyongsong Spinning, 105

labor complaints, 90
landed aristocracy, 103, 104, 106, 107
landlords, 19, 69
land reform

Farmland Reform Act of 1949, 112
Free China, 130
Provisional People's Committee of
    North Korea, 108
South Korea, 108–109
Taiwan, 129, 132
USAMGIK, 108
Leiden School, 147
Luzon Stevedore Company, 87

MacArthur, Douglas, 18, 84
Manchukuo
    Army, 53, 54, 58
    Manchukuo Military Academy
        (MMA), 58
    youth, 55
Manchuria, 20, 63–64
market price, 22–23
martialism
    nature, 51
    races, 52
    virtues, 52
Marxism, 126
maturity, 80
Meiji Constitution, 51
militarism, colonial, 49
    first wave, 50–53
    second wave, 53–56
    third wave, 61–63
militaristic-imperial program, 55,
    56, 69
militarization, 50, 57, 59
Military Law Academy, 160
Ministry of Agriculture, 25
minsheng, 133

naichijin, 57
Nanjing Decade, 129
Naomasa, Mizuta, 21
National Army, 66, 67
National Assembly, 109, 116
Nationalist China, 126
National Taiwan University, 128
nativism, 160
neighborhood associations, 26, 32
New Armies, 51
New Life Movement Chiang, 128
Northern China, 21
nuclear bombs, 35

occupational hazards, 88–93
October Harvest Uprising, 35, 38
Ohio-based Goodyear Tire Company, 78

Pacific War, 17, 20, 21, 26, 27, 83
Paik, George L., 107
paramilitary organizations, 54
patriarchal family system, 139
patriotic neighborhood associations, 27
People's Republic of China (PRC), 58
People's Republic of Korea, 19
Philippine civil service, 80
Philippine independence, 85, 88
Philippine-Ryukyus Command (PHILRYCOM), 85
Philippines William Cameron Forbes, 80
Philippine War Relief Inc. (PWR), 82
Posong Professional School, 105
postwar
　criminal reform, 184–186
　criminal reform system, 78, 170
　social welfare system, 182
　symbolic emperor, 184–186
　Volksgeist-ism, 156–159
price
　control, 22–23
　official price, 22–23
private universities, 101, 111
professional schools, 106
pro-Japanese collaborators, 19
provincial cooperative, 23
provincial food-ration cooperative, 23
Provisional People's Committee of North Korea, 108
public schools, 104

Qing Empire, 51

race, 53, 81–82, 94
Red Peasant Union movements, 37
rehabilitation, 170–171, 174
religious institutions, 113
Republic of China (ROC), 58, 125–126
　Chiang Ching-kuo, 142
　Guomindang, 125
　supplement, 126
　Taiwan, 127
　Three People's Principles, 126
Resolution Committees, 66–67

rice
　accounting system, 26
　collection, 25, 27, 30, 31, 36, 38, 39, 40
　cooperative, 22
　crisis, 17, 32
　famine, 22
　Japan, 20
　owners, 22
　rationing, 30–31, 33
　rice collection campaigns, 27
　rice-rationing system, 26
　Rice Taskforce Committee, 33
　traders, 22, 23
Rosenberg, Edward, 81
rubber industry, 79
rural society, 27
Russo-Japanese War, 52
Ryukyu Islands, 91

SCAPIN-93, 180
school segregation, 57
Second World War, 55, 77, 85, 86
Seoul Electric Company, 34
Seoul Government Property Bureau, 115
Severance Union Medical College, 105
Shuji, Izawa, 51
Sino-Japanese lexicon, 51
Sino-Japanese War, 21
socialism, 126, 130, 139
　cultural movements, 128
　education, 56
　revolution, 18
Southern China, 21
Southern Cholla Province, 17
South Korea, 17, 18, 62
　anti-communist alliance, 109–112
　higher education, 101, 105–107
　intellectuals, landlords to, 107–109
　land reform, 112–115
　North Korea, 108
　private universities, 115–116
　Pro-Japanese landed class, 103–105
　second life paramilitarism in, 64–65
South Korea Interim Government, 110
Soviet Army, 62
Special Compensation Act on Educational Foundations' Farmland, 113
standard of living, 81, 82, 88
starvation, 22, 30

state-controlled rice market, Seoul, 23
supplement, 136–137, 137–141
Suspended Indictment, 176
Suspended Sentence, 176
symbolic emperor system, 182–184

Taegu Insurrection, 35–36
Taisho democracy, 52
Taiwan, 127
   army, 54
   conservative revolution, China, 128
   economic growth, 137
   Guomindang (GMD), 126
   Japan, 51
   Korea, 55
   political rights, 52
   Republic of China (ROC), 127
   war mobilization, 66–67
tenants, 19
Thompson, Carmi, 78
Three People's Principles, 126, 127, 135
Tokyo government, 20, 21, 24, 25
Truman administration, 85
Trust Territory of the Pacific Islands
   (TTPI), 92
Tydings-McDuffie Act, 80

underground armies, 63
Union Christian College, 105, 109
United States Army Military Government
   in Korea (USAMGIK), 107
USAMGIK, 108, 110–111
US anti-Asian prejudice, 81
US-based sociologists, 140
US colonialism, 78
US federal buildings, 83
US military, 17, 30, 35, 36, 37, 38,
   78, 84, 89

engineers, 84
power, 78
US occupations, 17, 18, 29, 33, 37, 39
US-Philippine business lobby, 80
USSR occupations, 18

Visayan Stevedore Company
   (VISTRANCO), 87
Volksgeist-ism
   conservative, 160–164
   lineages of, 148–151
   Pancasila, 156–159
Volunteer Probation Officers Act, 179, 181
volunteers system, 53, 58, 60, 68

wages
   inequalities, 78
   racial, 81–82
warlords, 53
War of Resistance, 63
wartime
   colonial government, Korea, 40
   grain-control system, 18
   mobilization networks, 18
Weaving Company, 104, 105
welfare, 177–178
Wilson, Woodrow, 107

Yangsan police station, 37
Yi, Chen, 66
Yin Zhongrong, 137–138
youth
   brigades, 62
   leagues, 54, 55
   Manchukuo, 55
Yutang, Lin, 135

Zuolin, Zhang, 52

www.ingramcontent.com/pod-product-compliance
Lightning Source LLC
Chambersburg PA
CBHW062217300426
44115CB00012BA/2104